SHOBHAA DÉ

AN UNSUITABLE BOY

Karan Johar is one of the leading directors, producers and writers in the Hindi film industry. The son of much-respected film producer Yash Johar, who set up Dharma Productions in 1976, Karan took over his father's legacy after the latter's death in 2004.

An award-winning director, he started out as an assistant to film-maker Aditya Chopra on the sets of *Dilwale Dulhaniya Le Jayenge* (1995). Karan made his directorial debut with *Kuch Kuch Hota Hai* (1998) which went on to become a blockbuster. He has directed six major films and produced over twenty, all starring some of the biggest names in Bollywood. He recently made his acting debut in Anurag Kashyap's *Bombay Velvet* (2015).

The multitalented Karan also hosts one of India's most-watched celebrity chat shows, *Koffee with Karan*. He has dabbled in fashion design, and even done the costumes for films such as *Dilwale Dulhaniya Le Jayenge*, *Mohabbatein* and *Dil To Pagal Hai*.

An extremely popular and well-liked member of the film fraternity, Karan has come to be regarded as a spokesman of the industry. In 2007, he was chosen as one of 250 Global Young Leaders by the World Economic Forum.

Karan has recently become the father of twins, Yash and Roohi.

Poonam Saxena is the national weekend editor with *Hindustan Times*.

She has been a journalist for almost twenty years, first as a freelancer and then as the features editor of *Asian Age*. She wrote the popular TV review column 'Small Screen' for *Hindustan Times* for almost ten years.

Recently, she translated Dharamvir Bharati's iconic novel, *Gunahon Ka Devta*, into English (*Chander & Sudha*).

AN UNSUITABLE BOY

KARAN JOHAR

WITH POONAM SAXENA

Sdé
Shobhaa Dé
BOOKS

An imprint of Penguin Random House

SHOBHAA DÉ BOOKS

USA | Canada | UK | Ireland | Australia
New Zealand | India | South Africa | China

Shobhaa Dé Books is part of the Penguin Random House group of companies
whose addresses can be found at global.penguinrandomhouse.com

Published by Penguin Random House India Pvt. Ltd
7th Floor, Infinity Tower C, DLF Cyber City,
Gurgaon 122 002, Haryana, India

Penguin
Random House
India

First published in Shobhaa Dé Books by Penguin Random House India 2017

The views and opinions expressed in this book are the authors' own and the
facts are as reported by them which have been verified to the extent possible,
and the publishers are not in any way liable for the same.

ISBN 9780143423096

Typeset in Adobe Garamond Pro by Manipal Digital Systems, Manipal
Printed at Thomson Press India Ltd, New Delhi

www.penguin.co.in

Contents

Prologue

Today I finally feel liberated. I feel like I can take on anyone or anything. I don't want to be this person who is bound by principles, morality or reality, someone who has to conform to any kind of societal rules. The only time I'm tight-lipped is when I'm asked about my sexuality because it's my personal business and I don't want to talk about it. When I'm ready, I will. Right now I don't wish to. It's the only part of me I feel I've caged. But otherwise I feel alive. I'm forty-four and I'm ready for new challenges, new people. I'm ready to remove a lot of clutter from my life. When I walk into my office, I am so energized to do new things on a non-stop basis. I'm on the treadmill of life, running constantly. And the gears are in my hand, the levers are in my hand. I can go from one to ten, depending on what I wish. But I haven't reached this stage overnight. It is the result of all that I've been through over the years. I was asked the other day about my latest film, *Ae Dil Hai Mushkil*, and for some reason I felt the need to tell the truth. Actually it is a personal story. I've had two unrequited love situations in my life. One in my twenties and one in my thirties where I'd loved and not received that love back, and I remember how hurtful that was. It's worse than a toothache. It's worse than having a tumour in your brain. It's worse than having a wisdom tooth extracted. Your heart hurts. Some call it anxiety, some call it breathlessness. The second time it happened to me I was much older and I had to visit a psychologist and be on medication for several months. I kept getting these bouts of anxiety. My doctor said that the anxiety was a product of that depression which I hadn't acknowledged. My second love situation had really overstayed. There was the sense of being at the midpoint of your life with nothing happening in your personal life. There was professional growth, yes, but that comes with its own stresses and insecurities. And there was a general feeling of loneliness, emptiness, of being vacant, being burdened by the lack of love. Or the lack of companionship perhaps—despite being surrounded by people. I felt like I was going through something that required medication. Mere conversation was not going to help. My doctor put me on medication, monitored it, then slowly weaned me off it. I'm totally off it now.

It was the acknowledgement that was important. Sometimes we feel it's just a phase. We don't realize that in our times, this has now become part and parcel of our lives—depression, anxiety. I call it 'medical sadness'. It needs to be addressed, either through therapy or a psychologist, and it's important to know the difference. I just knew that I needed a psychologist. I'm quite self-aware. I didn't feel I needed somebody to walk me through the beats of my life. I felt I needed a diagnosis, not a discussion.

Now I don't go for the sessions but I'm still in touch with my doctor. Once every few months, I touch base with her. We're WhatsApp buddies. Not that I badger her with messages. She walked me through the writing of *Ae Dil Hai Mushkil* when I was feeling the burden of my unrequited love. She messaged me the other day, saying, 'Saw the promos. Feels really surreal, I feel a part of that.' Which she was.

With *Ae Dil Hai Mushkil*, I feel I've put out my first personal piece of work. I don't want to say it's an autobiography because there's a lot of fiction in it but there are scenes and conversations that are very true to what happened in my life. I'm pretty much Ranbir Kapoor in the film, and the film is all about him and his broken heart. There's a dialogue that goes: *'Rishtey jab jismani ho jaate hain toh kahin na kahin dosti mit jaati hai. Pyaar mein junoon hai par dosti mein sukoon hai aur main nahin chahti ki hamare beech ka sukoon kabhi chala jaaye.'* The person I was in love with told me, I'm glad we're not having sex. But I was also told, you're the most important person in my life, you're my family, you're my everything, you're just not my lover. This happened when I was thirty-five. It's taken me so many years to get over it. I realize that sometimes heartbreak is a luxury. You just lie in that spa of heartbreak for months.

Love is such an indulgent emotion. But I tried everything to get over it. I tried rationalizing it internally, I tried sitting with friends and discussing it (they told me I was being stupid, idiotic, nonsensical). But only you know what you go through. The only thing it did to me was that it made me feel alive. I never regret those years. (They gave me a feature film too!) There's a dialogue in the film: *'Ek tarfa pyaar ki taaqat hi kuch aur hoti hai. Aur rishton ki tarah yeh do logon mein nahin bant ti.'* I believe in that very strongly. That power of love is mine. To love someone is such a feeling of power, because even if you don't get that love back, you still have it. It could be a weakness, it could be a strength. It's how you look at it. I look at the love I had as a source of great strength. I built my company to the optimum fuelled by that emotion. It gave me some kind of energy. It hurt me, it broke my heart, but it also gave me power, made me feel alive. I don't regret it. It hurt only because what was said to me at that point was that this would be a relationship for ever, nobody could come in its way, but somebody did. A third person changed the dynamic. There's always separation because of a third person. Sometimes siblings change because one of them gets married.

But I'm finally over it because I put it out there. I wrote about it, I lived it, I shot it, I executed it. There are scenes, moments in the film that are completely me. The film is based on love and friendship. It's about how sometimes you can be in a situation where you can never translate friendship into love. Sex can change the dynamics. I never had sex with either of the two people I was in love with. The second person got married, moved country and now I'm not in touch with that person any more. The only thing that hurt me was that I was promised so much, but I never even got that friendship. Because of the third person who entered the picture. But the first person I was in love with is still very much a part of my life.

I feel a lot more internal today. It's strange—I used to be the most people's person; today I feel far more introverted. I don't feel the need for noise around me any more. I don't feel like going to a crowded party. I go because I have to; I've become less people-friendly. I'd rather sit on my terrace with a couple of friends and drink a bottle of wine and talk about my life and their lives. I don't want to be the life of a party no more. I feel bored. I've done it excessively for the last fifteen years. From the age of twenty to the age of forty-four, all I've done is surround myself with people. Now I don't feel the need to be over-reverential to seniority or to overly bond with younger people just to make myself feel that I'm relevant. You could call it disdain, detachment or just liberation. It depends on how you look at life. I'm happy in the confines of my own professional environment and the work I need to do.

This devotion to work also happens when you don't have children, a spouse or a love life. I'm constantly asked, 'Are you having enough sex?' Somehow, people equate being in the entertainment industry with having a lot of sex. But I don't want that much. Actually I don't care about it. I'm not one who switches on porn to feel happy before I pass out at night. People think that since I travel so much, I must be having a lot of sex. But it doesn't happen that way. A boarding pass is not a pass for sex. I'm not in love with anyone any more. I'm love-free, sex-free—completely free. I feel I'm not accountable to anyone and my mother has given me the strength to say that I'm not even accountable to her any more. I now have a child who I have to take care of and that's my mother. I feel like the patriarch of this company, the man of the house, running it as I want to. I don't want to please anyone any longer. I say 'no' a lot more easily than I ever did. And I say 'yes' with a lot more abandon than I ever have.

I feel the new emotion I've acquired is honesty, something I've not had in the last decade because I felt the need to not be honest in personal or professional situations. There was a time when I was very concerned about what other film-makers did. I was so bothered that others were making better films than I did—it was borderline jealousy, competition. I used to tell myself—acknowledge it, that way you'll get better. But I was not being honest. I was just doing the politically correct thing. Actually I was jealous. I used to sometimes wish their films wouldn't do as well as they did. I used to be troubled by Sanjay Leela Bhansali's brilliance. I used to be affected that I couldn't write a film like Raju Hirani. But now I'm not bothered. Now I feel happy for them if they make a great film. Today I don't care. If I hear a film has done well, great. Good for you. Hope you made lots of money. Great three hours of cinema. Bravo! Well done! Now move on.

I wonder what happened. I analysed it and wondered—is there a mojo that has been reduced? But that's not true because I'm alive in my editing room. When I was in the last stages of *Ae Dil Hai Mushkil*, my passion had not diminished a bit—but my preferences of life had. I don't care if my film has made 100 crore or 150 crore rupees or less or more as long as I feel I've made a good film and as long as it's made money for the people involved. I feel accountable to the people who've invested in me. I want to ensure that every employee of this company is catered to emotionally, personally and professionally. That's all-important for me. Other than that, no. I have no interest in accountability to the rest of the world. Do I want to broaden my horizons? Maybe. I'll see how it pans out. Do I want to attach myself to a studio? I don't know. Do I want to get into a web series? For what? I don't feel I want to give myself a cardiac arrest for no reason. If I feel like it, I'll do it. If I feel like making a film, I'll do it. If I don't, I won't. Sometimes I'll go wrong. Too bad. I hope I'll pay the price for it only so that I don't do that again. I've had a couple of duds recently and many successes. And strangely, my reaction to both situations was not extreme.

I'm a lot more detached from my professional zone than I was. This doesn't mean that I'm disinterested. I love what I do. But I'm detached from the eventuality of a product, the success that I used to give so much importance to. If it flops, it's fine, something else will work. If it's a hit, great, move on. Now I feel numb to both success and failure. The only thing that excites me is when I leave my zone and get lost on a trip, check into a hotel, sit in my own space.

So where am I at? As I said, liberated. Happy. And ready for the latter half of my life. There are some thoughts: Am I going to get married? No. Am I ever going to move out of this country? Never. These are things I already know. I know where I'm going. Am I going to be lonely? Perhaps. There's a lot of ambiguity, yet there's clarity. I'm almost excited because I don't know what will happen. Will someone waltz into my life, sweep me off my feet and will I be in love all over again? I don't know. It could happen, though I'm very cynical now and don't think so. I find most people very annoying and I don't think I want to share my bedroom with anyone. Even if I'm in a relationship, I feel we've got to have two separate bedrooms. And I'm not moving in with anyone, they have to move in with me. And do what I want to do. Am I going to be a sugar daddy? I don't mind. I'm open to that now. If somebody's going to be dancing to my whims and fancies, I don't mind. Am I open to loving again? I don't think I can do that level of intensity again. I'm too old. The drama of love has always excited me but I don't think I care enough now. I don't think I can love like that again. I feel you can go through it only twice in your life. I don't think there's a third time. The third time you just get married. Everyone has that one love story in their nascent years. Mine was a bit delayed. And then there's that one love story you have in your later years. If neither of them works out, then you go straight into your third zone—marriage or whatever it is that people do today, maybe move in together. I don't think my third dalliance is going to be as passionate as my first two. If something does happen so be it, if it doesn't I'm fine. If people waltz into my life organically, fine. I can't constantly keep in touch. I'm becoming a slacker even when it comes to text messages. I used to be so alert. Now I wish I could have a new number. I've become a reluctant social person. It used to be in my DNA. But I'm completely slipping. By the time I turn fifty, I might even become a recluse. I might shock myself.

There's one thing I am sure of though. After making *Ae Dil Hai Mushkil*, I do feel like I need to make a film every year. I loved it so much. Film-making is my primary and only passion. I love that one can play god when one's a film-maker. Giving instructions, being in control—these are now part of my persona. Even when I'm on someone else's set I feel like I should take charge! I'm not a control freak but I know that authority comes very naturally to me. I've always felt like I'm somebody people should listen to.

I feel like I'm walking into my next phase. There's a door opening and I'm entering. I feel there will be a lot of upheaval, a lot of drama, but there will also be a lot of silence which I will enjoy.

1

Childhood

I've always lived in Bombay. I was born and brought up in Malabar
Hill. We stayed in a building called Acropolis, which was in a
very upmarket, elite neighbourhood in South Bombay. The address
is entrenched in my head. Somehow, you always remember your
first address—it was 92 Acropolis, Little Gibbs Road, Malabar Hill,
Bombay 46. If you ask me the exact address of my new home, it won't
come to me so easily.

The building was in a compound—it was a regular building, there
was nothing special about it. We had a two-bedroom house on the
ninth floor, about 1000 square feet. As soon as you opened the door,
there was a narrow passage. My mom's and dad's room was on the left
and a few feet away was my room with a sofa-cum-bed and a desk. On
the extreme left was a tiny kitchen. And then there was a hall and a
little dining area. We had a wonderful view of the Queen's Necklace.
We could look out on the whole cityscape of Bombay.

My room was rather simple and basic. I had no posters on the wall
or anything like that. I was not that obsessed by any movie star to put
up posters in my room. I never was that person.

It was a tiny flat, but my parents were very social. They always had
friends over. My aunts were around a lot. My parents used to have these

great parties. The vibe of the house was especially inviting; there was a warmth about it that made people stay on. I believe very strongly in the energy of spaces. I am very susceptible to these energies. When I walk into someone's house, I immediately know whether I am going to be comfortable or not. Sometimes a close friend's house can be uncomfortable and a stranger's home inviting. It's really all about energy.

I was an only child and much loved by my parents. I remember being obsessed with my mother, which is a very Punjabi thing to do. My mother is Sindhi. My father, a Punjabi, was much older than my mother. He was forty and already bald and grey when he had me. He was almost the same age as I am now, when I was born. So my relationship with my father was always a bit like he was my grandfather. He was overindulgent towards me, the way a grandfather would be with his grandchild. Fathers are generally strict, but I never experienced that. My father was always loving and we were very tactile as father and son. He used to pinch my cheeks and I used to hug and kiss him. Very unlike what fathers and sons are supposed to be like. In fact, both my parents were very expressive emotionally.

I was a good, quiet, obedient kid. I never got into any fist fights. I never came back home with cuts or wounds. I don't have any of those stories to tell. I had one fall at the Hanging Garden right opposite our house. I fell off a swing, so I had some kind of an injury. I lived in a bit of a shell—now that I think of it. It was a protected, sheltered life.

I always felt different. I didn't feel like the other boys around me or the girls around me. I couldn't pinpoint what it was. I don't mean that I had a sad childhood. A lot of it is a blur, maybe because I have chosen it to be. If there had been anything called therapy then or even somebody to talk to, I might have actually felt better. But I clammed everything up a hell of a lot. I couldn't understand it.

I was scared of my mother, who was convent educated and valued studies. But I was never afraid of my father and I think I was so spoilt by him that I grew into this fat, round child (my father insisted it was puppy fat). But my mother was always worried about it. I had this constant craving to eat.

I was also much indulged by my aunts. My mother has a series of first cousins and all of them were air hostesses with Air India. Those days, being an air hostess was a highly glamorous profession. Actresses came second to them. I have a *maasi* called Pappu maasi, whose real name is Jyoti. Then there's Nalini maasi who cuts hair. She was one of the first people to cut hair stylishly in the city. And then there was Shobha maasi. These are the three maasis who were close to my mum. I grew up around these aunts and they were big influences in my life. They were all very stylish, well dressed and modern. They spoke well, were well travelled. So was my mother, though she was the most traditional of the lot. She was the go-to sister for all of them. My mother has no real siblings, no real brother or sister. These cousins were her immediate family. My fascination for the arts and glamour started with my aunts. It's something I've never really acknowledged. They all used to smoke and they were extremely glamorous. My mother was probably the most square of the lot. They often came back from their travels with the best bottles of wine, and things like cheese.

I longed for a sibling. I used to feel very upset when I saw other children's brothers and sisters. It really bothered me. But my mother couldn't have another child. She tried. But she had had a tough pregnancy with me, so when she got pregnant again, she had to abort the child because the doctor said she wouldn't be able to handle it and it could be detrimental to her health.

I think that's a regret she has because she feels things would've been very different for me as a child if I'd had a sibling. It was a lonely existence for me. I had complexes because of my weight, my being effeminate. It bothered me though I couldn't put my finger on it at that time. My dad was much older, so we didn't do the regular things fathers and sons do. And he was immersed in his work. Most kids my age had very young fathers. When I was eight or nine my father was nearly fifty years old. Everybody else had fathers who were a decade younger, if not more. They'd enjoy playing a sport with their dads. But all that didn't happen with me. A lot of my influences are from my mother because I spent so much time with her. I loved what she loved. But yes, there was a lot of loneliness. I always tell people not to make the mistake of having one child. It is just not fair.

Today you have technology and that can be such a big friend. But those days you had nothing. Today you can get away by being a single child. But those days I felt it was very abnormal not to have a brother or a sister.

I was always intense as a child. I was a good listener, which is why I became a good friend to many. Being an only child you kind of develop that quality; you start caring about other people's lives a lot because you don't have a sense of extended family. So other people's family stories, other people's sibling rivalries, fun times, whatever it may be, interest you tremendously. I remember always asking other people about their lives and their families. I used to compare other people's homes to mine, and my mother would get upset by that. I wasn't dissing our situation but whenever I went to somebody's home and saw siblings running around or a house full of people, it used to affect me. We saw some really good times in our house. But somehow I always felt a bit alone. It got to me more than it should have. I suppose because I wasn't like the regular kids. I didn't play any sport, my energies weren't being expended in any way. It was all getting bottled up.

I was overweight as a child and felt shy because I was so big. I was never part of the sports groups, where all the boys played gully football or cricket. So I used to hang out with the girls a lot. Girls always liked me. I think they felt comfortable around me and perhaps I also gave them the sense I was effeminate. I remember how that word used to disturb me no end. I also hated being called fatty.

But the word I hated the most was pansy. It used to irritate me and I had an aversion to it. You don't hear it much now but it was used a lot in the eighties for anybody who was thought to be effeminate. If someone called me pansy, the whole week used to go bad. For some reason it made me feel inferior, a lesser person. Older boys used to say it. It was not people from the school. Contrary to what people say, I was surrounded by a lot of compassionate kids. But it was different with kids from outside. Like once we went for an inter-school debate and there was a kid from Campion. We were in the preliminary rounds and I was sitting outside on a bench going through my points when he came up to me and said, 'God, you're such a pansy.' It shook my confidence. I went mad in my head. I couldn't perform. My debate was weak and we lost. And I realized that it had got to me.

I did have friends in my building though. I was very close to a Parsi girl called Farzana Muncherjee. She stayed on the seventh floor with her sister, parents and grandmother. They were like my extended family. I used to come back home and often go and play with them. Farzana had this hold over me because she knew that I was needy. And she took advantage of that sometimes. She's very much in my life today too. She is my rakhi sister and we have a strong bond. She doesn't understand the film business. She lives in South Mumbai with her husband. She moved back after living in Singapore and Hong Kong for a while. She is not a part of my day-to-day life but we still meet, maybe twice a year.

I grew up with Farzana. She has seen me through every phase. It is amazing how she gets me. Even now, she can be rude and nasty to me. And I take it because it's her. She has a kind of spunk in the way she says things. I was obsessed with Farzana. In a way, she made up for the sibling I didn't have. She would bully me. Whenever she wanted to leave and go back to her home, I would start crying. She was in and out of my house and I was in and out of hers. I still have an obsession with Parsi food because of her family.

I am not very religious, though I used to fake it. My father said a three-minute prayer every morning, bare-chested, with a towel around him. He used to do this 'combination prayer' which was really interesting because he'd start with a Sikh prayer, then go on to some Hindu chants and then it would go into some Dear Jesus kind of thing. It oscillated between three religions.

He would do this in front of a little temple we had. And he was the only one who did so. My mother, like me, pretends to be religious but she is not. She goes to the gurdwara about once a year. My *nani* grew up in a building called Shyam Nivas in Bombay, which has the city's most famous gurdwara in it. Both my parents had the gurdwara in common. But my father was a more proactive religious man. He was an Arya Samaji. He didn't believe in rituals. He didn't believe in *pooja-path*, he believed in the practicality of religion. But he always recited his little prayer. And I was very intrigued by how it oscillated between all the three religions.

Ours was a very cosmopolitan house. We all spoke to each other in English. There was no grandparent around. And my father was a modern, well-travelled man though he was a Punjabi businessman at heart, a film producer. And I think he got that from being self-made.

My father grew up in Shimla and then moved to Delhi (he lived briefly in Lahore too). After he completed his education, my grandmother took him aside and said, 'Run away, leave. Find your own destiny. You are made for greater things.'

She gave him money and jewellery and said, 'Go to Bombay and make a life for yourself.'

She'd faked a robbery in the house a week before that when she said her jewellery was missing. She had it all planned. And they sacked a member of the staff for the robbery! It was all plotted by her. My father didn't know this initially, till she told him the truth. She said she never wanted anyone to know that she'd given him anything. She wanted him to just vanish. She said she would handle his grandfather.

So he took the train and reached Bombay. The first thing he found himself staring at was the Times of India building. So he went in and asked around if any of the divisions were hiring. He was directed to one Mr Dubey who was a photographer with the *Times of India* those days. My father began working with him—for a paltry amount. That's how he made it to the sets of *Mughal-e-Azam* with Mr Dubey, who had gone there to take pictures. My father would usually just hang around. And then one day, Mr Dubey fell sick. So my father reached the sets to take a photograph of Madhubala. Those days—this was the forties—Madhubala would not allow anyone to photograph her but somehow she liked my father; she thought he was cultured and well spoken. So she allowed him to take pictures of her. She took him to her garden, and posed for him. His photographs of Madhubala were what got him more work in the company. His first job in Bombay was as a still photographer with the *Times of India*.

Subsequently, he got into films and became a production person. He worked with almost everybody in the industry. Then he finally landed a job as a production controller, which was his longest tenure. He worked with Navketan, Dev Anand's and Vijay Anand's company, for about twelve years. His biggest, longest and most loyal association was with 'Devsaab'.

Of course, one year later he went back home, and by then it was all okay with his father. They understood that he had made a life for himself in Bombay.

He started off living as a PG, then he began staying in a hotel called Marina, in Mahim, where he had a close friend, Rashid Abbasi, who I knew as Rashid uncle. They stayed together in this hotel for about nine years, till he moved to South Bombay and shifted into a rented apartment. He remained a bachelor.

In 1977, he actually gave up movies after being associated with them for over thirty years, and started an export firm. It was probably a better business opportunity for him but Goldie Bahl's and Shrishti Arya's father, Ramesh Bahl (who had a company called Rose Movies), encouraged him to get back to films. My father decided to produce films. He even approached Gulzar to direct a film for him but that project never happened. He then got in touch with Raj Khosla and that led to the casting of Mr Bachchan in *Dostana*. It was a Salim–Javed script. *Dostana* was his first film. And it was a hit. But it was his only hit.

After he got married, his office was near the race course in Mahalaxmi. It was a godown converted into an office. Every time it rained it would get flooded. You could see the race course from the office. It was a strange office; although it was a godown, it was carpeted and had those old ACs and fax machines. I have vivid memories of that office.

I used to go there a lot as a child and I used to hang around, and everyone would pull my cheeks. Later on, after my college, I worked there for a year or two, but got completely frustrated. However, I made my first film *Kuch Kuch Hota Hai* out of that office.

It was a rented place and we eventually let go of it and gave it back to the family it belonged to. In any case, in the last ten years we'd begun using it as a godown once again. It didn't make any sense to keep it since we were doing nothing with it. But yes, that was our first office.

My mother grew up in Kanpur and Lucknow, and studied in Nainital. She knew Amit uncle (Amitabh Bachchan) from college. Amit uncle was at Sherwood and she was at St Mary's. They were a gang of friends. I remember her telling me how she burst out laughing when Amit uncle told her he was going to be a movie actor. She said, 'YOU are going be in Hindi movies?' She knew his family background. He was a major poet's son, and Hindi movies were not considered to be culturally the most desirable thing.

My maternal grandparents were very conservative. My grandfather did not allow my mother to become an air hostess; it was too much for his traditional mindset. So she worked as Alitalia ground staff, went to Rome and studied Italian. She did all that before she got married.

My parents met at the race course and fell in love quickly, the quickest that I know of. My mother was about twenty-seven then and loved going to the races. She used to go every Sunday. My dad was thirty-nine and best friends with a lot of people in Bombay's 'social zone'. He also knew all the movie stars. He was like the Sea Link—he knew people at this end, and he knew people at the other end. He was very popular, the do-gooder, the one-stop shop for anything you needed. That was my father. You wanted anything in this world to be done, all you had to do was call Yash Johar and he would do it.

He saw my mother and, in true Hindi film style, chased her for three days. Initially, she acted very stuck up—he came from the film world, he was a production controller of movies (he had started working with Navketan by then).

They met in February, and my mother's birthday is on 18 March. My father called her and said he wanted to throw a party for her. Somehow she agreed. He threw a big party for her at Bhalla House which is in Pali Hill. It was owned by a man called Satish Bhalla who was a very popular man in Pali Hill. Everyone went to his house, from Dilip Kumar to Dev Anand to Raj Kapoor. So my father threw this big bash there and since he was the rakhi brother of Waheeda Rahman and Sadhana, all the top-notch actresses were there. In fact, pretty much everybody from the film industry was there. And in front of everyone, he proposed to my mother. She didn't know what to say! Finally she said, 'You'll have to meet my father.' So my father, who was thirteen years older than my mom, went off to meet his to-be father-in-law. But he was such a good man that my *nana* who was very stuck up about certain things, melted immediately. My parents were married on 20 May 1971 in the same Bhalla House. Their wedding photographs are full of movie stars. Leena Daru who was a film costume stylist prepared my mother's trousseau. It was a full-on filmi wedding. Almost everyone from the Hindi film industry attended. For my mother's side of the family, this was a totally different world from what they were used to.

I was born exactly a year later.

Though my father worked in the movies, my mother never really watched them. But ironically, all my love for Hindi movies comes from her. Even today, she comes and watches my movies or other people's movies only if somebody close to her calls her. But she loved Hindi film music. And that's what crept into my head and made me go completely cuckoo over Hindi movies and their music!

I did go through a phase where, like all other kids, I listened to Madonna, George Michael, and so on. Listening to music on your Walkman was a big deal then. For about two years I did this fake act of wanting to be like other kids and then I went back to Hindi film songs. I also read a lot in those days. I was obsessed with Enid Blyton.

I didn't grow up in the computer age or the mobile phone era. I remember the first time I saw colour on my TV was when I watched Wimbledon. There was this green patch on the screen, and I remember being riveted. I hated watching sports but I couldn't take my eyes off the screen because of that patch of green. I am from the generation that has seen the advent of the VHS, CD, followed by the DVD and LD. It was such an age of discovery. When I see kids today, I am amazed that they don't go through those beats at all—it's just all there for them.

But back then, the excitement of going to a *thelawala* and buying Archie comics! The excitement of going to one of those little provision stores that kept foreign chocolates and looking at a Mars bar or a Kit Kat or a Coke bottle with awe, and emptying your piggy bank—we all had piggy banks those days—and making sure you had 20 rupees to buy them. Buying the Coke can, bringing it home, staring at it for a while, then opening it with precision and taking little sips, and placing a plate on it so that it didn't lose its fizz. These are my childhood memories—pardon me that they are food related but those foreign chocolates and Coke cans were a very big deal those days.

My father travelled a fair amount on work. When he came back, I'd wake up in the morning and open his suitcase before he got up, to see what he had got for me. He would have come late at night when I was asleep; I remember that excitement, that Papa was back and his suitcase would have things for me. These were the little things that excited us as a generation, which are just taken for granted today.

I loved food. The food we ate was more inclined to my mother's side of the family, which is Sindhi. We had a lot of *sae bhaji*, khichri and mutton made in the Sindhi style. It was basic Indian food. And for years, we had a really good cook, Kedar, whose mutton was 'world famous'. Everyone raved about it.

And I was obsessed with eating.

I was very fat, so kids often called me 'fatty'. That just got me more into my shell. It used to bother me a hell of a lot but it never stopped me from eating. I believed there was no other way—I just had to eat for my own happiness. Now that I think about it, subconsciously or psychologically, my only friend was food. I had a relationship with food that helped me tide over all the other issues I had in my head. I needed to eat for comfort and solace. I still remember coming back from school when I was in the eighth standard and ordering from a hotel called Shalimar, which was just down the road. They made the best chicken *makhanwala* and naan. And the happiness I got when the food came in front of me and I ate it alone! Then there was Chinese Room, this little restaurant in Kemps Corner. I would send for chicken fried rice, sweet and sour chicken (which was my favourite) and chicken sweet corn soup. Just waiting for the food to come would make me happy. There was a lady called Azra Buryawala who made chocolates from her home and many a time I used to lie to her and say, 'Aunty, it's my birthday and I want your chocolate cake.' I would eat that whole one kilo cake on my own. I ordered it many times and the cake would come with a Happy Birthday Karan written on it, except that it wasn't my birthday at all. I would hide the cake in my room and demolish it. It cost about 300 rupees and I'd buy it from the money I'd got on Diwali and other occasions.

There was once an incident with a big box of Quality Street chocolate. It was sealed but I found a little edge where I could just peel off the Sellotape, open the box a bit and take out some chocolates. At the end of the month there was just one chocolate left but the box was still sealed. When my mother found out, I got a slap from her, one of the only two slaps in my entire life. The second slap was when she realized that I couldn't tie my shoelaces even though I was twelve. My maid always did it for me. When my mother saw this, she asked me, 'Can you not tie your shoelaces on your own?'

I answered, 'Of course, I can.'

She said, 'Show me.'

Then I had to confess I couldn't. I just couldn't make that knot. She slapped me hard and said, 'That's all you are going to do today. Tie shoelaces!'

But she didn't realize that I'd quietly go and make my maid tie my shoelaces. I just couldn't do it. Even today, I have a problem tying a knot. I do it but it doesn't come easily to me. (I put that scene in *Kabhi Khushi Kabhie Gham* . . . That fat kid in the film is a little bit of me.)

My father, of course, never raised his voice or his hand at me, ever. I was the apple of his eye. All I needed to do was shed a tear and he would melt. My mother, on the other hand, tried to be strict and enforce discipline. She was the one I was afraid of.

We had a club next door called the WIAA and it had a pool, a table tennis table and a badminton court. A lot of my life was spent at that club. We had a very strong club culture in our area. In the evenings, I'd go to the club, come back, watch TV, do nothing much, eat dinner early and go to bed. That was my school routine.

I never sulked but my mother loved to. I would get very upset when she did that. Even now I get very disturbed. When she goes quiet, it bothers me, I can't take it. Now I have trained her not to, but at that point she'd do it.

The only times I remember crying were when I wanted to go to Hindi film previews. The biggest showdowns I had with her were when I used to weep to see a movie. If the preview was at nine in the night and I had school the next day, my parents would say no—and those were the times I remember bawling, throwing a tantrum that I needed to see the film! My only access avenue was previews or when my mother allowed me to take our domestic help and go to the cinema. While she was never very excited about watching movies, my father, though he was a part of the movie industry, was also not a movie fan. Sometimes I don't understand how I have this fascination for cinema, though I know it started with music.

My mother used to listen to music on cassettes and she had this Akai music system. There were two songs that were my favourites—'*Lag Ja Gale*' and '*Ajeeb Dastan Hai Yeh*'. My mother was a big Shammi Kapoor fan—she loved '*Aaja Aaja Main Hun Pyar Tera*' and all those other hit songs of his.

All my knowledge of Hindi film music knowledge of the 1940s, '50s and '60s, I got from my mother. She used to play old LPs of Mohammed Rafi, Kishore Kumar and Lata Mangeshkar. Pick any song from the 1950s, and I will know the words. My mother used to hold my hand and dance to Elvis Presley numbers. She loved Elvis. She went to an Elvis Presley concert during her honeymoon with my father in Las Vegas and fainted. She fainted! My Punjabi producer father could not handle this happening on their honeymoon! But my mother was one of those fanatical Elvis fans; she also knew of the Beatles. Although not a movie buff, she loved watching Rock Hudson and Doris Day starrers. So there was the Hollywood influence too. My mother was quite a chick in the 1960s.

My parents used to have a party at Waheeda aunty's house on 18 March, every year, for many years. It was a ritual. Waheeda aunty had a house right behind where Salman Khan stays today. She has a bungalow in Bandra even now. A lot of stars would come. I'd take my neighbourhood friends with me and sit at the entrance with my autograph book.

But those days, Hindi films were not a big deal among the younger kids. It was not like today, when I can imagine kids oohing and aahing over a Ranbir Kapoor or a Shah Rukh Khan. But I was from the film world and I knew it was a big deal. However, kids around me were not like that. I grew up in a neighbourhood that was genuinely not aware of Hindi movies. Me? I was over-aware. I knew too much.

But my upbringing was not filmi at all, though my mum was close to Jaya aunty and Amit uncle, and I knew Abhishek and Shweta, Farhan and Zoya. We attended birthday parties together.

But I never grew up with film people. Most of my time was spent with rich kids. I always felt rich. But we were not rich. We were a middle-class family. My father was losing money in the movies, and making up with his export firm, which he ran alongside. He was like a middle agent for handicrafts that were exported to America and France. My father was not in the best place economically, yet I was always made to believe I was richer than I actually was. I always lived above my standards (and that continues till today) because I was the only child.

2

School and College

My biggest desire was to get into Cathedral School, because that was the pinnacle of affluence when it came to schools. But I was somehow so nervous that I messed up that interview. I refused to do anything. I was like a stone. They asked me to play with blocks and I refused. They asked me to open my mouth and I didn't. I just kept holding my mother's hand. I had poor social skills, which nobody would believe of me today!

I was five or six years old when I was denied admission to Cathedral. It was earth-shattering. Then my mother took me to Campion, which is an all-boys school. But there again, I did nothing. So she gave me a lecture and told me, 'You have to speak.' My next interview was at St Mary's. Nalini maasi cut hair, and I had seen her cut my mother's hair. I was so influenced by that visual that when they asked me what I wanted to be when I grew up, I said I wanted to be a hair cutter. My mother shouted at me and said, 'Couldn't you have said you wanted to be a pilot?' All the other boys wanted to be pilots. But I didn't.

I don't know whether my mother realized it or not, but I was always more inclined towards the arts. I was interested in my mother's saris. I would stare at what my aunts were wearing. I was fascinated by the handbags they carried.

My first thought was to say hair cutter. Because I thought that was the coolest thing in the world. At age six for a boy to have that kind of an aspiration was bizarre, especially in those days.

Obviously, I did not get into any of these schools. My mother wept, because for her education was the most important thing. She was shattered. I remember her sitting by the window, crying and yelling at my father: 'How can he not get into a good school?'

There was another top school called Green Lawns. So my father said he would ask a friend to put in a word. That's how I got into Green Lawns. It was a coed school. I remember the whole process of getting into my school uniform. I was very fat and my stomach stuck out.

Growing up, I had a few friends in my building. I was a funny child and used to say funny things. Both my parents had a great sense of humour, so I got that from them. But I never tapped into that side too much, because I was so shy. My mother always encouraged me to make more friends, because I used to make friends with great difficulty. She was concerned about me being so introverted and dependent on her.

My Nalini maasi had a daughter called Natasha and there was some talk about sending me and Natasha to a boarding school. I somehow liked the idea, because I felt that I needed to reinvent my life. I was eleven then. My mother had been to a boarding school when she was eight and a half years old. At the time when the discussion happened, I was all for it. Natasha and I were the same age and very close.

First, we tried getting into Doon School. I went for the exam. The principal then was a gentleman called Gulab Ramchandani who was my mother's uncle. I gave the test, but I was very bad at maths and got a zero in it. It was a multiple-choice test and you really can't get zero, so I don't know how I managed that! My mother got the letter about my results and again I saw her crying. Later on, I realized that I had misunderstood the format of the questions. I didn't understand that we had to pick only one of the options. Or maybe, I was just dumb as hell. The principal wrote a very emotional letter to my mother, and told her that he had tried his level best to get me through, but even he couldn't justify a zero in a subject to the school board and get me into Doon.

So then everyone said, let's put him in a boarding school closer to Bombay, in Panchgani. There was a school called New Era. Dimple's and Rajesh Khanna's daughter Tina (Twinkle Khanna), also somebody I knew as a kid because my mother was friends with Dimple, used to study there. Dimple suggested that Natasha and I could go there. So off we went. I was actually very impressive in my interview. The one thing I could do well, because of my aunts and my mother, was speak English better than most kids my age. So whenever I had to impress anyone, I could do it—if I dropped my guard, that is.

At New Era, I was put in Kanga House dorm which was for seniors, because I joined in the eighth standard. The school followed the Bahái system of education, and it had a motley mix of age groups. When I walked into my classroom, there was an eighteen-year-old and I just couldn't understand that. I remember feeling quite disoriented on day one. Then I got ragged that night which was fine. Some kids put me in the bathroom and locked the door. But soon they realized I was very scared and so didn't treat me too badly.

I met this kid called Ali; he was the only one who wanted to take care of me.

He asked me if my parents were dead.

I said no.

He asked, 'Are they divorced?'

I said no.

He said, 'Do they hit you?'

I said no.

He said, 'Then why are you here?'

I realized that this school had kids from different backgrounds who were trying to fit in. Or maybe, that was the perception I had. I remember asking Natasha—she was in another section of the school: 'Are you okay?' And she said, 'Yeah, it's a bit different but I'm getting along.'

But I was disoriented. On the second day, I realized I just couldn't do it. This was not me. What was I doing here? I had a sinking feeling.

I felt I couldn't stay there any more. I remember weeping loudly during assembly so that the principal would take notice. I was taken to the principal's room and was asked why I was crying so loudly. And I said, 'I want to go back home. I want to talk to my mother.' You were not allowed to make calls home because children had to go through this phase of feeling homesick. But I was too miserable. I wept so much that they allowed me to talk to my mother. And my mother said, 'You know, Karan, I was in a boarding school too, you must be strong and brave.' She gave me a big pep talk.

But the very next day I realized it was not working. I met Tina, who was very boisterous, completely in control, and very popular in the school. She'd already been there two years.

She said, 'Karan, do you have your tuck money?'

I said, 'Yeah, I do.'

She said, 'Then just run away!'

I said, 'But how can I just run?' I had never done something so drastic in my life.

I was not a naughty kid, I was the good boy, the quiet child, the introvert, the one who the teacher never knew existed in her class.

So I said, 'No, I can't do it.'

She said, 'Trust me, that's the only way. How much money do you have?'

I had around 300 rupees.

She said, 'There's a slope down the gate, you head down that slope, and go to the bus stop. The bus will take you from Panchgani to Mahabaleshwar, from there you can catch a train. Buy a train ticket to Bombay, to Dadar, and from there catch a cab and go home.'

I kept saying, no, no, no.

But she said again, 'Trust me, that's the only way.'

That night I couldn't sleep. Then I thought I should do that. I was dying to go home. I never knew that anything could happen to me if I went ahead with this hare-brained scheme. Imagine a kid just leaving like that. I wouldn't do it today. I don't know what made me do it then.

So I got up in the morning, took out my money, put it in my bag, got out of the Kanga House dorm and went to the gate. I opened it and for some reason I started running. I didn't know it was such a steep slope, so I slipped and rolled down. There were three watchmen right there at another gate. I was caught and brought back to the dorm. That morning, in the assembly, the principal actually said that there was this boy from Kanga House who was trying to run away but he'd been brought back. He told the children, 'If you try to run, you will get caught.'

He made an example of me. I was a mess that day. I had failed in my attempt. I was ashamed of myself. The school called my parents. My father came down; my mother had an angina attack—literally. She had to be rushed to hospital. My father came in his car to Panchgani. I still recall the moment. I was standing right at the slope, just like that scene in *Taare Zameen Par*, which, by the way, was shot in the same school. I wept buckets when I saw the film because it brought back such a flood of memories. I remember seeing my father in his red car, a second-hand Toyota Corolla (a car that always reminds me of my father). I ran up to him, panting and puffing because I was so overweight. 'I beg you, please take me home,' I kept saying.

He said, 'No, you must stay, Mummy has said you must try.'

Natasha and I went with him to this hotel called Hill Palazzo that weekend. Actually, my father wanted to bring me back home as much as I wanted to be home. But he was scared because my mother had warned him that he should not be weak and that I was too spoilt.

He fed me, took care of me, talked to me, asked me if there was any problem in class or in school. Saturday passed. Sunday came. On Monday, I had to go back to school. That Sunday night at about seven, my father came with some mangoes that he had brought from home. He began cutting them and giving me slices to eat. I was burning with fever because I had just built it up so much in my head. I had about 101 Fahrenheit fever. I was eating the mangoes and weeping. Even my poor father started crying. I hugged him and told him, 'Papa, please take me back home. I can't do this. I want to be with you, I want to be with Mummy, and I promise I won't eat.'

Because I was so fat, one of the things I said was that I would not eat for one month. For some stupid reason, I thought if I said I would not eat for one month, they would be happy. Which parent would be happy if their child didn't eat for one month!

My father called up my maasi and asked, 'Should I bring Natasha back, because I'm bringing Karan back?' She said, not at all. Natasha was much stronger than I was. Natasha said, 'I don't want to go home.' So Natasha went back to school. My father didn't tell my mother but he brought me to Bombay the next day.

We reached home and rang the doorbell. My mother opened the door, saw me, went to her room and banged the door shut. I will never forget that moment—the shiver of fear that ran through my head, my heart, my spine. And she herself was ill. My father knocked on her door, but she wouldn't open it. I knocked too, crying, saying, 'Mummy, please open the door.' Her validation meant everything to me. Eventually, I went to my room and just sat down there.

That evening, finally she called me. I don't think I can ever obliterate that conversation from my memory. Her opening line was: 'Do you want to be mediocre all your life?' Then she said, 'You're a mediocre student. You have no interest in sports. You don't make friends. Do I want to raise a child who never made any difference to the world? Do you want to make a difference to this world or not? You can do anything you want, Karan, but you have to do one thing well. Either sing well, or be a hard-working student who does well in economics, or play a sport well. But you don't do anything well. You don't want to. You just want to hold on to me. I cannot bear this. I cannot bear that my child is not good at anything.'

'What are you good at?' she kept asking me. 'Tell me, what are you good at?'

I looked at her . . . what could I say? She was right. She had always been positive, she would encourage me to try everything, to join a sports camp or an art class, but I would always leave it. For some reason, I was not motivated to do anything. I was so caught up in my own head about being overweight and effeminate that I was resisting any interaction with the outside world.

There was a spot in my house that overlooked the Queen's Necklace. It was a beautiful view. All our big discussions used to happen by this window. That was where my mother was sitting and speaking to me. I was sitting in a chair, crying. I used to cry almost every time my mother opened her mouth. It was not as if she would be screaming or shouting, but I would cry anyway. I cried a hell of a lot as a child. So she just said, 'Okay, fine, I'll put you back in the same school [Green Lawns].'

I had left Green Lawns to go to boarding school and my mother had to really beg the principal to take me back and tear up my leaving certificate. Because, technically I had left the school and it would have to be a fresh admission. But there was a change of principal. Sara D'Mello, who is now very actively into charity in Mumbai, was being replaced by a lady called Kiran Bajaj. Sarah D'Mello remembered that I was a very good, shy, quiet, well-behaved child, and she said she would pretend that Karan never left the school. She tore up the leaving certificate. So I came back to Green Lawns.

On my very first day in the eighth standard, I was a bit of a joke. Everybody said, 'But you had left the school!' I had been given a farewell party and here I was, back in literally five days!

Till the eighth standard when I went to the boarding school I was considered a big snoot in Green Lawns. I carried my own tiffin and I didn't speak to anybody. I had just one or two friends.

I was always in A division (2A, 3A, 4A, 5A). But due to a secretarial error they had put me in 6C, which was where I first met Apoorva, who is today the CEO of my company, Dharma Productions, and my closest friend. For some reason, in Green Lawns—not that it was a class or ethnic divide or something—A and B always had more, how do I say, kids whose parents were professionals, while C was all about new money. They put me into 6C by mistake. I knew the A and B kids.

It was a time when I was going through all my own traumas. So when I was displaced to 6C, I was miserable. One of the reasons for my going to boarding was that I was in that division. 6C was full of gregarious kids. All the people I know today, by the way, were from that division. There was this girl called Amisha Javeri and of course, Apoorva Mehta. All the 6C kids used to share their lunch—*khandvi* and *dhokla*—while my mother would pack ham and cheese sandwiches. They would ask me what I was eating and I would say, 'It's non-veg!' They were all vegetarians. They used to eat together, whereas I never talked to anybody. So I was doing miserably in class. My mother met the school principal and said that Karan was very unhappy (because I used to get back home and cry). I kept saying I wanted to be in 6A.

The 6C kids were a lively lot. They would get together as a group and visit places like the Elephanta Caves. Actually, they were fun. I was the one who was not. I was this South Bombay, elite Malabar Hill snooty kid. Nobody talked to me because I was this snob. The truth is, I had a complex. So to cover that up, my defence was to come across as a snob.

I remember the moment when Sara D'Mello came to class and said, 'Karan Johar is new in this class and nobody is his friend. Who will be his friend?'

Nobody put up their hand for a while and then Apoorva put up his, and I went and sat next to him. He said, 'You should share your tiffin with us.'

I agreed.

Then he said, 'But get veg food, okay?'

So my mother started giving me vegetarian sandwiches and rolls, and brownies, and I began sharing them with the other kids. Slowly, I got a little integrated into the class and I became quite close to Apoorva.

Then I went to boarding school. When I came back from boarding school—I was about twelve then—Apoorva and I became best friends.

He said, 'I really missed you, why did you go away? What is your problem?'

He, me and a boy called Sanjeev Binakiya became like a solid group. Sanjeev was the topper in class, Apoorva was also quite bright, and I was getting there. Apoorva always made me laugh. He is really, genuinely funny. Today, we work together on a daily basis, so I take that part of him for granted but he brought joy in my life during those years. I used to look forward to our telephonic chats after school when we would bitch and giggle about the teachers and other students. Literally giggle like schoolgirls on the phone.

Green Lawns had a club called Interact Club, run by a Miss Doris. It was all about elocution, debate, drama, for people who were interested in that kind of thing. School used to finish at two and the club would meet from two to four every Thursday and Monday afternoon. I had been observing this club for a whole year but felt too shy to be a part of it. The first day I rejoined the school was a Monday. I went to the club, wanting to go in, but for some reason, just hung around by the glass door—you could see right through it. Miss Doris was conducting the class, and she saw me.

She pointed to me and said, 'You!'

I kept staring at the class, there were about thirty kids inside.

She repeated, 'You, why do I always see you lurking in the corridor, why don't you come in? Either you come in or you go away! Don't just stand there and stare at what we're doing. Do you want to join Interact Club?'

I said, 'I don't know.'

She said, 'All right, just sit here in front of me. Today our activity is called Just a Minute.'

She brought out a big bowl which had little chits in it. (There is a scene in *Kuch Kuch Hota Hai* which is based on this.) Everybody had to pick out a chit and speak for a minute, extempore. You couldn't pause. She had an hourglass for the time. I was the last person to speak. Miss Doris said, 'Just come and do it. Try.'

My chit said 'Mother'—exactly what happens in *Kuch Kuch Hota Hai*. I was in a very vulnerable place, but I just started speaking. I don't now remember what I said, but I know that I made everyone clap. Nobody had heard my voice till then. But here I was funny and emotional.

And Miss Doris said, 'Do you want to join the club?'

I said yes.

She said, 'Okay, but then you have to wear the badge.' She gave me a badge and told everyone that the club had a new member now—Karan Johar.

So I joined the Interact Club. And I began loving it. Among the other children, there was a boy called Tapan Mehta, then Rohan Arthur and Bernard Paes. All of us were good at debates.

About two months later, while I was in class, a peon came and said the principal wanted to meet me. It was about one-thirty and school got over at two. The last class was left. I said I had a class, but I was told that the principal wanted to meet me urgently. My heart started beating fast—I was a nobody; nobody really knew me and now the principal wanted to meet me? And this was the new principal. So I went and found Miss Doris sitting there with Mrs Bajaj who said, 'Karan, Doris has something to ask you.'

She said, 'Do you know any poem by heart?'

I said, 'Yes, I know "The Highwayman".'

She said, 'Do you know every word by heart? Can you recite it?'

I said yes.

She said, 'Okay, don't recite it now. Rohan Arthur is sitting outside, call him in.'

I went and called him.

Then Miss Doris said, 'Today is the preliminary round of the inter-school elocution contest. Tapan Mehta has backed out because he has typhoid, so I want Rohan Arthur and you to go.'

I said, 'Now?'

She said, 'Yes, the school car will take you to the YMCA Churchgate. Go and recite the poem and we'll see if you qualify.'

I was nervous as hell. I called up my mother from school and told her that they wanted me to go for this inter-school contest.

She said okay.

So Rohan Arthur and I left. All the big Bombay schools—Cathedral, St Mary's, Campion, Bombay Scottish (incidentally, all these schools had rejected me)—were there.

A familiar-looking boy came up to me and said, 'Hey, I'm in Scottish, which school are you in?'

I said, 'Green Lawns.'

I was trying to place him when he said, 'You're Yash uncle's and Hiroo aunty's son, aren't you?'

I said yes.

He said, 'I'm Yash uncle's and Pam aunty's son.'

I said, 'Oh, you're Adi.'

I had seen him at birthday parties but I had not met him for about two years.

He said, 'I'm reciting "The Great Dictator".'

I said, 'Oh, I'm reciting "The Highwayman".'

Oddly enough, he sat next to me which was interesting for the way things happened later in life. But this was the first time I really interacted with Adi.

Anyway, I recited 'The Highwayman'. Both Rohan and I qualified for the final round. About thirty of us qualified from various schools, including Adi. But when the date for the next round came out, it clashed with his final exams' and Adi couldn't take part.

We had a month in which we had to write a speech. The topic was how drugs were deadly for society or something like that. I loved writing, so I wrote it. It was my mission that I should write a good speech.

The big day came. All the teachers from various schools were there. I can't remember if parents were allowed or not, but my parents were not there. Rohan and I represented Green Lawns. We all said what we had to. I thought I had done a good job. Actually, everybody spoke well. The standard was very high. It was a big competition. The judges included people like Pearl Padamsee and Shernaz Patel. For that time, for a school-level competition, it was a big deal. As they started announcing the results, I was all ready to leave. They announced the third prize, second and then the first prize. That was the time my eardrums went numb because I thought I heard my name.

'From Green Lawns High School,' they said, 'Karan Johar.'

I still remember sitting in the chair, looking at the ceiling in shock. I could feel somebody nudging me. I got up, and like a zombie, I walked up to the stage. I remember the huge cup that was put in my hand. I remember one of the judges hugging me. But everything else was a blur.

We came outside where Rohan's maid was waiting for us in a cab. So he, me, and that big cup got into the cab. We drove from Churchgate to my house. I rang the doorbell and my parents opened the door because I was late and they were getting anxious (those were the days of no mobiles). I stood there with this cup. My mother stared at me and I blurted out, 'I came first.'

She burst out crying.

I had never won anything till then.

My father took photos and phoned the entire world. I still remember him dialling people and telling them that Karan had come first. My mother couldn't get over it; neither of them could believe it. That night my father put the cup next to my bed, and all night I stared at it, thinking I have won this big cup! The next day, Mrs Bajaj addressed the assembly. Normally, she never addressed the assembly; it was always the head boy or a prefect or class head, but this time she came and said that for the first time in the history of the school, we had won an inter-school elocution competition and this feat had been achieved by a child called Karan Johar. She called me on to the stage and I was an instant star. If there was a shift in my destiny and my life, it was that cup. Coincidentally, the school's inter-house elocution was just two days later. I was not even in the running but I had won an inter-school competition! My house prefect came up to me and said, 'You're speaking the day after.'

From then onwards, I was in every inter-house and inter-school competition, not only in elocution but also debate and drama. It became a given that if Karan Johar was participating, he would win. I was winning everything. I became the most popular kid in my class. What I couldn't do in sport, I did on the stage. I was the best speaker in Hindi elocution, English elocution, in inter-house debates, inter-school debates—I was all over the place. My whole personality changed. I became more friendly, though I continued to have the old problems of feeling effeminate and large, but they became diluted and were suppressed by this feeling of elation that I had achieved something.

By the time of the tenth standard board exams, I had become a much better student. My confidence level had increased. And that translated into my marks. I was topping subjects (barring maths which I could never get my head around).

I had friends coming over. I was invited to all the parties. My life changed. I changed.

Looking back, I'd say the defining moments of my life were coming back from the boarding school, my mother's lecture, and winning that first cup.

Then came the final time I would be participating in a school elocution contest. I remember the head boy saying that this was the last time we would be hearing Karan Johar speak. I had reached that level of superstardom as a speaker. And my speeches were always very funny. At the end of that final speech, everyone clapped. When I got off the stage, I remember feeling very strongly that I was going to be famous. I remember this thought crossing my mind. I don't know why, but I just felt that I had some kind of aura that was transmitting itself. I felt that I had developed a kind of vibration, an energy that attracted people to me. What had happened was that the shift in my life had brought about a change in my own energy, in my own sense of self. Whenever I walked into a room I felt a lot more looked at, and many more people would come up to me than before. I'm not sure if it was just about my success in these elocutions or debates, but my aura had changed. I had become more confident in my own skin.

When I stood up on stage and performed, I felt like a movie star. The moments when I got a gold medal or won the first prize or got those certificates because of my abilities on stage were my biggest highs. I realized I enjoyed the spotlight. Shy and introverted as I was, and awkward about so many things, but when I went on stage I was very confident. I never had stage fright. I could completely blank out the audience in front of me and perform. I had that ability, whether you call it a gift or whatever.

The other high was when I acted in a TV serial after my board exams. That was also my first-ever meeting with Shah Rukh Khan. My mother said, 'Why don't you do something during your summer holidays?' So I enrolled in a couple of courses. Those days, computers were new, so I did a computer course. Anand Mahendroo, who is a TV writer and had made *Isi Bahane* and *Idhar Udhar*, was making a serial called *Indradhanush* at that time. He called my mom and said, 'I believe you have a really fat son.'

She said, 'Yeah, it's puppy fat, he'll lose it.'

He said he needed a fat boy for a role so could I come and audition?

He was somewhere in Lokhandwala. I was a Malabar Hill child, so for me it was the other end of the city. My mother said she'd send me with the driver. She didn't know what the serial was about or anything. So I reached at ten in the morning and Anand was in the edit room. I waited from ten to two. An assistant came and made me go through the lines, saying that Anand would take my audition later. There was a young man sitting opposite me, smoking, drinking many cups of coffee and doing a crossword. I found him familiar but couldn't place him. I was also shy and awkward, so I didn't look too much in his direction. Anand walked out at two and went straight to this person and said, 'I'm really sorry . . .' But this person said, 'No, I was just hanging around doing my crossword. I wanted to tell you that I don't want to do TV.'

Anand said, 'You sat here for four hours to tell me you don't want to do this serial?'

He said, 'Yes, I don't want to do it. I want to focus on films.'

I was seeing all this and didn't know what to do. Should I look away? I decided I should.

Then Anand came up to me and said, 'Oh, you're Hiroo's son, come along.' He added, 'Look at these guys, they think no end of themselves. You know this guy? He's Shah Rukh Khan, he was in *Fauji*, he's not even good-looking. This guy that I have, John Gardner, I'm renaming him Akshay Anand, he's going to be in my serial. He's much better. Don't you think he's better looking?

At face value, Akshay Anand was better looking than Shah Rukh! Anyway, what could I say?

Anand took my audition and I did the serial. I enjoyed it. But I remember one thing that really threw me off. There was an actor called Lilliput. He took me aside one day and said, 'You're a very good actor but you're very effeminate. *Log aapka mazaak udayenge*. Your hand gestures are very effeminate.'

That stuck with me. And I stopped acting. After that when I was offered some TV work I said no. I didn't want to come across as effeminate. I associated it with abnormality. Nobody said 'gay' those days but effeminate was the insinuation to make at that time. I was called 'pansy'—which is that you're not like a man.

And then came college admission time. I got into St Xavier's. But my mother had a meltdown about how boys didn't do arts. Apoorva told me, 'Come to H.R. College of Commerce and Economics, our gang is there.' My entire gang from 6C was there in HR. If I was not going to be able to do arts at Xavier's, then I'd go to HR. My father then managed to get me into HR. I was back with my school gang. Apoorva and I did all five years of college together.

Coloured clothes were what made me go through hell at the beginning of college. When you wear coloured clothes, all your body issues get enhanced, because in a school uniform, you could be different shapes and sizes, but basically, everyone looks the same. But when you get into coloured clothes and walk into junior college, that's when being overweight gets magnified. I realized I had to lose weight. So I went on this ridiculous Atkins diet, and I think my metabolism suffers till today because of that stupid diet.

College was a lot of fun because of Apoorva and our group of friends. By then, I had become even more social. Transformation happens. I was popular in college. Apoorva was the first among all of us to learn driving (I tried but failed miserably) and we used to go for long drives. It was a big thing those days. We used to go and eat ice cream, do regular things. Today when I hear of kids doing drugs, I think we were so innocent. I didn't drink. I never smoked. Drugs, not at all. They were nowhere on the agenda. What an innocent childhood and youth it was! We were a genuinely 'vegetarian' bunch. We were friendly, we went on picnics, to beaches, on trips to Mahabaleshwar, and ate strawberries and cream. We watched movies, went to plays. There was no such thing as alcohol or drugs, or anything decadent or debauched about us. Maybe there should have been! I am sure even in our time, there were kids who smoked and drank and did drugs. But we always thought they were the bad boys. It was a strange divide in my head. If you smoked and drank, you were not well brought up.

I was very popular, and participated in many extracurricular activities. I was someone who attended college. Others didn't but I was very diligent about it. I wanted that experience. I loved the idea that I could meet all kinds of people from all kinds of places, from all cultures and subcultures across the city.

Simultaneously, my father's film career carried on, though not very well. He had given about four or five flops and I knew we weren't going through the best of times financially. While I was in college, my father produced *Agneepath*, which although touted as a big hit turned out to be a big flop. My maternal grandmother had passed away and we had to sell her flat to recover the losses.

So while I was having a good time in college, I was also seeing my father's morale drop because he was going through a very bad patch professionally. What he lost in films he was compensating with his export business, but I saw him go through depression. I saw the film industry break away from him a little. I saw people not inviting him to parties and events, not giving him the best row at premieres. He would ask me to call up the cinemas to check on his seats. And invariably, his seats were not good. So I would end up going with a friend. He would not attend because I would tell him that the seats were not good. I saw his disappointment with the fraternity, though he tried not to show it to us because he was a strong man and did not want anyone to know of his troubles.

I started learning French at the Alliance Française. I thought it would help my father's business because he had a lot of clients in France. I thought that was pretty much my path, that I would join my father's business and work in the export firm. Movies were a no-no. My mother had drilled it into me that movies were the last place she wanted me to go. That was because we were having such a hard time in terms of money and dealing with the losses. My mother had made up her mind that that was not a zone she wanted me to be in at all. So the focus was on my father's export business.

I also joined public speaking classes at the Nazareth Public Speaking Academy, which was in faraway Dadar. An elderly gentleman, a teacher called Andrew D'Souza and his wife, Clara, used to do voice coaching classes. One day I struck up a conversation with him. He took me aside and told me that my gestures were very feminine, my hands flapped a lot and that my voice was very squeaky. He said that he and his wife did a lot of voice coaching. He said, 'We can coach you and I can bring a baritone in your voice.'

So I started going to them for voice classes. I didn't tell my father or mother about this. I told them I was doing computer classes because I had to pay the fees to the Nazareth academy. Somehow, I didn't feel they would understand why I wanted to do these classes. For two and a half to three years, I went there twice a week. My teacher would say, 'Imagine that you're living in a box, now make sure your hands don't get out of this box.' He would make me gargle every day, he taught me how to project my voice, and slowly, my voice started changing. What started with a forced baritone stuck, and today I still speak with a certain baritone. It's not my real voice, the baritone was brought into it by this couple. They became a big influence on me not just because of this one thing or the music—they would sometimes make me listen to opera—but because they also trained me to be a little more masculine. This was part of a process that I understood but which we never spoke about. Subconsciously though, my body language changed, it became a little stronger— Mr D'Souza told me that otherwise I wouldn't be able to deal with the outside world. Somehow, he put this thought into my head. I was not the most masculine kind of person but my voice changed, my hand gestures improved, and he gave me the confidence to be out there. I hid this part of my life from almost everyone. I felt that this was my thing and no one would understand what I was doing and why. I never told a soul. They were a wonderful couple. Then Clara died of a terminal disease. I was shocked. I hadn't met them for a month, because it was the summer vacation. Mr D'Souza became really sad after her death and stopped taking classes. But he had done his job, in a sense, by helping me immensely. Of course, only I could see the funny side when my father would tell everybody that I was doing computer classes!

Apoorva and the gang were Hindi film buffs. We'd go and watch every film together. I remember in the holidays of 1988 how I went running to watch *Qayamat Se Qayamat Tak*. I fell madly in love with Aamir Khan and Juhi Chawla. In 1989, I went for the premiere of *Chandni* because we were invited. Yash uncle and my father were very close. I was mesmerized by *Chandni* and *Maine Pyar Kiya*, and later by *Hum*

Aapke Hain Koun . . ! Both Aamir and Salman arrived on the screen
in 1989. Shah Rukh came in 1991, and I wasn't a fan of his at all.
Ironically, I liked him the least. But Apoorva did. I was Team Aamir
and he was Team Shah Rukh. There were girls who were obsessed with
Shah Rukh and there were people like me who were mad about Aamir.
I was not a Shah Rukh Khan fan because I thought he overacted. I
didn't like him in *Deewana*. And Apoorva used to say: 'Aamir is so
boring, what do you like about him?' We had these fights about Aamir
and Shah Rukh as if they were our relatives and we had to take up
cudgels on their behalf. They were very passionate fights. I had this
Parsi friend who told me, 'Shah Rukh has the cutest ass and an Adam's
apple to die for.' So when I met Shah Rukh later on the sets of *Dilwale
Dulhania Le Jayenge* and gave him Levi's jeans to wear, I told him that
this was what my friend had said about him. He was shocked. I told
him to open the front buttons of his shirt, because my friend had said
he had a really nice Adam's apple. I also told him that she said he had a
really nice ass but he didn't highlight it ever. 'So you should wear tight
jeans.' And he went, 'Uhh . . .'

Adi, I remember, nearly fell off the sofa because I said all this with
a lot of innocence. Shah Rukh went all red with embarrassment. But
it's so strange how everything pans out in your life. Now when I meet
Aamir, I tell him, 'You don't know how crazy I was about *Qayamat Se
Qayamat Tak*!' And Sridevi, my god, I was a retarded fan of hers. I never
put up any posters in my room, but if ever I had, it would have been
Sridevi's. I saw *Mr. India* about a hundred times. And *Chalbaaz* about
fifty times.

The other war we always had was about Sridevi and Madhuri. I
was Team Sridevi and Apoorva was Team Madhuri. He was always in
the opposite team. So this Hindi film mania was a big part of college.
Watching movies, then discussing them at length afterwards. Even
secretly dancing to the songs. I used to dance in my room to Hindi
movie songs. I attempted to dance to '*Hawa Hawai*' many times in my
room. I had a little mirror and I would stare at myself dancing. I was a
complete closet dancer.

I already had a sense of rhythm because of my mom. She used to hold my hand and make me dance when I was a kid. And I think Punjabis have dance in their DNA anyway.

Despite all this, it never crossed my mind that I could have a future in films. It had to actually do with geography, so to say. My friends were not from the movies. So I also looked at movies the way they did. It never crossed my mind that I should make a movie or act in a movie. I knew I couldn't act, I didn't have the physicality for it. And direction? I thought, me? Not at all. Then fleetingly I went through a phase when I thought I should be a comic actor because I had done plays. But this was just that—a fleeting thought. When I decided to direct a movie, it came as a shock to all my friends. They never saw it coming.

Yes, as a child, I was in the company of star kids. I knew Hrithik, Abhishek, Shweta, Zoya and Farhan. I was always closer to the girls, Shweta and Zoya. The boys were very bratty, especially Abhishek (he is four years younger than me) and Farhan. I never really got along with them. I never liked them. And Adi and gang always spoke a lot in Hindi. That was something I couldn't bear. I used to come back to my mother and tell her, 'Mummy, they speak only in Hindi! Don't send me to their house.'

She would say, 'What do you mean they speak only in Hindi?'

I said they were very filmi in their talk; that they would say things like '*Tune* Kranti *dekhi hai kya? Kitni acchi film hai!*'

I found this constant talk in Hindi rather downmarket and uncool. I told my mother that I would not talk to these kids.

I loved Shweta and Zoya because they were cool. Zoya was one of those full-on cool chicks, and Shweta was lovely, fragile, feminine, soft, very comforting to talk to. We used to chat a lot. I had fun times with Zoya but spent more time with Shweta because we used to go on family holidays together. When I was ten, I went with Jaya aunty, Shweta and Abhishek to Dubai for ice skating. Shweta and I would hold hands and ice skate, and Abhishek used to come charging into us and nearly break our bones. He was always like that. Shweta and I would sit quietly and bitch about him.

For me, Amit uncle was always this demigod. I looked at him with awe. But Jaya aunty was like a mom to me. However, despite knowing all of them, I always felt that I was not part of the film world. I connected with them as people. I liked and enjoyed their company. But nothing more. If anything, I always felt a lesser person in front of them. Because we were producers, and producers were not considered strong forces in those days at all. As a producer, you had to be extra nice to everybody. My father used to tell my mother to be nice to these people, because he was working with them and had to get his work done. So it was never a feeling of equality.

3

First Break: *Dilwale Dulhania Le Jayenge*

I was miserable. It was almost the end of college and I had decided to work for one year in my father's office. I realized that this was the life that my parents wanted for me but I knew I would get bored in an office environment. Understanding the technicalities of exports, the typewriters, fax machines, appointments, meetings, it was all so mundane. I thought, how am I going to do this, this is not who I am, I am not meant to be confined in this box they call an office. I was all about ideas. I didn't think of movies at that point but I wanted to try drama or advertising, something creative because I knew that was what I was.

In the last year of college, I had made a friend called Anil Thadani who's now a famous distributor, and Raveena Tandon's husband. He was best friends with Aditya Chopra who I had had fleeting encounters with in the past. Adi was in Sydenham, and we would sometimes meet in the train. He would catch the train to Juhu and I would catch the one heading home. We had had some conversations. Anil and I were very friendly because he knew my father was a film producer; and his father was a distributor, so there was a film connection. Anil used to call me for trial shows or previews which was where I started bumping into Adi. Over a period of time, Anil, Adi and I became really close.

We became a tight unit of three who would watch almost every film and then talk about it over dinner. Suddenly I found myself getting sucked into the world of Hindi movies, something which my mother didn't like at all. She loved Adi and his family, but she never understood why I was suddenly going off for late-night movie screenings and dinner, and talking for hours about those movies.

Adi's passion for Hindi cinema did not just amuse me, it amazed me. He told me how, when he was a child, he thought everyone in the world made movies. He didn't think there was any other profession. I thought differently because I was so removed from the film industry. But there was a subconscious, hysterical Hindi film fan hidden inside my large body, just waiting to come out. That happened when I met Adi, because his life was Hindi cinema. He has no other life, even today. He is obsessed with making movies and telling stories. I had never met a person like him. I was actually like him but I had repressed that part of me. Now when I look back, I think my parents had dissuaded me to such an extent that I had pushed it down even more. Adi brought it right up to the fore, and then it exploded. I remember there was a phase when all my South Bombay friends like Apoorva felt a little alienated because I was going a lot to Juhu and Bandra to meet Adi. But my whole life was being pulled in that direction. I realize now that at that point of time, I got a little distanced from my original gang. My school friends would meet, but I was more drawn to taking a cab and rushing to Juhu or Bandra at the drop of a hat to meet Adi and Anil. I could tell that I was drawn towards that world much more. Then I tried to combine both my groups of friends. Now when I look back, I realize that time, I was just following the beats of it. It's not something that I was consciously doing, it was just happening.

And they were overtly expressive about their love and affection for me. When you are making exciting new friends who love you, and who beg you to come over, you will feel drawn towards them. Nobody had done that to me before. Even though Adi is such an introvert, he opened the doors of his heart and home to me. I felt very loved. They thought I was a funny guy who had an opinion and was completely crazy about movies.

Even now, when someone I admire and respect shows so much affection, so much excitement about me, I don't know how to react. I am a little in awe of that emotion. Adi used to tell me that I had low self-esteem issues. Now of course, he claims I have high self-esteem issues, which is all rubbish!

Adi and Anil used to talk about the film business a lot. I didn't know that side of things—flops, hits, this distributor, that distributor, all these terms of the film fraternity, the business part of it. All this came to me at a much later stage of my life. I had lived my life away from it; my mother had kept me away. Now suddenly, through these friends, I was thinking of and talking about films all the time.

Though I used to go see films with Apoorva and my college gang, discussing films with Adi and Anil was quite different. They took it very seriously. They treated it like a business. They were in the film business, after all. Anil was a distributor's son. Adi was a film-maker's son. For them, films were not just mere topics of discussion. They wanted to know whether a film would be a hit or a flop. But they loved my take on things. I would react to a costume in a film, the sets or the art direction. And they used to say, but who is looking at those things? Nobody did in those days. And then I used to say funny things about what I thought of this actor or that actress. It was not that I looked down upon mainstream cinema. I saw all the *Himmatwala*s and all those crass Telugu and Tamil remakes avidly. But by the time I got to know Adi and Anil, Hindi cinema had entered into a new phase with a slightly different sensibility. This was around 1992–93. Often, when I saw the movies that they used to obsess about, I'd think they were rubbish and I'd say so. Like a film called *Sapne Saajan Ke*—it was a Rahul Roy–Karisma Kapoor movie—and I told them it was rubbish. They told me that I didn't understand and that it was going to be a big hit. I said it would be a big flop. And it was.

Soon they started entreating me to tell them what I thought. We used to have dinners and discuss movies till three and four in the morning.

Adi and Anil couldn't believe that a South Bombay boy who wasn't in touch with the movie industry had such strong opinions about Hindi movies. I knew all the songs; I was as knowledgeable as they were. My group in college was also kind of filmi, so I was with it—I had watched everything and I had strong opinions. During this phase of my life, I realized how much I enjoyed talking to Adi and Anil. With Apoorva and gang, it was more casual, it was part of a general discussion. But here, it was a big deal—if I didn't like a movie, I had to tell them what I didn't like and why.

I met Manish Malhotra at a film set and became really close to him. So there was this sort of film gang that had taken over my life. I made Manish meet Adi and Anil, because he was also from the film business. He used to come and tell us about heroines because he would be doing their clothes. So it was a happy gang of people who were discussing movies. All this was during my last year of college.

But I still hadn't thought of joining films—not till Adi asked me to.

I will always say that if I'm grateful to anybody, it's Adi, because he saw something in me that I myself didn't see. Neither did my parents. I didn't know I had it in me. Adi was the one who told me I was a film-maker, and why I was not doing anything about it. I swear on my life, my career, on everything, it had not crossed my mind. I never thought that I would be a film-maker, *never*. I had thought of fashion designing, and therefore costume designing was in my head somewhere.

After my college exam, I went away for two months to London. My mother felt I should travel. The whole idea was I would join Papa's business when I came back. I was there for two months and it was great. I discovered London. I walked on the streets, and felt a sense of liberation. I had a certain amount of money which I had to live within. My mother felt it would be good for me to handle my own life. I stayed with a relative. I would watch movies and plays. Those two months opened my mind out to the West because I hadn't travelled much till then. I was so busy doing a hundred things in my college, learning French, and doing a whole lot of classes. I remember there were two classes, one on import–export and the other on photography. You could choose a third for free, and I chose fruit and flower arrangement because I wanted to know what that would be like. I was a course junkie. I used to do a lot of courses. I was always rushing from one course to another. I liked to pack in my days with lots of things. I was not one of those kids who would loiter around. I was always focused about wanting to learn. I did import–export, and voice modulation. I used to do three hours of French a day, and attend college. It was only in my last year in college that I bumped into Adi and Anil, and my focus started shifting to cinema.

Anyway, I travelled to London, and came back in time for my results. As I walked into the college, I was called by the principal, Indu Shahani, who became the sheriff of Mumbai later (she also happens to be a relative of mine—my mother's second cousin's wife). She said, 'Sit down, I have some news for you. You've topped the Maharashtra board.'

I said, 'What?'

She said, 'You're a management student (because in commerce, you could do either accounts or management) and I'm so proud of you. The Bajaj Institute of Management has offered you a seat.'

I said I wanted a little time to think about it.

She said, 'Take your time but remember that Bajaj has given you a seat.'

I went back home, and there was elation in the house. My mother thought, wow, MBA!

There was much discussion. In the midst of all this, I said I didn't want to go to the Bajaj institute. I said I'd join Papa's business and see.

My father said, 'Why don't you go to France? You've learnt French. Do an additional course in French [I already had my *diplôme supérieur*].

And as I have a business there, I can get you in touch with people. Stay there for six months. We have an office there, why don't you work there as an intern?'

So it was all set up for me.

In the meantime, Adi had begun writing his first film, *Dilwale Dulhania Le Jayenge*. He came to me and said he wanted my inputs on the film. I was doing my paperwork for going to Paris at the time.

He said, 'I want your ideas.'

I said, 'My ideas?'

He said, 'I think you can help. I don't want to take advice from an old film person.'

My mother said, 'I hope you don't ruin this for him; it's his first film. He's such a big film-maker's son. What ideas are you going to give?'

I said, 'I don't know.'

Adi would come from Juhu to Malabar Hill which is an hour away and we used to sit every day, the whole day, for four weeks, and just talk. I would give my inputs, he would take notes. It was so much fun. He was writing the film, fleshing it out.

I was now three days away from taking the flight to Paris. One night Adi called me—we used to chat a lot at night on the phone—and said, 'You know, Karan, can I say something? Don't go to Paris. Assist me on the film.'

I said, 'Assist you on the film?'

He said, 'Why the hell are you not realizing that you were born to be in the movies? You're overdramatic, you're melodramatic, you're funny. The only thing you don't have is an interval because you have this non-stop mad energy. You're meant for the movies. You were always a big fan of the movies. You'll be a film-maker one day. Why can't you see it? Why don't you listen to me? Assist me, gain this experience and make a movie of your own.'

I hadn't thought of this at all.

So I said, 'No, no, don't talk nonsense. I can't, I'll speak to you tomorrow.'

Unsettled all night, I kept tossing and turning, thinking of our conversation.

My father used to wake up very early in the morning. At seven-thirty I went and sat with him. To my father, I could say anything; it was my mother I was afraid of. I said, 'Papa, what if I didn't go to Paris? How much money have you put in?'

At that time, he'd put in eight to ten lakh rupees. It was a lot of money. He had made a series of unsuccessful films; it wasn't as if the money meant nothing.

I said, 'What if I don't go, and assist Adi instead?

He repeated, 'Assist Adi? But he himself is making his first film. What will you learn from a new film-maker?'

Those days you were supposed to work with senior guys in order to learn film-making.

I said, 'Papa, I've been part of the writing process. I'm extremely attached to that film. I don't want to regret that I didn't give this a shot.'

He said, '*Karan, yeh bahut mushkil industry hai. Bahut saare paise chale ja sakte hain.* It's not dependable. Are you sure you want to do this?'

I said, 'If you allow me, I want to.'

Then he said, 'So much of my money has gone on people I didn't even know. You're my son. You're asking me for one year of your life. What is money? Even if it goes, it's fine. If it'll make you happy, I'm fine. That's all I want. But after a year if you feel *kuch nahin ho raha*, don't linger in this industry. At the right time, pull out and come back to the business or do something else. But don't linger.'

'Who's going to convince Mummy?' I asked.

He said, 'You leave that to me.'

And my father set up this whole act in the evening. He told my mother, 'I don't want Karan to go. Last time you sent him away, you saw what happened. I'll miss him too much. I'm also growing old now. I want my son to be around me.'

My mother got very emotional. Later, we told her about my assisting Adi, and she freaked out.

But my father said, 'Hiroo, give him this one year, *na. Kuch nahin hone wala hai.* He's not cut out for this industry. He won't be able to handle the sets.'

Since it was Adi, Yash uncle's and Pam aunty's son, my mother finally said yes.

This was how I began my journey in Bollywood, as an assistant director to Adi. I'd catch a cab, go to Adi's place, into the world of Yash Chopra's house. All they did and spoke about was movies. I was totally mesmerized by the *duniya* of Hindi films. And their level of passion. Yash uncle was passionate about food and movies. Pam aunty was also entrenched in that zone. For Adi and Uday, it was all about Hindi movies, Hindi movies and more Hindi movies. I was totally sucked into that world. Soon I started losing touch with my college friends.

I got into my job as an assistant: schedules, planning, prepping.

Then came my meeting with Shah Rukh Khan. After that meeting in Anand's office, I had met Shah Rukh once more. This time with my father at the shooting of *Karan Arjun*.

Adi took me to him, and he said, 'Oh, you're Yashji's son, I remember meeting you.'

At that time, he was deciding whether he should do *Dilwale Dulhania Le Jayenge* or not. Of course, he agreed. I had one or two meetings with him and then the big day came, my first day of shooting on the set. All the prep work hadn't prepared me for what it was going to be like. This was Filmistan Studios, and we were shooting with Kajol for the song '*Mere Khwabon Mein Jo Aaye*'. I was very close to Kajol, and she was very comfortable with me. But I was new to being on a set. Now on a set if you don't have a job to do or you don't know exactly what you're supposed to do, you feel like you're in everyone's way. It's like being on a station where everyone's running around, and you have to know where you're going. If you don't, you could be tripped on, you could be bumped into or you could feel completely disoriented.

I had done all the creative work with Adi but the on-set modalities were new to me. I was given the clap and I didn't know where to stand. So I was screamed at by the cinematographer for being in the way. Then I was given the responsibility to write the continuity but I didn't know which column to write what in because I didn't know what a camera was, I didn't know what a lens was, and I didn't know how to describe the shot. Uday was a big help because he had been an AD (assistant director) before on a film called *Aaina*. So he knew what to do. But I was lost. At three in the afternoon, I thought, this is not my world, I cannot do this. My father was right. My mother was right.

That evening when I was sitting with Uday, and we were drinking, Uday said, 'Why are you looking so lost?'

And I said, 'Because I'm not meant to do this. I'm going to tell Adi that this is a big mistake. I quit going to Paris, we let go of so much money, but this is not where I'm meant to be. I don't think I can do this.'

He said, 'It's just your first day.'

I said, 'No, it's not me.'

I had made up my mind.

But because the next day was a really early-morning call, I told Uday, 'You know, Adi is tired right now. But first thing in the morning, I'll tell him. I can't do this. It's a mistake.'

He said, 'Are you sure?'

In the morning I went to Adi and said I wanted to speak to him about something. He was rather stressed about the scene he was going to shoot. Plus, he'd just been told that that particular day Shah Rukh was coming to give one shot; his date had come through. He had to give that waving shot when Kajol imagines him outside her door when she comes home after her Switzerland trip. He was coming for just that shot. Adi was really stressed about how he should compose the shot. I tried to talk to him again but he said, 'Why are you stressing me out, speak to me at the end of the day.'

So at lunchtime I told Uday, 'I can't tell him right n

Uday said, 'Forget it, just go through the day. You'
one. Go through day two as well. Don't tell him.'

But I was ready to just get up and leave. So I said, 'Shall I just go:

He said, 'You can't just leave. He's your friend. He will be so upset.'

At lunchtime Adi called me.

He said, 'Listen, Karan, Shah Rukh's not happy with the guy doing the clothes. Can you go to the costume *peti* and get something unused? Get a sweater from Chandni's costumes for Shah Rukh for this shot.'

I was most excited. Chandni and Rishi Kapoor! I was a big fan of both.

After lunch, I went to the peti. I found this red-and-white sweater which I loved. I didn't like any of the other sweaters. But this one had a big hole. So now what to do? In the same peti, there was a blazer with an emblem on it. I made the costume dada remove that emblem and put it on that sweater, which I thought would look nice. And it did. The sweater actually looked kind of cool with the emblem. I was so excited. It was like I had created a garment. Then I hoped Shah Rukh would be okay with it.

Soon Shah Rukh walked in, being his easy, breezy, accommodating self.

He said, 'What a cool sweater! Why don't you only do my clothes, yaar?'

He told Adi, *'Itna achcha sweater badal diya hai.'*

I had also got two or three jeans which I had gone to the market and bought.

I told Shah Rukh, 'You wear very baggy jeans. You should wear tighter Levi's, they'll give you a better fit. [He used to wear Wrangler jeans.] Trust me, you'll look nice.'

He wore them, looked in the mirror and kind of liked what he saw.

He said, 'Why don't you do my clothes?'

So Adi said, 'Will you do that?'

And I said, 'Yeah, I'll be happy to.'

And then I suddenly felt I had a mission.

I thought, my god! Maybe this is my calling. I should become a costume designer. This is it!

I was so excited about doing Shah Rukh's clothes.

And then Adi said, 'Why just him? Why don't you take charge of the entire costume department of the film?'

'My god!' I exclaimed to Uday. 'This is it. Now I know what I'm doing in this film. I'm doing the costumes.'

He said, 'From an assistant director, you're going to become a costume designer?'

And I said, 'I'll learn, na.'

From then onwards I had a mission. But I was so attached to the film that I had one hand in the creative arena and one hand in costumes. Pam aunty and I would work on the women's clothes together. I would go and buy bangles from the Goregaon market and match them with bindis. Nobody did such things those days. The make-up artist used to get the bangles and the people who did the hair would get the other stuff. No one person sat and matched bangles with costumes. And the second half of *Dilwale Dulhania Le Jayenge* was full of Indian costumes. The production would give me a certain amount, but I would spend my own money and get better things. I'd also pick up things for the supporting cast—Faridaji, Himani Shivpuri . . . Kajol's clothes were being done by Manish Malhotra who was a friend. But I was doing the clothes for the other people in the film.

Then came the time when we were doing the climax in the month of April. There was a speech that Shah Rukh had to deliver to the father, *'Babuji, aap theek kehte hain.'* That speech.

Adi asked, 'What do you think the take of this speech should be?'

I said it should be like the Julius Caesar speech, you know, Caesar's an honourable man, etc. It should be sarcastic, it should be like, 'Yes, I'm a liar, so what if this liar loves your daughter like no one else. So what if I'm a *deewana*. So what if this deewana, *paagal*, liar, loves your daughter. I'm still a liar, still a liar.'

Adi liked the idea.

He said, 'Why don't you write it?'

So I sat down and wrote it and Adi took it from me and modified it. He kept 80 per cent of what I wrote and put in his own 20 per cent. And gave it to Shah Rukh. Now Shah Rukh always knew me as this aesthetically sound but very South Bombay person. He was very fond of me. I was very different from the other ADs. I spoke his language, I got his jokes. He used to find me really funny. I used to say these strange, funny things. I was a good narrator of stories.

When he came on set, he said, 'Adi, what a good scene, yaar!'

And Adi, in front of everyone, said, 'He wrote it,' pointing to me.

Shah Rukh looked at me and said, *'Tune likha hai? Hindi mein likha hai?'* Then he said, *'Lekin teri Hindi toh itni kharab hai, jaise tu baat karta hai.'*

I said, 'My written Hindi is good, not my spoken Hindi.'

He said, 'You wrote this scene?'

He asked me three times.

He said, 'I can't believe you've written this scene!'

He did the scene and from then on, I think something changed in the way he viewed me. He started taking me more seriously. After that, he would run every scene by me. He would act it out in front of me and I would give my opinion. Then he'd go and act it out for Adi. I developed a solid bond with him.

The moment he accepted me as a possible resource was the moment when Adi told him that I had written that scene. And I have to say that very few film-makers would give this kind of credit to an assistant in front of everyone. But Adi was so confident in his own skin and had such large-heartedness about him that he did. And that one incident changed the way Shah Rukh looked at me.

I enjoyed the company of the people I was working with. I loved Shah Rukh and Kajol. I loved Adi. I loved Uday. I liked the people on the set. I loved Yash uncle who was always there on the set. He reminded me of my father. It was strange but Yash uncle and I from the very first day struck this wonderful rapport which lasted till the very end. He was really like a father to me. I was very close to him. In fact, it took a very long time for me to deal with the fact that he's gone. Somehow, my father's death didn't shock me and shake me up as much, because he was diagnosed with cancer, but with Yash uncle I was just devastated. Even now, when I think about him I go into this trance because he was like my one-point contact on a daily basis. I would touch his feet every morning. With him and Pam aunty around, I never felt like I missed Mom and Dad. I'd been sheltered and protected all my life, but I never missed home because they made me feel at home.

I liked the work, the atmosphere, but I loved the people more. The work was great because I had been part of the writing process with Adi; I had seen him create the film in his head. So when I was standing there on the set, I could see the film unfolding in front of my eyes.

Seeing that oh, this scene was like this on paper and now they are acting it out like this, was just so exciting. I felt like I finally belonged somewhere. What I missed in not having a sibling or the loneliness I had felt, all that empty space was being filled by Hindi cinema and by these people. I had other friends I loved and I had had great times in college, but somehow I just felt more at home in this atmosphere. All my passion for Hindi film music, for Hindi films, was coming together. And this was probably my calling. I had never acknowledged it or addressed it. As a child I had continuously heard that 'Hindi films are not good for you, you lose money, it's not a dependable industry, look how much Papa has lost, you should have a stable job, a solid profession, or you should get into business.' I'd heard my mother say these things, and she was right. She was not saying anything wrong; she was guiding me in the right direction because we had burnt our fingers in the movie business.

I'd seen my father depressed, I'd seen my father upset, I'd seen him hurt, I'd seen him wronged by people. I was almost cynical about the movie business. But I had not dealt with this younger generation, nor had my dad. My dad had never dealt with a Shah Rukh Khan, who was kinda cool. He wasn't a regular movie star who had a regular secretary whom you had to work on and bribe to get his attention. He landed up at our house! He came and hugged me. I was just an AD, and my father was surprised that Shah Rukh had come to his AD's house for dinner with his wife, Gauri. My father said, '*Shah Rukh ghar pe aaya!*'

Shah Rukh and Gauri liked me. They used to pick me up and we would go out. And my dad would say, '*Tu kal Shah Rukh ke saath gaya? Very good. He took you out, he paid?*'

I would reply, 'Yeah, he paid.'

My father said, 'But you should pay.'

I didn't know how to explain to my father that it was cool with this generation. But, for my father, it was different. Somehow, I always felt my father had this need to look up to somebody, because he had been a production manager. Even after he acquired his huge producer status, at heart he remained a very simple production man.

My mother would go hoarse trying to tell him, 'Yash, when will you act like a producer and not a production manager?'

But he would just say, 'This is who I am.'

If a star was holding a bag, he would pick up the bag out of habit, and my mother would die of embarrassment. But it was his instinct. He would rush and do things like he had to do them, even if it had nothing to do with him. He was that kind of a man, the first man at the funeral, taking charge of everything, the first man at the wedding, taking charge of the wedding, whether he was related or not. He was like that. Everyone in the industry has a story to tell about him. He was the most loved and popular man because he was just always doing things for people unconditionally and selflessly. Ask any random ten people who have been in the industry for a while about him, and they'll tell you a story about him. Ask Salman, Shah Rukh, Aamir, any old actor or actress, and they'll have a Yash Johar story to tell. 'I was stuck in this place and he helped me.' 'I was in need of something and he came to my rescue.' I've got fed up of hearing 'Your dad did this for me, your dad did that for me.' He was the quintessential do-gooder and he did it selflessly without wanting any brownie points.

Looking back, I feel I have more memories about *Dilwale Dulhania Le Jayenge* than I do of any of my own movies, because it was my first film-making experience. I remember every costume and the thought behind it. I remember buying that leather jacket with Adi for Shah Rukh and contemplating whether we should spend 450 or 300 pounds on it, something we wouldn't even think about today! But at that time, I remember what a big decision it was to buy that Harley Davidson jacket. Every day of that film is entrenched in the recesses of my brain. I remember so many details. Kajol's make-up man not being there, and Kajol doing the make-up herself for the first five days, me combing her hair on the outdoor set because she didn't have a hairstylist. I remember interacting with all the character actors; it was a daunting task dealing with them. There was a girl called Chutki in the film, Pooja Ruparel; I remember dealing with her mother. I remember being so afraid of Amrish Puri. The first question he asked me on my first day was what time it was. So I told him the time. He said, 'No, what time is it in the scene? I have to set my watch accordingly.' I said, 'Well, it's a puja scene, so it must be around seven-thirty in the morning.' Then he asked me, 'What's the weather? Because I'll place my shawl accordingly.' I thought, oh god, I should ask Adi these questions! Should I even be giving these answers myself? I remember sitting with Shah Rukh and reading out the scenes.

I still remember the beginning of the Gurgaon schedule where we shot the song '*Tujhe Dekha Toh Yeh Jana Sanam*'.

Shah Rukh landed late at night. He knocked on my door at three in the morning when I was fast asleep.

When he came in, he said, 'Listen, Adi is sleeping, I don't want to disturb him. Let's go through the scenes.'

So from three to five in the morning, we sat with all the scenes of that whole schedule.

I remember Kajol had just started dating Ajay at that time and she would take me aside and confide in me. There were no mobile phones those days, so she'd have to go and make her calls.

Then I remember the London schedule, the Switzerland schedule. I remember the jacket I used to wear, I remember the jacket Adi wore.

That time, Adi was dating a friend of mine who had given me forty cards, and I had to give him one for each day of the outdoor shoot. There was so much romance on the set; it was like a film about love surrounded by love.

I was part of the costume division, so I'd sit with the costume dadas. Does it fit, does it not? We were a small crew—those days we didn't have large crews that went abroad. We'd be climbing up those snow-capped mountains with costumes in our hands, changing things at the last minute if the colour wasn't working.

And then acting in the movie myself. I was playing Shah Rukh's friend which I was forced into doing though I was quite happy about it.

How can you have any objectivity about a film you are so deeply involved with? It was Adi's vision and Adi's film, and we all loved Adi. I loved him from my heart; I could have died for him. I was that crazy about his vision. So when he thanked me at the Filmfare awards, I was, of course, weeping in my seat. He thanked his parents, he thanked Shah Rukh and Kajol, and he said my best friend, Karan Johar, without whom this film wouldn't have been possible. I remember being a mess sitting in my seat. I remember Abhishek sitting next to me with his mouth open, probably wondering, why is he weeping like this? I was so proud of *Dilwale Dulhania Le Jayenge*; the premiere was such a big deal, then it went on to become this legendary blockbuster, and it's still playing in the theatres. What a journey!

We were on this big outdoor shoot in Switzerland and London. By then, Shah Rukh and I were spending a lot of time together. Adi even told me, 'You know, he's growing very fond of you. You should think of doing a film.'

But I was all set to be a costume designer. Being a director was not on my agenda. I thought to be a director you had to work on the set for something like six years.

One day, we were just sitting around. I remember it was very cold, it was snowing. We couldn't shoot because we were waiting for some equipment to arrive. I was with Shah Rukh. He was telling me about his parents, about his life, about Gauri. By then, we had gotten really close. Shah Rukh was an insomniac, and I was all about pleasing him because I was so mesmerized by him. I kept thinking, 'The more time I spend with him, the more it'll nurture me.' So I used to be up with him till five in the morning, then report as an assistant in an hour's time. My sleep pattern had gone for a toss but I was high on the work I was doing. I was high on the film, I was high on this new phase I found myself in.

I developed a really strong bond with Shah Rukh more than with anyone else. Gauri had also come to the outdoor locale. Shah Rukh had introduced me to her as the coolest, funniest guy he knew. Gauri and I also got along well together. I spoke French and we were in the French part of Switzerland, so everybody in the unit was impressed that I could speak to people in the local language and even get better deals on farms to shoot in. The locals would get most impressed that this boy from India spoke the language so fluently. Yash uncle would take me everywhere for production meetings.

For Shah Rukh, I was like this Bollywood-born boy who spoke French, and had this sense of humour. Gauri was averse to film people but I was not plain filmi. I was cool.

One day, they gave me the day off just to take Gauri around because she was the star's wife. And it was the best day ever because I entertained her, I regaled her with my stories, I spoke nonsense. She came back and said, 'I want to get to know this person. He's the only person in the industry I've met who is so much fun.' Shah Rukh was so excited that Gauri liked somebody in the business!

So we were just sitting around that day, and he said, 'You know, Karan, you should direct a film.'

I said, 'You really think so?'

He said, 'You're a film director, you should direct a film. You have a very good instinct for writing. You're a very good writer. And you'll be a very good director, because all you need to do for that is to write. And if you make your first film, I will act in it.'

Kajol stepped in at that point and asked, 'What are you talking about?'

He said, 'I was telling Karan, that just like Adi, he too should be a director. And that if he does his first film, I'll act in it.'

Kajol said, 'Yeah, I too will do it, because it's Karan.'

He said, '*Chal*, we'll do it after *Dilwale*. The next film we do together will be Karan's film.'

I thought, they're talking nonsense, what are they saying? Me, a director? I'm just an assistant on this movie. I have a long way to go.

I said, 'After five to six years.'

'No,' said Shah Rukh. 'Immediately.' He was by that time working with my father.

I came home from that shooting stint, and my mother was very happy to have me back. I had been gone for two months. We were waiting for Papa to have dinner. When he came, he was so excited to see me. Then he said, 'You know, the strangest thing happened. I had a meeting with Shah Rukh for *Duplicate*. And he said that I don't want to do one film with you, I want to do two films. But the choice of director for the next one will be mine. Who is he going to suggest?'

I said, 'I don't know, I really do not know.'

So he said, '*Woh mujhe kal mil raha hai*. He wants to sign another film with Dharma.'

My father was excited and happy because Shah Rukh Khan was a big star and he was already doing *Duplicate*. And now he wanted to do one more film!

Anyway, that meeting never happened. Two or three months later, I was still assisting. *Dilwale Dulhania Le Jayenge* was on the cusp of release. One day, my father said to me, 'Shah Rukh has called me to his house. Today.'

He went for the meeting.

Next morning, when I woke up, my father called me and said, '*Shah Rukh paagal ho gaya hai.*'

I asked, 'Why?'

'He told me that you should direct the next film that he does. And he says he will start it right after whatever commitments he has.'

I said, 'Me?'

My father said, 'He was very serious. *"Aapki film mein karunga Dharma Productions ke liye, aur aapka beta direct karega." Lekin tune to ek hi film ki hai. Kya seekh ke aya hoga ek film se?*'

I said, 'I don't know. *Papa, woh aise hi bol raha hoga.*'

He said, *'Nahi, bahut serious tha.'*

Then my mother woke up. My father told her about it.

She said 'What? You, directing a movie? Now? But you've just worked on one film till now. What nonsense!'

I said, 'I don't know what he's talking about.'

She said, 'This is ridiculous.'

Anyway, the *Dilwale Dulhania Le Jayenge* premiere happened. Shah Rukh called me up after the premiere and said, 'See, it's October 1995. I'm giving you dates in October 1997. You have two years to write a film.'

I told my father, and he said, *'Kya bakwaas bol raha hai!'* Then he said, 'Don't assist any more now. Write.'

Adi told me, 'Are you stupid? Shah Rukh Khan has agreed to do your film. You know what that means?'

I said, 'But which film? What film? What am I making?'

He said, 'Shah Rukh has said you don't assist any more.'

I wanted to assist on one more film. But he said, 'Don't assist, write.'

I was overwhelmed. I thought, oh my god, Shah Rukh actually wants me to make a movie with him. A part of me was ready, a part of me pretended to be shocked. But in my heart of hearts, I think I knew—I can do this.

Suddenly, it seemed simple to me. It was strange, it didn't seem that daunting. I thought, you write a story, record the songs, shoot them, have cool people to execute things for you, get a director of photography. It's not so bad. I can make a Hindi film. *Dilwale Dulhania Le Jayenge* had been my training ground, my film institute.

Everything and anything I knew was from there. Actually, I didn't know much. Even today, I'm not very sound technically. I never got into that. For me, it was always about telling a story. I understood scale, I understood grandness, I understood what a cinema experience should be. I understand the whole beauty of celluloid, I understand the whole magic of taking a beautiful shot. I guess I was always inclined towards that aesthetic. But yes, my training ground was definitely *Dilwale Dulhania Le Jayenge*. I had visited a film set all of ten times in my entire life before that. These were visits with my dad, there was a bit of saying 'hello' to everyone, and that was it. It was the Chopras who inculcated that love, and ignited that passion. Whatever I know about how to conduct myself in a music sitting or on a set, I learnt from Aditya Chopra and then Yash Chopra because I also spent a lot of time with him.

Luckily for me, the magic happened again, with my film *Kuch Kuch Hota Hai*. Within a matter of three years, 1995 to 1998. Both films released in October, the same month.

The lives that Adi and I have lived after *Dilwale Dulhania Le Jayenge* are simply amazing. Where we started out and where we are now. Both best friends, both kind of responsible for the other. I may not have matched up, but then I went and made a film that was also loved. And today, both of us are still actively working, running two solid production houses. And we are still very, very close. It's a very layered equation, but the love is intact.

4

Kuch Kuch Hota Hai

I was supposed to come up with an idea for my first film and present it to Shah Rukh by January 1996. Nothing happened. In March–April of that year, Shah Rukh was shooting for a film called *Chahat*, which Mahesh Bhatt was directing, in Jaipur. He called me and said, 'Come and tell me your idea.'

But I had no idea. I kept thinking, what should I do? Then I thought, what have I not seen of Shah Rukh? It struck me that I had not seen him as a father. Sometime back I had seen an English film, *Jack and Sarah*. It was a British film, where this man loses his wife when she's delivering their baby, and he is left with his child whom he doesn't want initially, but eventually builds a bond with. He then falls in love with another girl. I liked that space—*biwi mar jaati hai, aur bachcha aa jaata hai, aur phir* Shah Rukh has to find another girl who completes the family. That was the idea I had. So I thought I would tell him this and buy time.

On my way to meeting him, I was thinking of scenes; it was then that the 'just a minute' scene came to my mind, about the mother and that chit. And I thought, what if this child gets a chit that says 'Mother' but her mother is dead? How would that scene be? By the time I reached Jaipur and met Shah Rukh, this was the only scene I had. I said to him, 'I see you as a father, I see this child . . . and . . . it's an emotional film.'

56

Then I narrated the scene about the chit. I improvised on the scene while I was narrating it. I said, 'She gets "Maa" and she stumbles, she can't say anything and then the father comes and starts saying that a mother is this, a mother is that. Your mother is your shoulder, she's your support, she's your strength. But a mother is someone we don't have. But we have me, and that's more than enough for the both of us.'

As I narrated it, Shah Rukh got very teary. I think he was thinking of his own mother. I had struck the right chord, and I myself got moved by the whole narration which I had just thought of while talking to him. I remember sitting on the white marble stairs of Rambagh or whatever palace it was in Jaipur, narrating the story that I had had no idea of until moments ago.

'I'm doing this movie,' said Shah Rukh. 'You should make a love story. Tell Kajol.'

I came back to Mumbai. I spoke to Kajol about it. She said, 'Yeah, whenever you're ready, I'll do it.'

I started thinking: both Kajol and Shah Rukh have said yes to me; are they mad? But they were quite serious. Shah Rukh had given me dates as well, October 1997.

With the hero and heroine finalized, I finally started the process of writing. What else could I do? Months passed, nothing happened. But by the end of the year I had to narrate a story. So I left for London for a long stay. Before I left, I met Adi, and he said, 'Why are you making a film about a father and a dead mother? Make a young film, you're a young boy, it's your first film. What is this father and dead wife and child?'

So I said, 'I have this other idea too.'

I was very taken up with Archie comics. I told him I had this idea which was about Archie, Betty and Veronica. A tomboy kind of girl, this other girl and a guy.

So he said, 'Yeah, write that.'

I went to London. I was trying to write the first half about Archie and the two girls, but I kept thinking, what happens in the second half? I spent two months in London. I had discovered the city earlier and I loved it. I lived in a rented apartment. My father had managed to get it at an affordable price. I was alone. I kept walking, writing furiously, thinking, going to Hyde Park, sitting there on a bench, thinking, thinking, thinking. I was really at my wits' end. I had these two ideas, but it wasn't working. What was I going to do? What was I going to narrate to Shah Rukh and Kajol?

One day, I was walking past John Lewis on Oxford Street when suddenly there was a eureka moment. I thought, I have two stories—one for the first half of the film and the other for the second. I have two stories but they are actually one film. I just need a flashback. The flashback is the college part. And the second half is where they're older, where the wife has to die. I went rushing to my apartment and started listing points. Then I came up with the idea that there would be these letters that the mother leaves behind for the child, and that would be what connects the two halves of the films.

I had to tell this to Adi.

I collected all the one-pound coins I could, went to this red booth right below my apartment and called Adi. I kept putting in the coins and telling him the story.

I said, 'The mother leaves eight letters behind for her daughter. When the daughter grows up, she brings his friend back into her father's life, this friend who was this tomboy he knew in college, while he had opted for the hot chick. But by then, that girl has been engaged to somebody else.'

Adi loved it. 'Karan, this is brilliant,' he said. 'It totally works. You should come back and flesh it out.'

By the time I caught my flight back, I had the first half in detail in my head. All the things I had grown up on, all my memories, went into the film. My love for Raj Kapoor was in the first line of the film: *'Mujhse dosti karoge?'* My love for Yash Chopra was in the second half, in the palatial house, with all the elements that I'd grown up watching, all the music that I had heard. My love for Archie comics, my fixation with the child finding her mother, all this just crystallized in my head and became *Kuch Kuch Hota Hai*. After I came back, I started structuring the second half. It took me two months. Finally, I was ready to narrate the story to Shah Rukh and Kajol. I did this at Shah

Rukh's old house in Amrit Apartments, and they were both transfixed. I narrated every single line. I had taken two assistants with me: Nikhil Advani, who had been my senior in school and had joined me after somebody's recommendation; and this kid Tarun Mansukhani, who later made *Dostana*. These were the only two people in my team. They took notes constantly, because I used to change the details every time. I kept improvising a lot of it as I went on, that's what I always do.

Both Shah Rukh and Kajol loved it. By now, it was March 1997, and Shah Rukh said, 'I'm still on for October '97.' With the script and the cast almost ready, I officially announced my first film. Adi gave it the title *Kuch Kuch Hota Hai* when he heard the story. We were a group of friends—Jugal Hansraj, Manish, Adi and me—and Jugal came up with the title song's tune. It all just fell into place seamlessly.

Kajol and Shah Rukh were a legendary love couple. So the hunt began to find this other girl. I approached my friend Tina Khanna who has always mesmerized me. She listened to the story, took three days to think it over, and then said, 'I don't think I should do this part, because Kajol will . . . like, you know. I don't think I can do this part. I don't want to do the first half and then not be in the film. And everybody will remember the film for Kajol and Shah Rukh, and not for me.'

Then I went to every leading lady in the business—Raveena Tandon to Tabu to Aishwarya Rai to Karisma Kapoor to Urmila Matondkar. But nobody wanted to do that part. I was very depressed. What was I going to do? But it's strange how life is so full of coincidences.

One day, Adi called me and said, 'There's a new girl in a promo for a film called *Raja Ki Ayegi Baraat*. A girl called Rani Mukerji. Just see that promo.'

Two hours later, Shah Rukh Khan called me and said, 'There's a girl called Rani Mukerji, and I've just seen one shot of her where she says, "*Raja ki ayegi baraat*". There's that one expression she gives . . .'

I thought, what's with this girl, that both these guys called me at different hours of the day and suggested her name to me? So I decided to have a look. I waited and waited, and finally that promo came and I saw her. But I wasn't sure. Adi said to me, 'Listen, she's doing a film called *Ghulam* with Aamir. She's got one good film. This film may not be great, but that is an Aamir film. Why don't you go and meet her? You don't have a choice anyway.' So I took Nikhil and Tarun again, and went all the way to Lokhandwala and beyond to meet Rani Mukerji. I rang the doorbell and it was opened by a five-foot-nothing little girl. She hadn't looked so short in the promo. I narrated the first half of the film to her. She said she'd take two days to think over it. I thought, even she's going to say no. But if that were so, I would be happy because she was a little dumpy. I also thought she was not right for the film. I started my hunt again.

Two days later, Rani called me and said, 'Can you come and meet me?' So I went back.

She said, 'How will you convince an audience that Shah Rukh loves me over Kajol?'

I said, 'Leave that to me.'

Then she said, 'You know what. I really like the part. I want to do the film.'

And I thought, she's saying yes? What should I do, because I'm not so sold on her? Manish had told me—he had worked with her—that 'she's short. How will you make her look sexy as a college bomb?'

Anyway, since she'd said yes, I thought, *chalo*, we'll work hard. Now I had to cast the other guy. Who was going to do that special appearance in the second half? I went to Saif Ali Khan and gave him a big narration.

He said, 'You know, this role is of an NRI. I want to play an Indian kind of role. I don't want to play this western, anglicized, hip, cool guy. I want to be more Indian, commercial.' So he said no. Then there was this actor Chandrachur Singh. There had been a little hype around *Maachis*. There was a lot of talk like 'he's a young Bachchan' and all that. So I called him. He said he'd get back to me in two days.

When he called me back, he said, 'Can you come to my house? I live in 7 Bungalows.'

Now I was a South Bombay boy; I didn't know 7 Bungalows was an area in Bombay. I thought he lived in seven bungalows.

So I said, 'But which one do you live in?'

He said, 'I live in 7 Bungalows, come here.'

I said, 'Yeah, lovely, but which one do you live in?'

He said, 'No, no, the area is called 7 Bungalows.'

He must've thought I was crazy. Anyway, I reached his place and narrated the story to him. He asked for two days. I went back after two days. But he said no. I was depressed again. I'd cast the girl, but who was going to do the boy's role?

One night I went to a party in Chunky Pandey's house. I had become friends with him through Gauri, who knew Chunky's sister-in-law. Everybody was asking me about my film.

I said, 'But I have to cast this other boy and I don't know who I'm going to cast.'

Salman Khan was there at that party.

He asked, 'What happened?'

His sister, Alvira, had told him that Karan was in search of an actor to play this other guy's role—a twelve–fifteen-day part.

Salman said, 'What role is it?'

I began telling him.

He said, 'Nobody's going to do this role. No hero will want to do this role. There's only one idiot in the industry who'll do it, and that's me. You know, my sister says you're a nice guy. Come and narrate it to me tomorrow.'

I thought, Salman Khan? Now who would have thought of it? My father said, *'Paagal hai? Woh kabhi nahi karne wala.'*

Salman was shooting for a film called *Jab Pyar Kisi Se Hota Hai* with Tina. I went to meet him there on the set.

Salman asked Tina, 'Why didn't you do the role that Karan offered you?'

She said, 'It was not good.'

Then Salman said, 'He's coming to me about a role, that role is also not good.'

I sat with him the whole day. He took me home. I met his mom, who I knew well. Everyone said, *'Arre, Yash aur Hiroo ka beta aaya hai.'*

Salman said, *'Picture likhi hai usne. Narrate karne aaya hai.'*

So I went to his room and started the narration. I gave a very sincere, heartfelt narration of the first half. I used to give very theatrical, opulent narrations. This was my first film, so I put my heart, soul, muscle, everything into it.

After one and a half hours, Salman said, 'You want some water?'

I said, 'Yeah.'

He went out, brought some water and gave it to me. While I drank, he looked at me and said, 'Superb narration, yaar!'

I just choked on that water and said, *'But aapka part toh second half mein hai.* You've not heard your part.'

I got scared. I started thinking, I hope he's not thinking I'm narrating Shah Rukh's role to him.

He said, 'No, I know what your film is going to be all about. But I'll do it for you. And more than anything, I'll do it for your father, because he's the nicest guy in the movie industry.'

I looked at him and said, 'You're doing the movie?'

He said, 'Yeah. You pay me what you're paying Kajol.'

I said, 'But I wouldn't be able to do that.'

Then we reached some kind of agreement.

'But I'm doing this film for you and your father,' he said again. 'Mainly for your father. Go home and tell Yash uncle that I'm doing this for him.'

So I walked out in a daze and called up Adi. Adi, too, was surprised. 'Salman Khan is now doing the part? Do you know the cast you have now? You have Shah Rukh, Kajol, Salman and a new girl.'

And that's how the cast fell into place.

Early in the morning, at six-thirty, on the first day of shoot, I came out of my room and found my mother sitting in the hall. I said, 'Why are you awake so early?'

She said, 'I wanted to get up before you go.' Papa was getting ready to leave with me.

I said to her, 'Come for the mahurat shot.'

But she said, 'I haven't slept. Come and sit here.' Then she held my face and said, 'You know what you're doing, na? You know where to put the camera?'

I said, 'Yeah, Mama, I know.'

She said, 'Even now, it's not too late. If you don't want to do this, don't. I'm very scared. You have to know what you're doing because it's a very big thing to make a big film. And look at the cast you have. You are sure you know where to put the camera?'

I said, 'Yeah, yeah, I know.'

She said, 'You're fine, na? You'll do this?'

I said, 'Yeah.'

She hugged me and I left. I reached the set, and we were to shoot the song 'Koi Mil Gaya'. Farah Khan was choreographing it. Kajol called me to her van and said, 'Karan, you're a very soft person. And in film-making, it's not easy. You need to be a leader. You need to be authoritarian; you need to control the set. So I have a great idea. When you reach the set, for the first five minutes you scream at me. Whatever you do, you scream at me.'

I said, 'How will that help?'

She said, 'Because, you know, I am the biggest spitfire. Nobody dare scream at me. You know how I am. If they see you screaming at me, everybody's going to take you seriously.'

I said okay.

At the set, everybody was there doing rehearsals. Then I screamed at Kajol, 'Just focus, Kajol! Keep your focus, okay? You have to get the steps.'

She said, 'Yeah, yeah, I'm really sorry.'

Everybody turned to look. But when Kajol smilingly went back to her mirror, I turned around and burst out laughing.

Shah Rukh said, 'Have you gone mad? Why did you scream like that?'

Then I said, 'No, she told me to.'

All of us just couldn't hold our laughter. So it completely defeated the purpose.

But somehow, that kind of cemented everything. I was okay, because I was always a bit of a leader. The confidence I had developed in school leading a team to a debate or whatever helped. I was fine.

I was in the most exciting zone of my life. The work was good, the actors were cooperative. I don't have any story of struggle in the making of that film because it was a smooth experience. The shoot started when it had to and the film headed towards release at the right time.

In the midst of all this, *Duplicate* released right before *Kuch Kuch Hota Hai*. And it was a big flop. All the distributors of *Kuch Kuch Hota Hai* pulled out of the film. They thought I hadn't been able to help my father although I was on the sets of *Duplicate*. But it was not a film that excited or interested me. It was not the zone I was in, creatively. I had had nothing to do with it, barring helping out here and there whenever Shah Rukh asked me to. The film bombed. At that time, we were shooting in Ooty for the summer camp part of *Kuch Kuch Hota Hai*. My father was very upset. When the distributors pulled out of the film, Yash Chopra, who knew what my film was all about, stepped in and took over a lot of India territories and the overseas, because he had faith in me. He felt that I was making something special because Adi had told him that this film was going to be a hit. So my father got immediately compensated because Yash Chopra stepped in at the right time.

Adi was a big help when I was editing the film. He sat with me through the edit. I remember the first half was ten minutes too long, and Adi came and cut it for me. Then I took charge of the second half. I went through a bit of a struggle while editing it because it was a long film. I had to crunch it down, hold the emotion. Finally, we came down to the adequate length of the film. When the film was ready in its rough-cut stage—before it goes into post-production, which is background music and other things—nobody except Adi had seen it.

We had a screening for my mum and dad. It was just the four of us—Adi, me, my mum and dad. They were nervous as hell. A lot of money had been put into the film. A lot was riding on it, because my father had dealt with so much financial loss, even with *Duplicate*. This was something of a last-ditch attempt. If this went wrong, we would not be able to afford making another film.

I had started feeling the pressure once *Duplicate* bombed. But I had a strange kind of confidence in my film, although I was really afraid too. I felt if this film went wrong, we would have to sell property or take other drastic measures. My father had taken heavy loans, and put a lot of our equity at stake. It was a 14-crore-rupee film at that time. That was a lot. Especially for a new director.

We were watching the film at a preview theatre called Dimple. After it finished, my parents couldn't get up from their seats. Adi got up, I got up, and then my mother and father got up. I could see my mother's feet and hands trembling; it was an emotional film and I don't think Mom and Dad could believe that what they had just seen was made by their son.

I held my mother's hand, she hugged me, and my father just broke down. The three of us wept for something like forty-five minutes. I've never seen my father cry after that. I've seen him upset, I've seen him depressed. But I've never seen him break down like he did that day. Adi quietly stepped out. There was one production person alongside, and he realized it was a moment where we had to be left alone. Seeing my father cry made my mother even more emotional, because we had never seen him like this, weeping like a baby.

Then he sat down, we gave him some water, but he was crying so much that he couldn't even bring himself to say, 'I'm so proud of you'; every time he opened his mouth, he would choke. And finally when he said those words, he broke down again. He just kept crying for forty-five minutes or so and it was an embarrassing sight. He was sixty-five and to see him break down like this was something new for me. I'd always seen him as a strong leader, a survivor.

Adi walked in after a while and asked, 'Does this mean you liked it?'

My father replied, 'It's the best film in the world. My son has made the best film in the world.'

He just kept saying, 'It's the best film in the world.' And that was all.

As for my mother, she said, 'I can't believe my son made this movie!' She kept saying, 'I cannot believe my son has done this. He created this world, and this movie.' She hugged Adi whom she had always been very fond of.

Soon after, we got down to the post-production work, and getting the film ready for release. Everything was on track. A film called *Bade Miyan Chote Miyan* was also releasing on the same Friday. It was a Diwali release.

My father decided that he was so proud that he wanted to have a premiere. On Monday, we were writing out the cards, dispatching them through production. My maasi had come to the house to help us. I went down to drop her. My mother was alone at home, even the servants were not there, all of them had gone out. The phone rang. My mother picked it up, and it was a call from the underworld. A man's voice said, 'Your son's wearing a red T-shirt, I can see him right now. And we're going to shoot him if you release this film on Friday.'

For some reason, they didn't want the film to be released that Friday; we didn't know why. It was a call from Abu Salem, and my mother was shaking with terror. She put the phone down and ran towards the door. She pressed the lift number, and I was coming up. As I came up those nine floors, she was going through really tough moments. When I reached, she just dragged me to the room and said, 'You have to call the cops. This call has come and they said they're going to shoot you, they don't want you to release your film this Friday . . .'

That evening, my father, Shah Rukh, the cops, Adi, everybody was there. The cops advised us, 'We will protect you but you have to go ahead. You can't show your fear. You have to have the premiere on Thursday.'

But my mother said, 'What does this mean?'

We were a simple family. We'd never had the underworld calling us to stop the release of a film. We'd never dreamt that something like this could even happen to us.

My mother said, 'We don't want all this nonsense.'

But we did have the premiere at Liberty. They put me in this small room, to keep me safe. The industry who's who came. It was a full turnout because my father's goodwill was so strong—everybody wanted *Kuch Kuch Hota Hai* to be a hit, for his sake. It was the first—and possibly the last time, I think—that the industry had felt so positive about a film's release. It was because of my father. He had so much love going for him.

I had always had a dream that Shammi Kapoor would come out of a car to attend the premiere of my film. I told my mother, 'You know, I'm going to see it come true. Shammi Kapoor is going to get out of his Mercedes car and attend this premiere.'

But they had taken me into this room. My mother and father were outside. My mother was so upset because Shammi Kapoor was going to come and I would not be around to witness the moment.

'My son's dream was to see Shammi Kapoor get out of a car and come for his premiere,' she kept saying. 'But because of this situation, he has to be cooped up in a room; they're not allowing him to come out.'

Shah Rukh said, 'What nonsense!'

He went inside and dragged me out. He said, 'I'm standing here in front of you. Let's see who shoots you. I'm standing right here.'

I said, 'No, no, no, my mother was . . .'

He told my mother, 'Nothing's gonna happen. I'm a Pathan. Nothing can happen to me and nothing will happen to your son. He's like my brother. Nothing's gonna happen.'

So I stood there, and Shammi Kapoor came in a Mercedes just like I had imagined. I had my moment. But my mother was very scared.

She said, 'Now go back inside. We can't do this. I'm too scared.'

So I went back. Throughout the screening, my assistants kept coming to tell me, 'Oh, they laughed here,' 'Oh, they did this,' 'Oh they did that.' But I couldn't go outside because of the threat.

While everybody enjoyed the film, I was sitting alone in that little room, with two security guards outside. I wanted to know what had happened. The film had ended, people were leaving but the security guys weren't allowing me to meet the industry. And then Nikhil and Tarun came, followed by the whole team. They said, 'Karan, the entire industry clapped. They stood up and clapped. You got a standing ovation.'

And I said, 'Well, I didn't see it.'

They said, 'There was euphoria, and they were asking for you.'

Literally, 'a star is born' moment had happened!

That night, Mum, Dad and me flew out of the country because the cops said, 'All of you should leave Mumbai. You'll be safer anywhere else.'

We took a flight to London. The film released. We were away, disconnected, in a rented apartment in London. We went to see the film in a local theatre, but it was not the same. My mother was so scared. I felt it had reached a point where she was hoping the film would flop so that it would go off the radar.

On the Monday after the release, I got a call from Adi.

I asked, 'How is it doing? What happened on the weekend?'

He said, 'What do you want in this world?'

I said, 'What do you mean?'

He said, 'What do you want to buy?'

I asked, 'What nonsense are you talking?'

He said, 'Your picture's not a hit.'

I said, 'It's not?'

He said, 'No, it's not even a super hit.'

I said, 'If it isn't a hit, it can't be a super hit.'

Then he said, 'It's a blockbuster, Karan. People are going crazy. Your advance booking lines for the next week are longer than your first week's. Wake up your parents, it's a huge hit.'

I went barging into my parents' room. They were asleep. It was early in the morning. I woke up my parents and said, 'Adi just called, it's a blockbuster.'

My father woke up and started calling distributors in India.

We had never given a hit film, not since my father's first film, *Dostana*, in 1980. That was a gap of eighteen years. From 1980 to 1998, my father never had one hit film. All of them had flopped. He had seen eighteen years of failure as a producer. He had never heard the word 'blockbuster' associated with any of his movies.

I don't know how I felt. I don't remember being very happy, but now when I think about it, I feel a sense of elation. We were in London, so I missed those first four weeks.

When I came back to Mumbai, the euphoria had subsided. But over a period of time, when I meet people, I realize the impact *Kuch Kuch Hota Hai* has had on their love lives, their kids. I saw girls with the same hairband as Kajol's, people wearing cool chains, buying those Shah Rukh T-shirts. All these things that I had created were intrinsically part of my South Bombay aesthetic and sensibility mixed with my love for Hindi cinema. Added to it was my desire to tell an emotional tale. *Kuch Kuch Hota Hai* was undoubtedly the most honest projection of who I was.

5

Early Film-making Years

When I look back, the most uneventful part of my life was between *Kuch Kuch Hota Hai* and *Kabhi Khushi Kabhie Gham* . . . I had missed out on all the excitement of my film's release and early run because of the underworld threat. I had somehow become the representative of a small new brigade of young film-makers. There was Aditya Chopra who had come before me and there was Sooraj Barjatya. But both of them were low-key and introverts. I was the only one who was a bit of a speaker. I gave interviews. I think people realized I could speak when I gave those acceptance speeches at various award shows. So people took note of the fact that here was an articulate young director. I was about twenty-six then. I came across like somebody who could make good copy. For a film director to be articulate and communicative was a new-age phenomenon. So I did a lot of press and built a lot of relationships with the media. I was so excited about what was happening in my life. I was happy to be in the limelight. It's something I've never shied away from, even today. I realize that it's a big-brand offshoot. Today, when I look back, I think I set a certain precedent for things to come. I brought the director out of the closet, pun not intended. I started that movement of bringing the director into focus. Directors were talked about in the 1950s and '60s.

There were big names like Guru Dutt, Bimal Roy and Raj Kapoor. In fact, it went right up to Subhash Ghai. Then there was a slump about discussions of directors. They were not really at the forefront of things. I think I changed that. I say this with a huge amount of modesty—it was not intentional, it was just an extension of my personality. I like to speak, and I made sense when I spoke, and I spoke a lot, and was out there giving interviews to newspapers and various TV channels. I remember the first-ever show I did was for Sanjana Kapoor. She did an Amul show for which she called me. And I said things that were interesting, sometimes funny, candid and irreverent. So it kind of built up. I built that equity subconsciously. It was not something I did purposely. It just happened.

In the meantime, I kept accumulating awards as the *Kuch Kuch Hota Hai* euphoria continued. But I think my personality doesn't allow for things to go to my head. I think it's my upbringing. When I look back, I don't know why I never developed any arrogance. I handled success really well. When you have a sense of low self-esteem, and when you achieve success, there's relief more than arrogance. There's relief that this is now my home for life. Now I can't be pushed out of this domain. I can linger here for a long time because I've done one solid film that will be considered a landmark in Hindi cinema. I feel that people from the fraternity realize that I have a lower level of arrogance than people from the outside, because when people come from the outside to Bollywood, they have no reference to context. They think that this is me, I've done it, and rightfully so. They have a certain kind of inbuilt arrogance which I think the fraternity children don't have because they have seen the ups and downs. I'd seen so much failure that I knew that success and failure go hand in hand. You can be successful one Friday and the next week things could work against you and you could be off the radar. The one way to keep yourself afloat is to have your own way of being.

Earlier, I had this innate need to be Miss Congeniality. I wanted to be Mr Popular, loved by one and all. I had a huge need and desire to be liked by everybody. I worked towards it, to be nice to members of the media, to be nice to the fraternity, to be nice to actors. Also, I was meeting people as an entity in my own right for the first time. I was so excited to belong. I think that's what I wanted to communicate. I was very excited—that when I meet Sridevi, she'll know who I am. When I meet Mr Bachchan, he might take that extra minute to talk to me because I've done something worthwhile. When I meet superstars of yore, they'll bless me with, 'So proud of you, we knew your father.' And then the actors of my generation—I can hang out with them. It was more exciting than anything else. I think arrogance isolates you. When you blend in, you're a part of the scheme of things, which is what I wanted to be. I didn't want to have a high-handed attitude, I wanted to be that accessible, amiable, affable person, and I sometimes play-acted the part, to fit in. I also created a certain personality type which stuck only because I wanted to blend in. I didn't want to be this aloof, distant film-maker. I wanted to be a socialite film-maker, and I think I did everything in my capacity to make that happen for me. I attended parties, I hung out, I made a conscious attempt to get in touch with people, plan dinners, outings, social events. I was completely in the thick of it all, and I loved every bit of it. When I look back at that phase in my life, I realize that was the time when I was actually building this personality type, which then became a part of who I was, for very many years.

After the success of *Kuch Kuch Hota Hai*, what immediately happened was that our economic status changed. We moved to Bandra and bought a larger apartment. The cars changed, and I got myself a driver. I didn't have one during *Kuch Kuch Hota Hai*—I used to drive to the sets in a Maruti 800, and I'm a terrible driver. Earlier, I used to share a driver with my father, and that changed. The clothes changed, the watch on the wrist was a little more expensive. My mum always says I'm middle class in my head, I can't change that. So she was still kind of watching her moves in terms of her expenditure. But there was definitely an economic growth. I'd say that was the first upside that my mom and dad saw. My father was an exceptionally simple man. He was never somebody who wanted material things. My mother and me are the type who enjoy the good life. So we definitely leveraged the financial rewards that came by as a result of *Kuch Kuch Hota Hai*. As far as the mood and morale go, my father was so proud and excited, embarrassingly so. At parties, he would embarrass me, pinch my cheek, and introduce me and say to the other person, *'Tune* Kuch Kuch Hota Hai *dekhi? Kitni bar dekhi? Do bar to dekhi hogi.'*

And I'd say, 'Why are you saying this, Papa?'

Then he'd say, *'Toh kya hua?* Dev Anand once told me, "It's your trumpet. If you don't blow it, who will?"'

So I just let it be. He was seeing that level of success after nearly two decades, and he deserved to enjoy it. And my mum was very happy buying her new diamonds. Mum, Dad and I travelled; we went on a holiday again after six months. Meanwhile, I had started writing my next film.

We were at Adi's shoot for *Mohabbatein* in the outskirts of London. Mum, Dad and I had gone for that outdoor shoot and that's where I narrated the central idea of *Kabhi Khushi Kabhie Gham . . .* to my parents. I wanted to make the Ramayana but in a modern milieu. One of the brothers is sent away, like being banished from the house. And the younger brother goes and gets his brother and *bhabhi* back. The Lakshman character was actually Hrithik.

I felt, why not make a family film. I was obsessed with the image of having six stars on a poster. Like *Kabhi Kabhie* had an array of stars. I was a huge Yash Chopra fan and I wanted a poster that had a host of stars on it! Leading movie stars all together in a big, mammoth family saga.

My parents reacted very strongly to the characters. They loved the idea, they loved what I was trying to do with it. I kept developing it. Then I wrote it with a friend called Sheena Parekh. I met Sheena through a common friend; she was a Harvard MBA and all that, so she had a different take on things. But it was nice to collaborate with her. We started writing it together. I took off for a month or two to London. It became my retreat to get away from Mumbai, and to write. We developed the script in detail; I decided I wanted the Bachchans to play the parents, and Shah Rukh and Kajol to play the older brother and wife. Hrithik was a friend at that point of time. I knew him as a child; I met him through Adi and Uday, and that whole gang I had gotten close to. And Hrithik was a very close friend of Uday's. So I used to hang around with Hrithik a lot. I saw that he was very sincere about what he was doing. He was training for *Kaho Naa . . . Pyaar Hai* at that point. I bumped into him at Manish Malhotra's store. He'd come with his mother for something.

And on a whim I said, 'Listen, I want you to do my next film, and play the younger brother of Shah Rukh.'

He then called me, asking, 'Did you mean what you said?

I said, 'Yes, I will come to you with the script.'

Two nights later, I walked into the *Bombay Times* party, and saw Kareena Kapoor. She was eighteen, and looked like she was already a movie star. She had just been signed to play the lead in *Refugee*. She was supposed to do *Kaho Naa . . . Pyaar Hai* but she walked out of the film, and became Abhishek Bachchan's heroine in *Refugee*. But the way she stood in that party, it was as if she had already released five blockbusters. She had that attitude which I wanted for my character Poo. And I said to myself, this is it. I've found my Poo. I decided that Hrithik and Kareena should play the younger lot.

So I went to my dad and said, 'I want Amitabh Bachchan, Jaya Bachchan, Shah Rukh, Kajol, Hrithik and Kareena.'

He asked, 'All in one movie?'

I said, 'Yes, that is the cast.'

He said, 'Why Hrithik? He has not even released his first film. *Kareena ki kitni film release hui hain?* Take someone more established.'

I said, 'Have faith, this is the correct cast.'

It was just my instinct on Hrithik. So my father said okay.

I had spoken only to Shah Rukh about the idea. He had said, 'Yeah, cool, whatever you want to do, it's your film.' He was completely cooperative and supportive.

I called Amit uncle and said, 'I want to meet you.' I went to his house and told him about the film.

He said yes. 'It sounds great. Of course, I'm on and very excited and happy.'

He was shooting for *Mohabbatein* at that time. There had been a little dip in his career. But this was also the time when his show *Kaun Banega Crorepati* was on its way up on TV. But he was in a zone where he was not getting the films he wanted to do, it was that interim zone.

I got out of the house, called Jaya aunty again, and said I wanted to meet her officially. I offered her the role, and she said, 'Okay, give me a day.'

I didn't want to approach them as a couple. I wanted to approach them as two entities.

Shah Rukh called, and I told him, 'Listen, the Bachchans are on.'

And he said, 'Cool, great!'

The only one I was not sure of was Kajol because she had just gotten married to Ajay, and there was a lot of talk that she didn't want to act any more. I called her and asked her where she was shooting that day, and she told me she was at Filmistan Studio. 'Why?' she asked.

In the afternoon, I went to meet Kajol at Filmistan and she was all set to say no to me.

She said, 'I know it's for *Kabhi Khushi Kabhie Gham . . .*' I had told her about the movie earlier. Then I told her about her role and she said, 'Listen, I can't say no to you. I can't not do this. I'll die if you sign another heroine.'

I had actually decided that if Kajol said no, I'd go straight to Aishwarya. I had the feeling that Kajol might refuse. But here she was, saying that there was no way in hell that she was not going to do this film. She's a very possessive girl, and she loved me.

So, that was done. Hrithik I had already told. I called him again and said that we were on, and he was really excited. He said, 'I can't believe it!'

My last meeting of the day was with Kareena Kapoor. Yes, I signed all of them on the same day, all six of them.

I wish it was as easy today, to sign six movie stars for a film in one day. But it's not possible, not for anyone.

Shooting *Kabhi Khushi Kabhie Gham* . . . was the easiest thing ever. The only problem in the shoot was that *Kaho Naa . . . Pyaar Hai* had released by then and Hrithik was this new star. People had started comparing him to Shah Rukh. It was unfair, because he was too junior, and Shah Rukh was already such a big star. But that was a phase when one or two of Shah Rukh's films had gone wrong and the media had started projecting Hrithik up there.

When I'd signed him, *Kaho Naa . . . Pyaar Hai* hadn't released. But by the time we started shooting in September 2000, it was already a certified blockbuster after its release in January that year.

The negativity that crept in was not justified or correct, and it was really sad. I felt Hrithik was the only one during the course of the shooting who needed a little hand-holding. See, the Bachchans didn't have that equation with him. Shah Rukh was a bit distant at that time because of everything that was happening. Kajol was Team Shah Rukh. So I felt I needed to hold his hand a bit. And we developed a really good friendship. We got close to each other—he was a bit of a lost child in this whole lot. And Hrithik, anyway, is slightly awkward around people. He's not the most people-friendly person. Now he's become a lot better.

Apart from that, it was the most fun I've ever had on set. It was a dream. There were no problems whatsoever. There was not a single ego clash. No actor wanted a scene changed, there was no insecurity, nothing.

If you see *Kabhi Khushi Kabhie Gham* . . ., it's a star vehicle. Everyone has that big scene. Everyone has a big introduction. If one has a comic scene, then the other one has an item song. It's actually a well-balanced screenplay, which is why there was no problem. You know that Hrithik and Kareena are the youth factor in the film, so they come in and sing two big songs in the second half. Shah Rukh and Kajol have the two big songs in the first half. Then they all have one big song together.

It was a blessed screenplay that gave everyone equal importance. Even now, when you think of the movie, you don't realize who's better than the other, you just talk about the movie. No one says, oh, Shah Rukh stole the show or Kajol did. It's everyone's movie. You remember Hrithik for what he did, Shah Rukh for what he did, Kareena for her Poo, Kajol for her gregarious Punjabi girl act, the Bachchans for the gravitas that they provided as parents. There was no inequality in roles. When I look back, I wonder, how the hell did I get away with this film?

I didn't have to 'handle' anyone. In such a success-ridden industry, everyone automatically places all their faith in you if you've had success, and they expect you to do your job. You've made a blockbuster, you have to make another. It's as simple as that. And I was so excited, I thought I was making *Mother India*.

It was after the film released that I got the first knock on my head. In the course of the shoot, there was no problem. The film was looking great. The visuals were engaging, the music was big. Everybody who came on the set said, 'This movie is going to be it! Oh my god, it's like a saga! *Yeh toh* Sholay *hai!*'

Each set was bigger than the other—whether it was the set of Chandni Chowk, or the '*Bole Chudiya*' set, or the '*Shawa Shawa*' set. Or the song we shot in Egypt, or the big homes we shot in, the helicopter shots, the big star cast. Everything was monumental.

I had all the money in the world to play with. I had become this spoilt, overindulged child who just felt like spending all that money. The budget at that point of time, in 2001, was Rs 50 crore, which is equivalent to today's 500 crore. It was an all-time-high budget. No one had ever, in the history of film budgets at least, spent Rs 50 crore on a feature film when the total remuneration of the cast at that time was 6 crore rupees. The money was all spent on the movie. It was humongous.

Today, if you make that exact same film with the same cast, it'll be unaffordable and you won't be able to release it, because there's no way you can recover that kind of investment.

So the film was made and it released on 14 December 2001, on the heels of 9/11. But I had got my first blow when I saw *Lagaan*, and subsequently *Dil Chahta Hai*, which had released earlier that year. There was a part of me that got a little afraid. I felt, suddenly in that year, the syntax of cinema had changed. And Aamir Khan had brought about that change.

When I went to see *Lagaan*, I thought it was going to be a disaster. It had everything wrong, that film. But *Lagaan* banished all the myths of Indian cinema. I saw it and I thought, shit, my film is not that great, mine is not this kind of cinematic experience, it's just a commercial film. Then I saw *Dil Chahta Hai*, and realized that this is what the new cool was. Up till that point I was the cool guy, because I had got Polo Sport and DKNY into my films. But my film was wannabe-cool. What was really, intrinsically, authentically cool was Farhan Akhtar's depiction of urban youth, the way they dressed, spoke, the mannerisms. My sensibilities were mixed up with those of the film-makers of yore—Yash Chopra, Subhash Ghai, Raj Kapoor. I wanted to make a film that did the numbers. *Lagaan* released in June on the same day as *Gadar* and did the same numbers. I thought, what happened there? *Lagaan* changed the tide of Hindi cinema. Two months later, in August, came *Dil Chahta Hai* and it redefined, or created the new cool, for hairstyle, clothes—all the things that I was known for. And then came my film, an over-the-top, overly opulent, in-your-face mainstream family saga that seemed so full of effort. My worst fears finally came true.

The film released three days before Eid, which was on Monday. Eid was on 17 December. Those days, there were no multiplexes, it was just single screens. A trade analyst wrote about the film and his last line was '*Kabhi Khushi Kabhie Gham* disappoints, and will entail heavy losses to all concerned.' As it had opened to 50–60 per cent houses, it would make the 'investors unhappy'. These were the words, I'll never forget them. They resounded in my head. My parents had gone to show the film to the President of the country at that time. Like Alia Bhatt, I can't remember the name of the President.

One day after the release, I was alone at home. We had this magazine that came every Saturday—it arrived as scheduled. I read it and started weeping. Niranjan Iyengar, my friend, called me at that time to tell me excitedly that he was at a birthday party where the kids were performing to the 'You Are My Soniya' song. And he heard this meltdown on the phone.

He came running to my place and asked, 'What happened?'

I said, 'I think I've made a big flop.'

My father had fleetingly said that if this film didn't run, we would have to go back to our old house. Yash Raj was doing the film on commission. And we had overseas rights—which was a big part of the picture—on commission. We were doing a lot of territories on our own because it was such an expensive film. We had taken risks ourselves. So I suddenly thought, have I just screwed it up for myself? What have I gone and done? I loved the film. But yes, it was, as Rajeev Masand said, 'old wine, new bottle'. I was not used to such words. I had been accepted after *Kuch Kuch Hota Hai*—there had been a flurry of compliments. I was not used to criticism yet. Now there were reviews which said, 'nowhere close to the magic of *Kuch Kuch Hota Hai*', or 'in your face', 'over the top', 'over-opulent', 'not as cool as *Dil Chahta Hai*', 'nowhere close to *Lagaan. Lagaan* remains the film of the year', and things like that.

I was feeling deceived, betrayed, shattered. Niranjan, instead of taking me to a doctor, took me to a psychic, Sunita Menon, who was the celebrity psychic at that time. There I was, sitting in the waiting room of a psychic, weeping.

When Sunita Menon saw me, she asked, 'What happened to you?'

I said, 'My picture is going to flop and we'll be moving back to our old house, and I've ruined it all.'

She asked me to calm down. 'You'll be fine,' she said.

Then I called Anil Thadani, my college friend. And Aditya Chopra.

Adi said, 'Just calm down, it's before Eid. Wait, we'll see on Monday, na.'

I said, 'No, I've made a disaster.'

Anil said, 'You know what, just wait till Monday. Will you calm down?'

That Sunday was miserable. I said to myself, if everything goes well, I'll give up non-vegetarian food, I'll walk to Siddhivinayak. Idiotic things I vowed in my frustration.

On Monday morning, I was nervous. I remember leaving the house, heading towards the office, scared, waiting. Those days, advance booking used to open for the second week on Monday; it was not like today, the climate was totally different. Then Anil called me and said, 'I need you to come to town, I have to show you something.'

I asked, 'Why?'

And he said, 'No, I need to show you something. You have to come to Liberty Cinema.'

But I got stuck in traffic. I told the driver, *'Kitna traffic hai, horn bajao. Anil mujhe Liberty mein mil raha hai.'*

He said, *'Baba, traffic toh hil hi nahi raha hai.'*

I then rolled the window down and saw a cop. I asked, *'Bhaiya, ye kya hai? Itna traffic kyun hai? Ye jam kyun hai?'*

He said, *'Woh advance booking ki line,* Kabhi Khushi Kabhie Gham . . . *ke liye.'*

I just looked at him. Then I asked, *'Ye wali line?'*

He said, *'Haan, woh pata nahi abhi picture release hua hai. Itna bada line hai ki police ko bulaya hai, crowd control ke liye.'*

I got out of the car and started running towards Liberty.

I met Anil Thadani, all out of breath, and he said, 'Have you seen this? This is what you were crying over the weekend for. Your picture is a blockbuster, screw the reviews. People are clapping in the halls!'

It was as big a hit as *Gadar*. It did double the business of *Lagaan*. But it never got the respect at that time. I remember Screen Awards had a Jury Award, which was an industry award. My father's rakhi sisters,

Waheeda aunty and Sadhana aunty, were on that jury, and I was not nominated in the Best Director category. My father took it to heart.

I said screw it, I'm not attending Screen Awards, I'm leaving the country.

I went away. I was like a sulking child who didn't get his candy. That entire year, I was very depressed.

Kabhi Khushi Kabhie Gham . . . remains my biggest hit, but for me it was my most depressing time. I went to London to get away from it all. I landed there, and got this message: *Lagaan* Oscar nominated.

I thought nobody's going to remember *Kabhi Khushi Kabhie Gham* . . . because *Lagaan* became the toast of the town. That's what happened that year, you see. Today, nobody remembers that *Kabhi Khushi Kabhie Gham* . . . came out that same year. Now it's on television every week.

Kabhi Khushi Kabhie Gham . . . has been the biggest success for Dharma Productions. It has given me more money than any other film because every two years, some rights are negotiated. Everyone in the world knows *Kabhi Khushi Kabhie Gham* . . . as the go-to Bollywood film of this country. It's true. It's got the biggest brand value in Germany, in France, in Ireland. People across the world know this film. It has global love. But that year it broke me, and I am still getting over what I went through that year. In some ways, it brought me down to earth. I came crashing down, and maybe that was the best thing, because had that not happened, maybe I would've become some crazy person.

I felt I had so many stars in the film, I had done so much, I had spent so much, I should've made a great film. I didn't think of whether the film was good or bad, I just thought that nobody liked it. I felt ashamed, which was so stupid when I look back. Now I'm very proud of it. But back then I was not. People would tell me they had seen the film ten times, but I could only think that so-and-so critic didn't like it, so-and-so reviewer didn't like it and that I didn't win any award. I attached so much importance to those awards and those critics. But at that time, only I know what I went through.

I felt the need to justify the film to everyone. I felt the need to say, 'Oh, but do you know it did double the business of *Lagaan*?'

People at that time didn't know so much about a film's commercial earnings, and they'd say, 'Really, it did better than *Lagaan*?'

And I would think: Why is he acting shocked? Why is he acting surprised? It did do better than *Lagaan*. So what if *Lagaan* got nominated to the Oscars. Mine did double the business.

In this industry, perception is reality. There are so many mainstream movies about which people will say, 'But I hated it. Who likes that movie?' But those films have done the numbers. There is a certain urban audience you surround yourself with, who may not have seen a blockbuster, but will love *Udaan*. Yes, *Udaan* is great, *Lunchbox* is spectacular. But you make some cheesy commercial film, people are like, 'Yeah, whatever.'

I was going through that, to the point that I thought I had to make a cool film. I was very charged. I thought, even I'm cool, I've grown up in South Bombay, I've got that affluence, I have that exposure. How can Farhan Akhtar be considered the coolest director? I will write a cool film. That's how I began my journey to write *Kal Ho Naa Ho*.

But I was a bit shaken. I didn't want to go on the set as a director. I kept thinking that if I directed now, I might do the same thing again. Let me write a cool film, let me shoot from somebody else's shoulder. So I chose Nikhil Advani, who had worked with me on two films, to direct it. I started writing *Kal Ho Naa Ho*. First I wanted him to write it. I gave him the central idea: A man dying. An angel who comes into people's lives.

But I wanted to tell it interestingly. I wanted to do voice-overs, which was a new idea. I wanted talking-to-the-camera which is what *Kal Ho Naa Ho* is like. I wanted to do it in a modern, cool way. I decided I would shoot the film in New York, not London, because now I was obsessed with New York. I had made a trip in between and I felt like New York should be a character in the film. Also, nobody had yet shot an entire Hindi film in Manhattan. I wanted that New York vibe—people rushing about with coffee cups, and everyone in their New York city clothes.

I decided I was going to make this cool, hip film in New York, but with a traditional heart. So I started writing. I loved the process. In fact, I believe it's my best screenplay. I went to New York and sat there for three months. I sat in Central Park, stared at people, wrote the film, came back to Mumbai, narrated it to everybody, selected the cast. In fact, I wrote it with the cast in mind.

My first problem was with Kareena. She asked for too much money and we had some kind of a fallout at that time. *Mujhse Dosti Karoge!* had just released, directed by Kunal Kohli.

She said, 'Aditya Chopra's assistant, Kunal Kohli, has made this flop, so Karan Johar's assistant, Nikhil Advani, is not to be trusted either.'

The weekend of that film's (*Mujhse Dosti Karoge!*) release, I offered her *Kal Ho Naa Ho*, and she asked for the same money that Shah Rukh was getting.

I said, 'Sorry.'

I was very hurt. I told my father, 'Leave that negotiation room,' and I called her. She didn't take my call, and I said, 'We're not taking her.' And we signed Preity Zinta instead. Kareena and I didn't speak to each other for almost a year. For a year, we looked through each other at parties. It was very idiotic. She was a kid; she's a decade younger than me.

Then came a function, organized by the police, where I saw Kareena and gave her a semi-smile, but she looked away and so I looked away too. I thought, how dare she behave like this with me?

Anyway, finally Saif, Preity, Shah Rukh and all of us went to New York. My father had already done a lot of prep work. He had made three or four trips to New York, and he had gotten really exhausted planning the film because we had to deal with unions—it was basically a new kind of zone we were operating in. And I wanted to do all the formalities and get all the rights properly. I was also grappling with the fact that I was not a film-maker on this film, I was just the writer. I was letting go.

It was hard. When I look back, I feel I should have never given anybody else the chance to direct this film. Now I would never make the mistake of writing a film and giving it to another director. Today when I write that I'm the director of this film and that film, and I don't have *Kal Ho Naa Ho* there, it bothers me. I just feel terrible I didn't direct it. I don't know why I gave it away. It should have been me all along. I deeply regret that the film does not have my name on it as director. Because in spirit, in heart, perhaps in execution, it's completely *my* film.

But then I had met Nikhil's mum once, and she was so proud that her son had been given this big platform, to direct this big feature film, and I felt it was karma. The film was not mine any more. It was his. I was almost going to call him for a discussion once. Then I stopped myself. I wanted to say that 'Nikhil, I think I should direct this film.' I was advised by close friends to do the film myself, as I was passionate about its writing. But I couldn't bring myself to do it.

All these thoughts were there before the shooting of the film. I could have done anything and gotten away with it. Maybe I would have upset him, but he would still have been with my company. But I couldn't do it. The emotional side, or the sensitive side of my personality, stopped my ambitious side. That's what invariably happens with me. I sometimes place people above the work, which you should not, because it is your work. Film is about energy. Now when I look back, I feel I should have done it. I don't know why I didn't.

But I really have only the fondest memories of him. There are two people who trained me in camera—Aditya Chopra and Nikhil Advani, even though he was my assistant. It was tough during the making of *Kal Ho Naa Ho*, things were turbulent. It had to happen because there was an inherent conflict between the writer of the film who was on set and the director who was executing it, but more than anything else, because we had a history before that; we rose above it. Today we are in touch and we're friendly though we're not friends. I know he respects me and the company. He's been a part of my journey and I can safely say that that journey hasn't ended. There's something there.

Anyway, in the middle of the *Kal Ho Naa Ho* shoot, my father began losing a lot of weight. We all thought it was the stress.

But it wasn't.

6

The Death of My Father

In 2003, we were going for a big outdoor shoot for *Kal Ho Naa Ho* in June and July. We had already shot outdoors for eight days in Toronto with Preity and Saif, but we had to come back earlier because Shah Rukh was supposed to have a surgery. On that outdoor shoot, I had met a coffee-cup reader, a lady called Rita, who was make-up artiste Mickey Contractor's friend. She did my coffee-cup reading and said some very accurate things about me. But one thing stuck in my head. She said, 'Beware of the month of August. Beware of the first two days of August, because you might get some kind of news that might shake up your life.'

Anyway, the shoot started on 15 July, and my father was very stressed out handling everything, including the tension between Nikhil and me.

Then July ended. And I kept thinking, god, August is going to come, something's going to happen. I kept feeling that some explosion would happen, maybe Nikhil would erupt, maybe Shah Rukh would get upset. I was so worried. Anyway, 1 August came, but nothing happened. I thought, this is the best day of the shoot. We were in New York. The weather was great, the sun was out and we completed all our work.

On 2 August, we were shooting Saif's introduction scene in an office area when my father walked in.

He took me aside and said, 'I want to talk to you.'

I said okay.

I looked at his face again and said, 'Give me two minutes. We'll take this shot and break for lunch.'

When we broke for lunch, my father took me to a little room where it was just him and me. It had a glass window and we could see what was happening outside.

'What happened, Papa?' I asked.

He was silent. I looked at him and—I have no idea why these words came out of my mouth, I have no explanation—but I looked at him and said, 'Do you have cancer?'

He looked at me and said, 'Did Sam tell you?' Sam was the general manager of the hotel where we were staying. He was an old friend of my father.

I said, 'No.'

Then I asked again, 'You have cancer?'

He said, 'Yes.'

I just sank, literally sank into a chair in the room.

But he was very strong. He said, 'If you've noticed, I've been losing weight, I've been eating only khichri–dahi.'

My father had told Sam that every time he swallowed, it really hurt. And that this had been happening for two months. He kept thinking it was merely a case of a sore throat. Meanwhile, he had also lost about six kilos. My mother thought it was because he was so stressed out about the shoot. We put it all down to the shoot. None of us could think of anything else.

Twenty days before my father spoke to me, he had gone to a GP, who, as a precautionary measure, had sent him to an oncologist. They discovered a fourth-stage tumour in his oesophagus. He had done all his tests, and now had to start radiation. Sam told him that the doctor had said that if Dad didn't tell a family member, they couldn't go ahead with the treatment.

My father was not planning to tell me at all. The bank where we were doing business and the hospital where he was going for his tests were next to each other. So my father would take the car, get off at the bank, walk two blocks, and go to the hospital to do all the tests just to make sure that the driver wouldn't tell anyone that Mr Johar was visiting a hospital every day. He hadn't told any of us for about three weeks. When he gave me this information, he had already been diagnosed with fourth-stage cancer.

I left the shoot and went to Sam who took us to the doctor. He explained the entire situation. Right after that, my father said, 'Don't tell Mum.'

I said, 'No, you cannot do that. You're starting radiation. You have to tell her.'

The next day he was to start radiation, which is the stage before chemotherapy.

So he said, 'Then I'll tell her.'

I still remember that day. I was sitting in a room; in the hall my father was telling my mother, and then I walked towards them; my mother hugged me and of course, she was in tears. I held her hand tight, and I could feel her hand shivering in mine.

I said, 'We have to be strong and positive for him because he's going to make it.'

And she said, 'Yes.'

We cried, and let it all out.

In a sense, it was like our whole world had fallen apart. We were a strong unit of three and it was like one-third of it, the epicentre of that unit, was crumbling. Actually, the enormity of the situation didn't hit us at that moment.

But that night, when I went to Shah Rukh's room—he was very, very, very close to my father—it really hit me like a ton of bricks. Farah Khan was there too.. I told Shah Rukh. He broke down. Then I realized the reality of what was happening, because he wept like a baby. He held his stomach, and he just wept and wept, as if from his core.

He cried and said, 'I've lost one father, I can't lose another.'

He just kept saying that because he used to treat my father like his own. He used to call him 'Tom uncle', you know, with affection. I was so shocked at his reaction; I had gone numb. I couldn't find the tears, because I couldn't believe it. We were in an outdoor location, we were shooting a film, and my father was diagnosed with cancer in New York . . . What was going on?

I called up Rita, that coffee-cup reader, in Toronto.

I said, 'Can you fly to New York?'

She said she'd come.

The whole crew, you could tell, had gone into shock. My father was very clear that the work had to go on—it could not stop.

The next day we went to the hospital, and met the doctor who was an American gentleman.

He did some tests on my father and said, 'What are you doing in New York? How come you're here?'

I said, 'We're here making a film.'

He said, 'Oh really? What is the film about?'

My father said, 'It's about a man who comes to New York because he's dying. He's come for treatment.'

The doctor said, 'You're serious? This is the story of the film?'

My father replied, 'Yes. What is happening to me is what the film is about.'

And I thought, trust my father to have a sense of humour even at such a time.

We started the treatment. My mother was there, so were my maasi and my mother's first cousin. There was a support system, and the whole crew was there to help my father go through the beats of the treatment. For the first three days, my father was very strong. But I found him a bit quiet three or four days later. One day I went into his room in the hotel and he was sitting alone staring at the photograph that both he and Mom always carried with them. It's one of all three of us—and they're hugging me. I have the same photo too.

I put it aside and said, '*Papa, kuch khaana hai?* You hungry?'

We had been instructed on the specific foods to give him, and he had to keep eating. But his appetite had gone down because of the medication.

He said, 'No,' and then he mumbled something.

I said, 'What happened?' and he said, 'I don't want to leave you and go. I don't want to leave you all and go. I don't want to go anywhere.'

I said, 'No, you're not going to go anywhere. Why do you say that?'

He said, 'No, I don't want to leave you and go. I can't leave you and go. How can it happen? I have to see you married, I have to see you grow, I don't want to leave you.'

He kept saying, 'I don't want to leave you and go.' He said it about ten times and then he broke down.

I had seen my father cry only once before this—when he saw *Kuch Kuch Hota Hai*. In my whole life, I saw him cry only on these two occasions.

I went and closed the door, and—this happens to me in extreme situations—I became very strong. There is an innate strength that just comes out of me. I'm overly sensitive, and I can cry a lot. It's my way of expressing myself and I always feel like it's soul cleansing when you cry.

But in situations like this I don't break down. I take total control. I said, 'Papa, you're going nowhere. We're doing the treatment, we're doing the radiation, you're going to be fine. Everything is going to be fine.'

I meant that from my heart. Rita had come to New York by this time. I went to her room right after this.

I asked her, 'Is my father going to make it?'

And she said, 'Ten months, Karan. I don't think he's going to make it. Unless there's a miracle, he's not going to make it.'

I said, 'Okay.'

We went through the beats. I would go every day to the set, and on the chemotherapy days I would take him to the hospital. By then he had finished radiation, and done two cycles of chemo.

Then the outdoor shoot finished. All through the chemo, there was a lot happening around us. It was a unit of eighty people, and everybody used to come and sit together after pack-up and chat. Everybody was trying . . .

When Pam aunty went through a bout of cancer, she had dealt with a Dr Noorie in New York. So she had already put us through to the doctor. He was very positive. They are always very positive in New York. He kept saying, 'It's fine, you're going to be fine, and there's a great chance that you're going to make it.'

We were releasing *Kal Ho Naa Ho* in November. We had shot the film in June, July, August, and in September I had to shoot the songs, make the promos, and so on. So I had to head back, while my father continued the treatment in New York. That was the time Kareena Kapoor called me. It was August. We had not spoken for nine months.

She called and said, 'I heard about Yash uncle.'

She got really emotional on the phone, and she said, 'I love you and I'm so sorry I haven't been in touch. Don't worry.'

We sort of patched up at that time.

I came back to Mumbai, and got into the thick of getting the film ready for release. Meanwhile, my father's treatment was going on. We had changed the doctor and now a Sindhi gentleman, Dr Suresh Advani, was treating him. It was a hectic time, caught between the chemotherapy and releasing *Kal Ho Naa Ho*.

The film released in November to great feedback. My father, who was back by now, was doing his last couple of cycles of chemo in Mumbai.

The film was our third hit in a row. They called it the hat-trick of Dharma Productions. It went on to get a lot of love and became a cult film. Critics liked it, and so did the audiences. *Koi . . . Mil Gaya* released the same day, so both were touted as films of the year. The award season started, and my father was such a loved man—he started getting all the lifetime achievement awards. Filmfare, Screen, Zee, IIFA (International Indian Film Academy), all of them honoured him. People performed to his songs, he got so much adulation. It was a time full of tears and pride and applause. His voice would kind of crack every time he spoke. He was also a little weak by then.

I think my best moment was in Singapore, during IIFA, when I made a speech about fathers and sons. I remember the speech so well:

Fathers and sons, probably one of the most emotionally deep, human relationships. Probably one of the most intense human equations. Words alone cannot describe what a father and son feel for each other, simply because there are such few words in this relationship. So much is left unsaid between the two of them. Communication, or rather a lack of it, always broadens the gap between the two of them. There's always a gap between a father and son, always a gap between a name and a surname. I've always asked myself and today I address this question to all of you sons out there: Why did you stop hugging your father after a certain age? Why did you stop expressing, and being affectionate to your father after a certain age? Why is there this inexplicable awkwardness between a father and son? Why are all your emotions, your innermost thoughts, your tears, always reserved for your mother, your sister and then your wife? Why? Because you then become a father, and then you bottle up, just like your father did, and this vicious circle continues. Who is going to break this vicious circle? I realized, and I'm sure this applies to all of you as well, that, like everybody else, I too had issues, minor issues with my father, like every other son. You could call it a generation gap, you could call it a difference of opinion, you could call it anything. But what I also realized was that I was subconsciously being the man my father is. I was talking like him, feeling like him, loving like him—I was just being him. I then realized that a father not only gives his son his name, he also gives him his personality. So somewhere, if you have a problem with your father, you actually have a problem with yourself. Ladies and gentlemen, I've had this realization and this opportunity to express myself, and I wish with all my heart, that one day you do too. My father is my conscience, my father is my strength, my father is my support, my father is my hero. I don't say it often enough to you, Dad, but what better than this global platform to say, I love you. I love you very, very, very much. And I wish I could love you as much as you love me, but I don't think I'm capable of such unconditional love. I love you. You are my world.

And then Amit uncle, who was there, said: 'Ladies and gentlemen, I think whatever needed to be said about Mr Yash Johar, his son Karan has very ably done. There are very few fathers that have sons like Karan, and there are very few Karans who have fathers like Yash-ji.'

All through this time, my mother stayed very positive, but the PET scan we did in February or March, came up with this clutter. It was lit up like a Christmas tree. So it had spread. The doctors said that it had not gone to the liver. When it touches the liver, it's not a good thing. It was still centred around the lung but it had spread, it was not ebbing. There were other clusters. He had developed prostate cancer by now. I didn't tell my mother, I didn't even tell him. But that's when I knew that it was not looking good at all.

I was very strong those last few months. I actually have no individual recollection of that time. I just remember being very strong through it all. I suddenly felt like I had become the man of the house.

My mother, who is a very emotional person, was very strong as well. She was rock solid. I derived a lot of strength from her. She would get teary but I never saw her break down. I think it was because we knew that if we all broke down, it would kill him. All Dad worried about was Mom and me, and our response to his cancer. We were such a close-knit family that the thought of not having him around was not a thought we could bear. Somehow I had not accepted it, but I was preparing myself for it in my own strange way. And yet fighting and trying everything possible, whether it was alternative treatments, homoeopathy, or doing the *mrityunjay jaap* on the side. I was desperate and tried anything and everything.

I made that speech about fathers and sons in Singapore in June 2004. He passed away twenty-one days later.

We had come back from Singapore and his treatment was still going on. He was consuming medication orally. The doctor didn't advise us to do any more chemo. On 16 June, he went to see *Lakshya*, Farhan's new film. For some reason, I was somewhere else, and I couldn't go to the screening. It was an industry screening, where they had called Javed saheb, and a lot of other people. He went, and met almost the entire industry. He came back, complained of a headache and went to bed.

Very strangely, I have twice had this instinct about something.

The first was when I looked at my father and asked, 'Do you have cancer?' and the second time was when I told my driver, Anwar, that night to stay back. I have no idea why I did that. I just felt like he should wait at home. By that time, I had not driven at all in ten years.

At six in the morning, the maid came and woke me up. *'Papa bimar hain, kuch keh nahi paa rahe.'* I went running to his room. Mom was asleep. He was looking for something, I didn't know what. He was breathing heavily. He was wheezing and he kept rummaging about, as if searching for something.

I said 'Papa!' and then quickly called up the driver and said, 'Take Papa down.' I wanted to rush him to the hospital because he was wheezing, and yet he kept looking for something. 'Papa, what are you looking for?' I asked, but he wouldn't tell me. Every time I held him, he pushed me away. I wanted to drag him out of there. The servant too had come by then, and we were trying to take him to the car, but he kept pushing us back. Finally, I realized that he was looking for a pen. He took out his will, and signed it, because he had made some change and he wanted to make sure he had signed on it.

And then he collapsed. It was as if he'd clung on to all his energy just to sign that will. My mother and I rushed him to Lilavati Hospital. They had to immediately put him on the ventilator. There was one particular injection that was an organ reviver. Dr Barve, who is Amit uncle's doctor too, was in charge of him in Lilavati. He gave him that shot. He said it had a 30 per cent chance of succeeding, because his lungs were giving way. But it didn't work. Then Anil Ambani came up to me. He was a very close friend of my father. He always treated him like his own father. It was not like they had known each other for very many years, but he had built up a kind of rapport with my father in a short period of time.

He came to Lilavati, took me aside, and said, 'I've spoken to the doctors, Karan. It doesn't look like your father's going to make it. Clinically, he's already dead. Keeping him on the ventilator is delaying the inevitable. Trust me, the doctors are afraid to tell you this. They don't know how to put it to you but this is the reality.'

I called my mother in, she broke down, and I held her and said, 'We have to just . . . allow this.'

She said, 'We should go inside the room. I want to talk to him.'

We went in. We sat on the bed and both of us said, 'Don't worry, we'll be fine, Papa. You go . . .'

They took him off the ventilator, and subsequently, all his organs failed. He passed away on 26 June 2004.

My father was a man who used to take charge of every single funeral. It could be anybody's; he was the one who did all the arrangements. But I didn't have the capacity to do that. Anil Ambani was like that angel who took charge. My father was an industry figure, and had had a lot of love. He had known people for about four to five decades. So his funeral had to be proper. Anil Ambani took charge of everything. He did the planning, organizing, he did it all mechanically. He's a very, very emotional man and he was very emotional about my father. But he did it. Amit uncle and Shah Rukh were there, everybody was. Everyone who was going into the room was just breaking down. Shah Rukh, Adi, Yash uncle, all my family and friends, it was a blur for me. I didn't see anything, I don't remember, I just know that Anil took charge. It was the most important thing for me. I had to give my father the right send-off. My father was an Arya Samaji, so he had already told me: 'When I go, I want the electric crematorium, and I don't want any fuss.'

What he'd said was in my head. Amit uncle, who's a very traditional man, asked me, 'Are you sure?'

I said, 'Yes, my father asked for it.'

He had wanted it and I wanted to do exactly what he had wanted. Of course, I knew that his ashes had to go to Haridwar, because the entire Johar family has records there, for centuries. But everything was a blur. The only time I think I was really, genuinely aware, was when his body came to the house and there was a fly that was buzzing around.

Then we went to the electric crematorium. We didn't take my mother because she couldn't have borne it. People kept saying that women didn't go to funerals, but I just didn't want my mother to be there.

I will never be able to do an electric cremation of anyone I love, because it's like putting somebody into an oven. Putting my father into that oven, the sliding in and sliding out, the insensitivity of that ritual just broke me into a million pieces. I sank to the ground and wept. I kept saying, 'He can't go into an oven and come back out like that. That cannot be the end of my father. It cannot be the end of such a life. One of the nicest people in this world cannot just go into a tray and come out like this.' That was what really broke me, and I kept thinking, is this what life is all about? That you live, you put so much of your heart and soul into your work and other people's lives and relationships; you create this equity that is outstandingly powerful and earnest and sincere, and you amount to this? This is what happens to you in the end?

When you have a funeral pyre, there is something pious about it, but this electric cremation—I kept saying, 'No, this cannot be, you have to come back. You have to come back and say you're more worthy than what just happened. No, you can't go.'

That's what happens when lives go, you cannot believe it. Death is such a finality. In the end, you just amount to dust. Bones and dust. Spiritually, you go into a realm, to a soul space, but that's not something that was visible to me. My father was finally dead and gone, and I had to deal with it with all the strength that I had built up in those ten months. That shield I had worn to protect my mother and myself had just crumbled. It just fell apart.

I remember coming back to the house, and there were people I had to meet, but I just went into my room. There was a tiny closet there. I went inside, closed the door, sat down and wept. I just wept and wept. I think it's the last time I've ever cried like that. People were banging on the door outside, but I said, 'Leave me alone, please give me twenty minutes. I don't want to meet anybody.' It was like a shriek. I was clutching my stomach tightly. I just couldn't believe what had happened. I don't think his death made me feel like that; but that ritual, that electric cremation, just broke my heart. It made me realize that it can be so trivial, the end, you know. It can amount to absolutely nothing.

Eventually, I stepped out and went to Mum.

It's been over ten years now, but she's just degenerated, she's an emotional mess. She's always shaking and vulnerable. Her health has taken a turn for the worse in the last decade. She's never been able to get over it. I always say that when you get a marriage right, the loss of a spouse can be much worse than the loss of a parent. You get over the death of a parent, but you cannot get the death of a spouse out of your life.

It's so strange how marriage today has taken such a beating as an institution. But that generation got it right, my parents became each other's soulmates, companions, each other's strength, support, everything. I really feel that my mother is half of herself today, because she feels she's lost a part of herself with my father. A big part of her spirit died when my father died. Her zest for life, her excitement for things . . . I don't think I can ever repair that, because for me to repair that, I would have to get my father back. And that is not a possibility. So I think I lost two parents on that day. I lost my father's body and I lost my mother's spirit.

7

Taking Over Dharma

In the *chautha* observed by Punjabis, after the father's death, the son takes over, and is made to wear a *saafa*. It was an extremely emotional moment for me, this feeling of taking charge, being responsible. I remember there were about five thousand people in front of me. It's like I was doing it on stage. And I thought: I have to live up to the expectations of my father. I have to run the company, I have to take charge. What am I going to do? I don't have a sibling, I don't have an uncle, I don't have a cousin, I don't have anyone to help me. What am I going to do?

I had nobody. When my father passed away I hadn't even understood the modalities of the business. I was just the kid who was given money to make movies. I had no idea about cheques, FDs, equity funds, investments, paperwork, income tax, chartered accountants . . . nothing. I was like this bimbo on the loose, who knew absolutely nothing. My father had always treated me like a star on set. I was like a prince who had been given a kingdom without any of the responsibility. I never had to worry about a single thing.

When I came back after the chautha, which was the fourth day after the death, I went to the office. It was a Sunday. I sat there in a chair, staring into nothingness. I remember I kept thinking, what am I going to do?

Then I called Apoorva, who was in London at that time. He was the kid who had put his hand up for me in class. It was time for him to put his hand up for me again.

I went back into that space when my principal had walked into class and asked, 'So who'll be Karan Johar's friend?'

And Apoorva had put his hand up. I felt like it was time for that same question to be asked again. Apoorva was in London, working for Yash Raj films. He was handling the finance for their distribution office in the UK. I called him and said, 'I have a big favour to ask of you. Can you come back and, you know, run this company?'

He had just bought a house in London, he was with his wife, married, and settled. But he came the next day. He left everything overnight, and moved to Mumbai bag and baggage. It was an entire shift of life. Can you imagine—a couple who has lived in London for six years, just moving overnight to Mumbai?

The next day in office, a man walked up to me and said, 'I'm your chartered accountant, though we haven't met.'

That kind of summed up my existence. I had not even met the chartered accountant of the company. That very day, I also got a call from Anil Ambani.

He said, 'I have something to give you.'

I said, 'Okay, I'll come to you.'

But he said, 'No, I'll come to you.'

He came to my office. Apoorva had arrived by then. Anil gave me a letter written by my father. It was a very practical letter, with details of bank accounts and investments, lists of go-to people, the properties we had, the people I could trust, the people I couldn't. He mentioned the names of two people in the office he felt I should sack. He'd written out the names of the chartered accountant, investment consultant, etc. It was like a Bible for me to follow.

He had never told me he had given such a letter to Anil Ambani. I was a bit zonked looking at the letter. It wasn't an emotional letter at all. It was a very practical letter signed by him, with lots of details. That letter became like a guide that Apoorva and I followed right through.

Anil was a big support because we had a lot of inquiries about our investments. It was pretty much like starting from scratch. Apoorva was totally new to the company, and to the industry and its ways. Today, of course, he's a veteran, he knows everything. But all those years ago, we were like freshers out of college running an entire company about which we knew nothing. People in the office were very supportive, especially the older employees, who had all loved my father dearly.

But it really was about starting all over again. My primary thought was this: I have to build this company the way my father would have liked it.

He was someone who'd taken baby steps but I wanted to take bigger, stronger leaps. I wanted to make this company one of the largest, most reputed companies, under my father's banner, Dharma Productions.

A lot of people suggested that we collaborate with some other studios or get someone to do a takeover. There was a lot of discussion. But somehow, some part of me said, no, we'll run Dharma on our own.

When I look back I can't believe how it's all turned out. There have been big highs, a few lows, but at that time it didn't seem like we would be where we are today.

There was a film called *Kaal* which was being directed by one of my assistants, Soham, who was with me on *Kabhi Khushi Kabhie Gham* . . . and *Kal Ho Naa Ho*. This project had started when my father was alive. I had decided to give Soham a break. He was writing a horror film, and I don't get the genre at all. But he had worked with Ram Gopal Varma before, and came from that school of cinema. We had already done the prep work on that film while my father was alive. He'd been a bit averse to the film because it was not the quintessential Dharma film.

We had somewhat changed gears. Before *Kuch Kuch Hota Hai*, my father had made all kinds of movies. There was a film called *Gumrah* which was inspired by a Thai film. There was *Duplicate*, a quintessential '70s type of caper potboiler, an action movie. I was the one who had brought in the romance with *Kuch Kuch Hota Hai*, *Kabhi Khushi Kabhie Gham . . .* and *Kal Ho Naa Ho*. So *Kaal* was very much against the grain of what we had created in the last five years.

After my father passed away, I told Apoorva, 'You know, we need to make a small film that we produce ourselves. And we can learn from whatever mistakes we make.'

Apoorva had never worked as a CEO of a film company. I had never run a company on my own. So I thought this was a good idea. Apoorva agreed. And we set out to make *Kaal*. I don't get that space of horror films, so Soham cast John Abraham, Ajay Devgn and Vivek Oberoi. We also got Lara Datta and Esha Deol. It was a film set in a jungle and it was about tiger spotting.

As it was being made, we did learn from our mistakes. We had a few bad pennies in the company, and oddly enough, their names were mentioned in the letter my father had written to me. He was right about all of them. In fact, he was right about everything in that letter. So we sieved out the people who we thought were siphoning money, or the people who were trying to take us for a ride because they thought that here were these two boys who didn't know what they were doing.

There was a sense that Apoorva was all at sea, and I—I was in the ocean. Apoorva is a very bright guy. He is an MBA but the film industry is not about modalities, it's about dealing with people. Apoorva is too much of a Gandhian. He's very correct, for him black is black, white is white. He doesn't understand grey. And unfortunately in the business part of this industry, we all live in the grey—like any other industry. He gets legalities. He thinks you draw up a contract and people should abide by it. But the thing is you can't write down all the clauses. I may not have had much training in film-making but I had that street-smartness. I just didn't have the sense to manage accounts and money. I was never ever good at that. My instinct about people, about a film, and generally about the business is very strong. But my handling of money, controlling costs, understanding the technicality of investment, etc. are zero. Even today, it's zero. My sense that one should buy XYZ property will be right, but how to go about raising the funds to buy that property I won't know. I have a sense of which film to back. But how to get the money to back that film? That I don't know.

We self-funded *Kaal*. We took a bank loan. That's pretty much how we run the business even today. Unless a studio takes charge of a film, in which case they buy your film. We are in the midst of heading towards a studio but are currently still a production house. I feel we are in a very unique place. We are not a quintessential studio like UTV was, yet we are not just another production house. We churn out an x number of movies. Some films are self-funded, as in bank funded, some are funded by a studio, like *Yeh Jawaani Hai Deewani* or *2 States,* both of which were sold to UTV. Films like *Student of the Year, Agneepath, Humpty Sharma Ki Dulhania* were self-funded. So we have done a combination of things in the last decade. In these ten years, we've dealt with every studio—Fox, Sony, UTV, Eros International. We have also got into co-productions. At that juncture we made *Kaal*. As Shah Rukh and I were joined at the hip literally and since this was our first endeavour, we collaborated to make the film.

Though horror was not my space, I go by my gut about a person. I liked Soham. I liked him as a person and thought we were going to make a film within a certain budget—because he was kind of production savvy too.

About nine months after my father passed away, in 2005, I was down with jaundice. When *Kaal* was being shot, I was ill. I was at home for a month and a half. I got a lot of time to think. I think this was also the time when I really mourned my father, lying in bed, alone. It was a cathartic one and a half months for me. Anyway, I had gotten weak, jaundice saps you of all energy. It was a combination of the disease and all the pain and baggage I was carrying, which hadn't found a release so far.

It's not that I cried throughout that month and a half of jaundice, but it was an emotional period for me. You have to just lie down when you have jaundice. You can't get up, your movements are restricted. There is no medication, no pill you can pop since your liver is weak. You can't even take a headache tablet. So those forty-five days of lying in bed gave me perspective. It got me to deal with my father's death and also gave me a lot of time to think about what I wanted to direct next, and where I wanted to take the company.

So the jaundice was almost, well, it's awful to say this, like a godsend.

Meanwhile, *Kaal* got ready and I got to see the film. I am very scared of horror films. I hate them. But when I saw *Kaal*, I wasn't afraid at all and that got me scared because I realized it was a terrible film. What would I tell Shah Rukh? I called him up and then went and met him. I told him I was going to record two songs. We were making a song-less film at that time, trying to be all avant-garde, but at that point I decided, nothing doing, we are going to add two songs. We put in an item song in the beginning with Shah Rukh and Malaika Arora. And at the end credits, we put in a song called '*Tauba Tauba*'. We made the film really hot with the songs. Suddenly it became exciting. It got a huge opening when it released and then it tanked after five days. But we made enough money in the beginning for us to stay afloat. That's when I realized that, yes, I can market a film. I can change the tide of a film a little bit by doing certain clever things.

Anyway, after *Kaal* I went on to develop *Kabhi Alvida Naa Kehna*. When my father was alive, I was writing a love story set in pre-Partition times. But the canvas was too large. It was supposed to have Shah Rukh, Ajay, Rani and Kajol. It was about two homes, and it had a Hindu–Muslim angle. It was a very strong subject, and would be called *Kalank*.

But at the last minute I pulled out of it. I started thinking of making a more intimate film. I wanted to do something bold. When my father died, it was an emotional downer. But I had professional freedom. I suddenly realized that I could do what I wanted. Dharma was my company. My father had been a very traditional man. He may never have allowed me to make a film about infidelity. But I wanted to make it. And I wanted to be very modern about it because there was so much talk about marriage being a crumbling institution and how divorce was the new marriage and infidelity was a part of every home. I experienced it around me, with friends, with family. *Arth* had always been one of my favourite films, so was *Silsila*. I wanted to make an urban film about infidelity and I decided to base it in New York again because I realized if a man and a woman in India had an affair, and if you wanted to show them prancing around, well, it wouldn't be possible to set it in India. Because here, in every cafe, shop or hotel, you will bump into a friend or a relative. That is how insular we are as a society. But New York is the kind of city you can get lost in. If you want to have an affair in New York, it's possible. But you cannot be frolicking around Mumbai city with your lover if you have a wife or husband at home.

I wrote *Kabhi Alvida Naa Kehna* with Shivani Bathija. When the film released, it evoked completely polarized reactions. There were people who were very angry and there were people who completely related to it. I realized my mistake. While the core strength of the film lay in its narrative, I had tried to stick to the whole Karan Johar formula, the big songs, the big sets, the largeness, which the film didn't need. It was trying to be both things. I should have chosen just the bold part. Yes, it would have probably still evoked polarized opinions, but it would have been true to its theme. That is a mistake I made. I think I messed up that film. This is the one film I wish I could direct again and I will, one day. I feel very strongly about its narrative and I still think it's got some of my finest moments as a director.

At the time when it released, a lot of scenes in the film were, I realized, uncomfortable viewing for many couples. I remember a couple came up to me and said, 'If my wife says she liked it, I would say why did you like it? Similarly, if I say I liked it, she'd say what did you like about it?'

I think every dining table in the country that week of its release was discussing *Kabhi Alvida Naa Kehna*. Why did Shah Rukh behave the way he did? Why did Rani have to leave Abhishek? He was such a good husband.

I was so angry that I kept trying to tell people, 'Can't sexual chemistry be a reason for people to leave? Maybe she wasn't aroused by him. He may have been a great guy but she was not turned on by him. She found a crabby, crotchety, angry man attractive.'

But in this country we are the first ones to judge people. We don't realize that textbook morality doesn't work for us, or for our situations at home. I would think, you fool, in your own house this is happening, but you'll judge my film.

I got very wound up during that time. I remember leaving the country a month after the film was released.

Kabhi Alvida Naa Kehna did exceptionally well overseas, while it did average business in India. It did well in the cities but the small towns rejected it. I had people writing emails to me, saying, 'You were the family guy. From loving your parents to leaving your wife, what kind of a departure is this?'

And I would say, 'I made a film I wanted to make.' I was defensive about it. I was annoyed and irritated that my film didn't create the stir I wanted it to. Actually, it had created a stir but it hadn't created a box office storm. When I went abroad, everybody was talking about it. They were talking about 'this scene' and 'that scene', 'that moment is so true', everybody was discussing it animatedly, vociferously, and I remember thinking: Did I make a good film? Or did I not make a good film?' I am still confused because even today I get so much feedback on *Kabhi Alvida Naa Kehna*.

Like I said, there were many people who loved the film and there were many others who didn't. I remember a lady walking up to me at Imax Wadala, a cinema in Mumbai, and saying, 'I took this person whose husband had left her, to a Karan Johar film to lighten up her spirit, brighten up her day. After watching the film she's been crying all day.'

I said, 'I'm so sorry, ma'am.'

Subconsciously, after my father passed away, I think there was a sense of freedom. Now when I look back, I think I broke through. When my mother saw the film, she told me, 'Your father would never have allowed you to make this film.' And I realized what a strong influence he had on my morality, on my sense of being, on my sense of character. But I am a modern person brought up in a certain society that accepts, understands and doesn't judge these situations. And I felt infidelity is a given. It's around you. It is a reality. Why are we brushing it under the carpet? I would rather face it and put it out there.

I wanted the couple to be with each other in the end. The only thing is I feel I directed Rani too sad. And I made Shah Rukh too angry. I think these were the mistakes I made. Apart from this, I feel the syntax of the film should've been more intimate, and that's something I really hold myself responsible for. And I wish I had directed Rani less guilty. She played it too guilty only because of me.

While we were filming *Kabhi Alvida Naa Kehna*, everyone was awkward, barring Abhishek who had this completely white character. All the others were walking the path of grey.

Preity Zinta was this overambitious character. She kept asking me, 'Why doesn't he love me?'

I would say, 'He loves you, Preity, he loves you as Shah Rukh Khan loves Preity Zinta the friend, the person, but the character does not love your character.'

Then she would say, *'Nahi, mujh mein kya kharabi hai?* Why doesn't he love me?'

Then Rani would say, 'Arre, give me one scene to justify my behaviour.'

I'd say, 'No, Rani, there is no justification.'

She would say, *'Itna achha husband hai. Main kyun affair karoon?'*

Shah Rukh would be awkward. I'd never asked Shah Rukh for more than a second take in my entire career; he's never taken more than two takes for anything. He and I have this synergy, we just get what we want. But there was one scene where he's on the phone, and Preity Zinta asks, 'Dev, who are you talking to?'

And he says, 'I am just coming.' That's it. But he couldn't do that scene. He was just so embarrassed.

He said, 'I can't do this. What is this nonsense!'

I said, 'Shah Rukh, you are not having an affair. The character is having an affair. Can you not understand this?'

The only person who was cool was Abhishek.

Even Mr Bachchan would say, 'Karan, what are you making? What is going to happen? What are you doing to me?'

And I'd say, 'Amit uncle, I am casting you as a slightly overtly sexual older man.'

Then he'd laugh and say, 'You have come to the right person.'

He has a great sense of humour and he was loving it. He loved his clothes. He loved the flamboyance of playing Sexy Sam. But the core characters like Shah Rukh and Rani? I could tell they were awkward and uncomfortable. I remember Adi calling me when I was in America and asking, 'Karan, are you sure you want them to sleep with each other in the film?'

I said, 'Yeah, why?'

He said, 'Karan, please trust me, this country is not going to like it.'

So I said, 'Adi, at that age of their lives, how can they not have sex with each other?'

I remember I was shooting a song in New Haven with Shah Rukh, and I told him, 'You know, Adi was saying this.'

He said, '*Tu soch le*. We haven't yet shot that scene. We can shoot it like *The End of the Affair*, with Meryl Streep and Robert Redford, where they go to the hotel room, they try to make love but they don't, they stop, and there is a sad moment where they sit and just hold each other's hands.' He said we could do it like that and it would be more emotional.

But I was in this bohemian headspace, trying to be completely above it all.

So I said, 'No, they have to fuck. They cannot be crying in a hotel room. I am so sorry I can't do this.'

Adi told me, 'Trust me, it will create a storm.'

I said, 'Maybe, but I don't want to do that.'

What Adi was saying was right for the box office. What I was doing was right for my thought process.

What he said was bang on target for the mainstream audiences of this country at that point of time. But I was not willing to listen. I had that whole scene in my head. So I shot it like that.

The thing is, at first Kajol was signed for Rani's role. I wanted a slightly older woman, you see. Casting Rani with Abhishek was a great pairing because they had just done *Bunty Aur Babli*. So they were like a cool, fit, young pair. She was to have been about five to six years older. So she felt he was like a *bachha*, a child. But that part didn't come through because Rani and Abhishek were too much of an integrated couple. If Kajol had been playing Rani's role, you would've believed that she was slightly older and therefore not getting what she wanted out of the relationship. And that this other, tormented man fulfilled her desires. That was actually how Maya was written. All her energies go into her OCD because her life is actually lacking in something.

That's why Abhishek tells her that '*Tum is ghar ko hamesha saaf karti rahi, lekin sabse zyaada gannd tum hi le aayi ho is ghar mein.*' That's what he tells her in anger.

The whole film was too much for this country. We even had a bit of a bout with the censors because they wanted to give it an adult certificate. But there was no sex in the film! They said the film was thematically adult.

Shah Rukh thought I had gone mad but he did it. Shah Rukh and I have that *rishta*. But I was so convinced that I could pull it off. It was a bold thing to do, it was a chance I had to take. Now when I look back I am glad I did it. If I ever remake *Kabhi Alvida Naa Kehna*, I would do it somewhat differently. That's the only film in my career I will direct again and make it better even though I like a lot of it. There are scenes like the dining table sequences where Amitabh Bachchan realizes that he is not joking. I also love the moment when the two women cross the road. That was like opera. It was so dramatic. There was a lot of madness in that film.

Anyway, once the film got released, it was the most tumultuous time for me. I got a combination of bravo, well done (I remember Rajeev Masand gave me a four-star review; and I don't think he has ever given me a four-star review) and shocked reviews. The moral ones, the so-called trade analysts and pundits said, 'What the hell is wrong with Karan? He has gone mad.'

There were people who told me, 'You've lost your father, you've lost your marbles. Your father was a traditional, rooted man. The banner was called Dharma Productions. We had Ganesh as a part of our logo.'

I was all about the pooja, the family, the correctness, the virtues, traditions and family values. And here I was breaking every conceivable norm. It was as if by making Shah Rukh Khan cheat on his wife on celluloid, I was doing the biggest injustice to cinema. *Kabhi Alvida Naa Kehna* was mounted huge. Nobody actually knew it was about infidelity. Those days it was not the way it is today, where everyone knows what a film is about.

Now I get irritated when people come and say that 'Your best film is *Kabhi Alvida Naa Kehna*. We hated it then, but we like it now.' Then people were newly married, but today they know that the shit can hit the fan in a relationship.

But at that time, it was almost like the country had gone up in arms about infidelity. Somebody said, 'How can you endorse infidelity?' I said, 'How can you endorse something that's already sold out? Infidelity is a reality of life. You find me one marriage that has opportunity and hasn't succumbed to it.' Cynical as that sounds, it's part of urban life. Marriages go through ups and downs. But people don't like to see it on screen. They experience it at home, brush it under the carpet and move on. There's a huge latent hypocrisy in our society. Especially in a country and culture like ours. We don't like to acknowledge infidelity. I have a simple theory. I'm one of those people who feel that if you want to save your home and marriage, don't consider sexual infidelity as infidelity. Sometimes consider it as an error, forgive and move on. Turn your back if you need to. I mean it for both men and women. In fact, I find more and more women succumbing to it and sometimes I feel so proud. I'm friendly with a lot of couples, so I get to hear both sides of the story. And it's quite amusing to me when I hear that the husband has done his bit on the side and the wife is doing it too. I think this is interesting!

My only advice is: Make sure your spouse doesn't know. Sometimes you do love your spouse but you're not necessarily turned on by them after two decades of marriage. So they come back with guilt and a present. I'm not married, so I can say it lightly, and I'm sure married people would not take this as lightly, but unfortunately I'm one of those people who've heard too much. When you're single, unattached, all you do is hear about other people's love stories, traumas, problems, and all the nonsense that goes on in a relationship. My friend Kajal Anand (Putlu) and I talk many times about how happy we are being single. She says, 'Just look around us!'

People often say that I surround myself with couples in unhappy marriages and that's why I hear these stories. No. That's not true. I went to a school reunion. There were twenty-five of us, not from the film industry. They had corporate backgrounds, they were working professionals. Out of the twenty couples I met, twelve of them were divorced, eight of them seemed unhappy, and all the men were bald. I thought, thank god for my hair and my single status! I was so amused at this reunion. Every second person was divorced. There were second wives, ex-wives . . . I thought, what's happening? All the people who had been the most earnest, strait-laced, committed students were all with second wives or had broken marriages. I thought, is this the reality of our times? It's not just the film industry but it's also outside. Is divorce the new marriage? I don't know. It's really strange. Where is that old-school resilience? Or the old-world commitment to the institution? Is it now a thing of the past? I ask myself this all the time when I see so many marriages succumbing to the finality of divorce. Is there a shift in the ethos of our times? Is the level of tolerance reducing? I don't know. I can observe this because I'm single. When you're single, people somehow like to pour their nonsense on you and you too have no choice but to hear it. So you listen. And I've always been a good listener. It doesn't make me sad. It certainly amuses me at times. At the same party I've seen the wife at it and the husband at it, and I'm amazed to see how

widespread it is now. They go back home and they're normal? How do
they live this life? But who am I to judge what they're going through? If
they're happy with their life and pretending that nothing is happening,
then why am I getting so wound up? I've seen so many marriages
crumble around me—I hate to say I'm almost used to it.

Kabhi Alvida Naa Kehna was also the toughest shoot in my life. We
were combating weather. It was too big an outdoor project; it was
Apoorva's first big film. We were all a bit lost. And we were doing all this
without my father. Everything that could go wrong was going wrong.
There were production issues. I was learning, Apoorva was learning.
It was at that juncture that Apoorva even questioned his decision to
come back. He felt it was impacting our friendship, which he felt was
more important to him than anything else. His position, the money,
the status or the power, nothing could ever override the affection and
friendship that we'd shared up to that point for nearly twenty-five years.

He kept telling me, 'Karan, I am losing the friend I have in you.'

We were close friends but what happened was that he began
instilling anxiety and fear in me. He was the one coming to me with all
the bad news since he was the one in charge. And I just wanted to block
that part because I wanted to direct the film. I was trying to run away
from all the problems he was bringing.

He told me, 'Listen, I have to address these problems. It's not all
good times, you know, there will be stresses.'

In the running of a shoot abroad, it is so easy to have a production
meltdown. Some requirements are sometimes not met. When I
wrapped up a shoot, I didn't want to meet him because he would tell
me about all the problems and issues, and I was too used to my father
taking care of them and not bringing them to me. But why should
Apoorva do that? We were equal in age. I, too, had to shoulder them.
I didn't have my father any more but subconsciously I was looking for

that person who would take charge like my father used to. But Apoorva was also learning on the job, it was not his fault. And he needed me on board. I had to tell him, don't do this, do this, because I knew the industry better, he didn't. Now he knows everything. But then it was his first time.

We had a long chat at that time where he felt that 'nothing is worth losing a friendship. It's not what I want. I'll go back.'

I said, 'You can't do that. I need you.' I had nobody else.

So we went through that phase. I realized that when you work with somebody on a daily basis, it is tough to go back to being the best friends that you know you are. Especially when there is a different dynamic. Now I was the one leading the company, and Apoorva was working for me. Though he was doing much more than I was in terms of day-to-day modalities, etc., there was a shift in the dynamics. I had to address that.

We have managed to work together over the years, but it has been at the cost of our friendship. I don't think we are what we used to be. We're very close—Apoorva is like a member of the family. But we used to laugh together—Apoorva used to make me laugh and he is still capable of making me laugh. But somewhere, this equation has changed. He has grown in status, he is the CEO of our company. Nothing in the office can move an inch without him. He totally runs the show but we've lost track, which is unfortunate. It's been the biggest downside of him being here. And he knows it. We've talked about it, his wife always brings it up with me and feels really bad that we don't have that friendship any more. We don't socialize with each other. It's hard to when you are working the whole day. Every time we meet, we only end up talking about work. So that's why we've chosen different paths. We know the same people but we don't land up meeting each other socially. Of course, if anything happens, like if my mother goes into surgery, Apoorva is there first. If there's anything in my personal life, he is there next to me, rock solid. When I am unwell, he'll be in my house. When the doctor's there, he will be there. So he is in every way like my brother. But what happened was that we moved from being best friends to this sibling dynamic. Because of his position, he's taken on the role of an older brother, and I am the indulged younger one. He takes care of all my issues. But we've lost that friendship, which is a loss. This is something that bothers him and it bothers me, but unfortunately there is nothing we can do about it. Because now, too much time has passed. And the beginning of that was on the sets of *Kabhi Alvida Naa Kehna*, where we realized that things were not going to be the same ever again.

8

Consolidating Dharma

After *Kabhi Alvida Naa Kehna*, we moved on to other films. *Dostana* was directed by Tarun Mansukhani, who had been my first assistant on *Kabhi Alvida Naa Kehna*. Ayan Mukherjee and Puneet Malhotra also assisted me on that film. So the *Kabhi Alvida Naa Kehna* crew had a lot of potential directors.

Ayan Mukherjee is Kajol's first cousin and Rani's second cousin. I didn't meet him through them though. My meeting with Ayan Mukherjee was actually rather hysterical. He is Ashutosh Gowariker's brother-in-law—his wife, Sunita's, half-brother; they have a mother in common.

I had finished *Kal Ho Naa Ho*'s screening and I was standing outside when a young, lanky, awkward-looking boy came up to me and said, 'I really liked the representation of homosexuality in the film.'

I said, 'Oh, thanks.'

He said, 'Really, so how did you think of this? I have never seen this representation in mainstream cinema.'

I said, 'Well, it's what it is.'

That was my first meeting with Ayan.

Then I met him in Goa with my friends Pooja and Aarti Shetty, Manmohan Shetty's daughters. Aarti wanted to assist me, and she's now

My parents on the day of their engagement

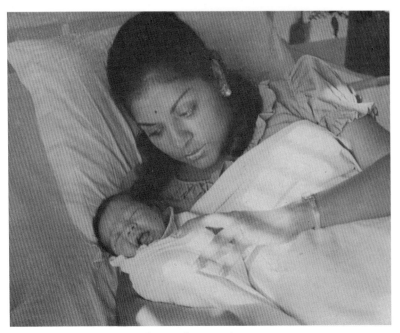

Newborn in the arms of my mom

On my first birthday

In Ooty during the outdoor shoot of *Dostana*

In our house in New Delhi with Dad at the age of seventeen

With Mom in New York, 1999

With my college gang in Mahabaleshwar at age eighteen

With Kajol during the shooting of 'Sajanji Ghar Aaye' in Kuch Kuch Hota Hai

Shooting the title song of Kabhi Khushi Kabhie Gham . . . with Jaya aunty

With Gauri and Aryan during the making of *Kuch Kuch Hota Hai*

In conversation with Yash uncle who had
come to wish me on the first day of *Kabhi Khushi Kabhie Gham . . .*

With Farah Khan while shooting 'Bole Chudiyan' for Kabhi Khushi Kabhie Gham . . .

Shooting the climax of Kabhi Khushi Kabhie Gham . . .

Behind the scenes: with Hrithik and Kareena on the set of *Kabhi Khushi Kabhie Gham* . . .

Behind the scenes: with Farah Khan during the shoot of
Kabhi Khushi Kabhie Gham . . .

Shooting a song sequence for *Kabhi Khushi Kabhie Gham* . . .

Behind the scenes: *Kabhi Khushi Kabhie Gham* . . .

Shooting at Blue Water Mall, London, for *Kabhi Khushi Kabhie Gham* . . .
with Amit uncle and Jaya aunty

With Abhishek and Aishwarya during the shoot of *Koffee with Karan*

Behind the scenes: *Kabhi Alvida Naa Kehna*

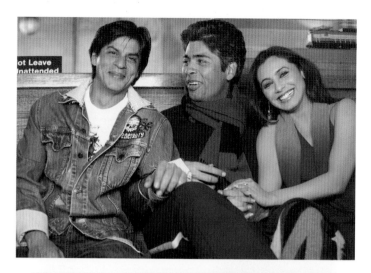

With Shah Rukh and Rani while shooting *Kabhi Alvida Naa Kehna*

Behind the scenes: *Kabhi Alvida Naa Kehna*

With Dad during IIFA, June 2004, when he received the
Lifetime Achievement Award

Behind the scenes: *Ae Dil Hai Mushkil*

A still from *Ae Dil Hai Mushkil*

At home with Mom

Behind the camera

one of my closest friends. She knew Ayan; in fact, they both knew him well. So Ayan came and had breakfast with these girls and me. And I thought, oh, this strange person has arrived again. He kept staring at me, and I thought it was a bit weird. So Aarti told me, 'I think he wants to assist you.' I thought, whatever, there is no way in hell I am going to take this weirdo. Then I got a call from Aarti saying that he really wanted to assist me, had taken my number, and could I just let him message me? I said, 'Okay, let him message me.'

So he sent a message and I read the message and immediately called him for a meeting. I had never read a message that had so moved me, made me chuckle, and then made me emotional. It was the most beautiful message. I can't remember it now. It's no longer on my phone. But I remember I was blown away by the message. It was all about how he wanted to assist me.

I said, 'Meet me tomorrow at two in the afternoon.'

When I met him, the first thing I told him was, 'You're a writer. You'll write, whatever else you do.'

He said, 'I want to assist you and it's really one of the things that I want to do.'

I said, 'Yeah, okay.'

I knew immediately there was something about him. Because that message was just outstanding. I wish I had archived it, knowing his trajectory later on in life.

That was how I hired Ayan. He was twenty-three-something and he was a bright kid. He has a spark about him. Ayan can be irreverent and obnoxious in a way that you will always forgive him. He will never ever upset you. He's got that knack of saying the most irreverent things, but you'll pass them off as pleasantries. He's got that knack. Anyway, he came on board.

Soon after, I started on my journey of giving breaks to these budding directors. It started with Tarun Mansukhani and Rensil D'Silva. Tarun made *Dostana* for us, an idea of mine that he developed. I always wanted to make a film on the story of two boys who pretend to be a gay couple to get accommodation, and Tarun built on this story. Simultaneously,

I asked Ayan to come up with a script. He did a coming-of-age tale, which he tentatively titled *Wake Up Sid*.

I had an idea for *Kurbaan*. It was my story that I gave to Rensil to develop into a screenplay. So these three projects started one after the other. *Dostana* released in 2008. I knew there was a director in Tarun. I thought the same of Ayan. I liked Rensil's style of writing. He had written *Rang De Basanti* at that time. *Kurbaan* didn't go on to do well but I liked his headspace nonetheless.

Dharma Productions had started opening up and finding wings. *Dostana* did really well, *Wake Up Sid* got a 10, and *Kurbaan* didn't work. Subsequently, we had a film called *I Hate Luv Storys* directed by Puneet Malhotra, who was an assistant of mine. That did really well and we developed a great rapport with UTV. We started understanding the game—the distribution and marketing of films. There was also a sea change in the way the industry was operating. *Dostana* was one of our highly marketed movies. I understood that our strength also lay in marketing. I have a good mind about how to project a film, 'platform' it, and position it. It's not just about making a product, it's also about how you pitch it to the consumer, the cine-goer. I felt I had a knack for that.

We gave *Dostana* an interesting promo. We said, 'From the makers of *Kuch Kuch Hota Hai, Kabhi Khushi Kabhie Gham . . ., Kal Ho Naa Ho*, comes another kind of a love story. *"Tum gay ho."*' So we made a little fun of it. It was an interesting gimmick. Then I felt that we needed to present John as sexy. So we marketed him in those yellow trunks. And we made that image go viral. There was Priyanka looking superhot in her bikini, and we introduced the whole homosexual angle with a lot of fun. We positioned the film for the youth.

I remember when Karan Malhotra (who later directed *Agneepath*) came to me to assist (I eventually took him in as my first assistant on *My*

Name Is Khan). In the first three weeks of his job, he was very shy and quiet. Karan has a strong and stern kind of personality. After three weeks, the ice finally broke and we started interacting more. I also take a while to open up to new people around me. I am a bit shy. It may sound strange but I am. I am awkward around new people. It takes me a very long time to get used to somebody new in my office. I also maintain a conscious distance from the people I work with unless they are my friends. I believe that's the only way you can keep objectivity. Karan told me a very amusing thing later. He said, 'You know, I never thought I would get the job because I thought you hire only good-looking, well-dressed people.'

I said, 'What? You actually thought that!'

When I launched the careers of all these young film-makers, I started sensing that Dharma was gaining ground as a production house-cum-studio and that my instinct in spotting talent was mostly correct. Dharma's brand value was already strong, and we had begun consolidating it. Actors were excited to work with us, and we had gained a certain stamp of quality.

But I still feel like we're finding our feet. We're in the driver's seat for sure, but we're still combating the bumps on the highway. We suddenly have divisions and departments, and work is being delegated to teams. For me, even the fact that we're on email loops with each other is a big movement. We have always been an informal, boutique production house, used to barging into each other's rooms. Apoorva is the only one in the office who has a strong dress code. He observes corporate wear from Monday to Friday, and on Saturdays he'll wear a T-shirt. The rest of us all look like ragamuffins.

The decision to move to our new office in Andheri was because we were running out of space in our old one in Khar. It had been a bit like a cottage industry, and Apoorva felt the need to make it a little more corporate. I thought we would never be able to create the same love in this big space. From 7000 square feet we have gone to 27,000 square feet. It was a huge leap to take, geographically and otherwise. But we didn't have a choice and now we've made it our own. I feel that I set the vibe.

I'm always all over the place. I'm never in my room. I hate my room. According to feng shui, my room had to be elevated which, as it turned out, was not a good thing because the first thing I did was fall. That was the way I introduced myself to this cabin. Because of feng shui my room is in the corner of the office and I feel very cut off. It's meant to be the hotspot. But it doesn't make me feel hot. I just feel I'm in a spot! But otherwise I love my office. It is my *sukoon ghar*. Even though it takes two and a half hours of my day to commute, I feel very happy and proud that this is mine. I feel like I created it. And despite the new move, there are a few things Dharma will always be: accessible, amiable, affable—the three As. That's us. I don't take myself seriously, so no one else does either—in a good way. No one calls me sir. Some of the ADs are really young, barely twenty-one, twenty-two years old. When they join, they are scared and nervous, but soon enough, I start cracking my stupid jokes with them and they relax. I ask them to call me Karan. I'd feel old if they called me sir. I want to stay young.

That's the vibe in the organization.

Dharma has a great vibe. People who work in the company have been around for years. We're friends first and colleagues later. There's a lot of buddy bonding. Believe it or not, all the directors of Dharma get along with each other. Occasionally, we do gatherings. When we screen any film, we make all the directors come and see it. And everybody comes with the right spirit. There may be an underlying spirit of competition and one-upmanship, but, by and large, there's love for the company. Dharma screenings are full of Dharma love. It's our motto—good dharma and karma. I don't mean that in a cheesy way. It really comes from the heart, from the energy that my father created and spread, which I decided to absorb and spread further. I'm not sitting prissily on top of some kind of food chain at Dharma.

People just hang out at Dharma. The other thing is that there's no such thing as keeping a secret here. The gossip channel is always on, and that comes from me perhaps! If we find one AD is in love with another AD, everybody will chat about it and everybody wants to know. The gossip on a film set is very exciting, and everybody is interested to know all about it. I think that too comes from me!

When I decide what films Dharma will be making, I follow my instinct as a film-maker. Much as we may try and deconstruct it, there is a tag that comes with Dharma films—they're associated with gloss, good music, a feel-good emotion. There's an expectation of these qualities when we make a Dharma film. We do try to break it. I've made a violent film like *Agneepath*, a martial arts film, *Brothers*. We presented *Baahubali*. We presented *Lunchbox*. I made a film like *My Name Is Khan* that didn't have those prerequisites. Yet, people associate us with movies like *Yeh Jawaani Hai Deewani*, *2 States* or *Humpty Sharma Ki Dulhania*. No matter what we do, even when we follow a different path, we end up getting more known for the quintessential feel-good, good-looking film. Somewhere, there is the Dharma brand that comes out. People say they like the way actors look in our films, they like the music and the costumes, the way it's all shot. There's a certain aesthetic associated with Dharma films—this can be great but also annoying. Sometimes, you feel like you've done so much that's different, but why aren't you being acknowledged for that?

It's exactly like the problem I face as a film-maker. No matter what I do, even if it's different, people say, 'Oh, you make family films.' No, I don't. I made one family film. Or they say, 'You make love stories.' No, I don't. I made one love story. I don't get credited for anything different I do. It's the same problem with the company. Ayan is now making a film about a superhero which will be a trilogy. Karan Malhotra wants to make *The Immortals of Meluha* which is part of Amish Tripathi's Shiva trilogy. We're now trying to upgrade our thought process. We're trying to get into the franchise film space by integrating Indian mythology with computer graphics, which, I think, will work really well in terms of the scope that cinema offers. *Baahubali* was a step in that direction. I decided to take on *Baahubali* because I felt it was a film that should be watched by a national audience.

I have always been a big fan of the director S. Rajamouli. When Rana Dagubatti, who is a friend, told me that Rajamouli was making *Baahubali*, I landed up at Hyderabad to meet him. I told him I thought his film deserved national viewing. With this kind of scale and opulence, all of India should experience the film. Why should it be released in South India only? And I believe very strongly that in terms of quality, technique and storytelling, it's not down south but it's up south. Rajamouli is a master storyteller. I've followed most of his work—*Magadheera, Eega, Maryada Ramanna*—and they are all amazing films. I knew he was making this big motion picture, an epic film, the largest motion picture ever made in India, budget-wise, scale-wise, opulence-wise, story-wise. I was keen to present it to the whole country. Luckily, he was completely on board. He is a great man to work with.

I didn't know anything about the story, and had just seen images and certain sequences. He made a five-minute computer presentation to me about what it looks like. Till I released the film, I didn't know how the film was going to end. I had no clue. I saw it like a member of the audience. But I had faith in him and belief in the world he was creating. I felt that if we positioned the film correctly, it would work. When *Baahubali* was finally released across the country, it got an opening of Rs 5.5 crore because it had the Dharma branding as well as the fact that we presented the film to the audience in a certain way. The first thing I said was that let's call it 'India's largest motion picture'. Why should you want to pay 400 rupees for something unless it entices you in some way?

That was what I did with *Lunchbox*. I think I have a marketing instinct. When *Lunchbox* came to me, it was a tiny film, and I thought, what is the peg that will intrigue anybody beyond the fact that it is an off-mainstream film? The line I gave was 'Can you fall in love with someone you've never met?' This line was not on any other poster—it was meant just for the Hindi release. We added that line because I felt it would make people curious about the film. Of course, the film had great actors, but it was considered a 'festival film', it was considered art house. These are bad words in commercial terminology. The feeling is that, oh, this is a festival picture, must be boring. That is the subtext. Today, of course, many more are excited about good content because there are certain urban multiplexes that react to these kind of films, but you have to position the film properly. Otherwise, it'll just get lost. You have to energize the exhibitor. A lot of work goes into releasing a film.

Our industry is finally emerging as an industry of the producer or the studio. It used to be an actor's industry, it still is in many ways, and superstardom always reigns. So Salman Khan will defy all sensibilities, and all business models. The audience just wants to see him. But it is now the age of the producer or the studio because they are the ones who are giving the money. If they don't fund you, you can't release the film. And I'm proud of that movement. Because, the empowerment of any film finally comes from the money you put into its projection, its promotion, and the platform it gets. This happens only due to a studio or a producer. If a studio is efficient at it, it works well for the film. On the contrary, if they slacken they can actually ruin the product. You have to nurture a film. *Lunchbox* and *Baahubali* are good examples, because these were films that could have easily got lost. *Baahubali* could have done really well in the south and nobody from anywhere else would have seen the film. It needed to be positioned. After that, so many films have come to me, but it doesn't work every time. I have to believe in it. *Ghanti bajni chahiye*. I saw *Lunchbox* in Cannes, and despite the naysayers, I persisted. I said, 'You are all wrong. It's a commercial film. It'll do a restricted number but it'll get liked by the audience. There is a thirty-five–fifty-year-old audience that is going to bite this film. I was moved by it. It's a wonderful, tiny film, and it must be seen. Yes, it won't do phenomenal numbers, but it'll do enough to be called a success, and it did. It ran for three–four weeks, had a very healthy lifetime, and everyone made money on it.

The producers have to be creative to push a film. Any studio that is not creative is going to dissolve into nothing, vanish into oblivion. If you chase just the money, you're going to fall into a bottomless pit. You need to balance creativity with commerce. A studio has to think like a creative producer. People are not going to pay up if the content is not strong. Eventually, they're going to come and see your film only if it's good. You can make a lot of noise in marketing, but if your product is not good, nobody is going to come. The audience is always smarter. Every consumer is born with an instinct. Whether they want to see your film or not, or buy your soap or not. It is a sixth sense every consumer has about the product you are selling. It is almost like they can smell a bad film. And they can sense a great one. So you can't take a consumer for granted any more.

You can't do a hard sell by just putting in an item song, for instance. Out of thirty such songs, one works. Or two. 'Chikni Chameli' in Agneepath worked phenomenally. You have to take a big-ass movie star and completely deconstruct her. Katrina had never done a song like that. She's sexy but had never danced to an item song sporting an ethnic look. The song has been emulated thirty-five times since, but it hasn't clicked. Invariably, an item song that's integrated with the film will work better. 'Badtameez Dil' in Yeh Jawaani Hai Deewani worked with the audience because it was a part of the film. The lead actor was doing it. Sometimes, to create that big energy and big vibe, it has to be integrated with the film. When it's a little distant from the film, the audience senses it.

With My Name Is Khan, I tried to win over the critical audiences who thought I couldn't make a different kind of film. I made it for just that reason. I wanted to make a film based on a social cause because that is what those kinds of people like. Of course, I believed very strongly in it. I am one of those people who is very open-minded about religion. I don't have any prejudices. When there's talk about Islam and terrorism, and the association between the two, I believe there are larger political reasons for everything. You can't generalize about a religion. There are millions of people across the world who are Muslim, who are suffering on account of a faulty perception, and I felt very strongly that I wanted to tell that story. But I also made the film for a selfish reason—I wanted to make a film with a social message, and win critical acclaim for it. *My Name Is Khan* did eventually go on to bring me critical praise.

Looking back, I feel I went wrong with fifteen minutes of that film. There was a whole hurricane angle that didn't work at all. I pulled it off really badly, but I thought the intention of the film would tide it through. I wanted to win the Best Director award. And I won it. I got five-star and four-and-a-half-star reviews.

My Name Is Khan was a heavy film. To get the point across, something tragic had to happen to the family. We did debate whether the child should die or get handicapped—those discussions were quite macabre, actually. We eventually went with the decision to kill the child. I myself advised many pregnant friends at that time not to see the film. I knew it was disturbing. I tried very hard to tone down the sadness of that moment, but it wasn't possible. When Kajol breaks down in that scene, it is very disturbing. And that's why I didn't make it the interval point. I wanted the interval to be elevating and then to absorb the sadness into the second half, going into elevation again. If the child's death came right at the interval, I felt you may not have wanted to go back in. Today, perhaps I would not be able to pull off that same film. Today, I would not be able to kill off a child in a film. But at that time, I felt I could. It's always about the state of mind you're in at that moment.

After *My Name Is Khan*, I began feeling the need to take a break from anything heavy. I also started fearing that I was becoming mildly irrelevant to the youth. They didn't know me. The youngsters, the teenagers, were not aware of me. I feel if you need longevity in your career, you can never afford to be irrelevant to the youth. You have to be able to connect with the youth and this is something I would tell any businessman, any entrepreneur or anyone in the creative field. Today, Amitabh Bachchan is relevant to youngsters because of what he's done perhaps as a quiz show presenter, or by doing a film like *Piku*, or for his flamboyance, or dress sense. There is something young about Mr Bachchan even at seventy-three. He's on Facebook, he's on Twitter, he's interactive, and the youth are connected to him. He has made himself relevant. And that's something I always want to be—relevant to the youth.

So on my fortieth birthday, I made up my mind that I would release my youngest film yet. Probably my worst film creatively, but it would be fun, cute and happy. I didn't want to move any movie mountains. I needed to make a young film and decided that if I had to create the talent, I would have to direct this film. *Student of the Year* was designed to be a launch pad for three kids. And that's what it was. I wanted to make an energetic young film with sport and music and dance, like a high-school musical. That was the template in my head. I wanted the eleven-, twelve-, thirteen-, fourteen-year-olds to see it. I didn't care about anyone above twenty-one. My demographic was eight to twenty-one. That's what I was chasing. I didn't want the mummies and daddies to watch this film. I knew them, they knew me. But I felt I didn't know the kids any more. And after *Student of the Year*, I became immediately relevant to them. I love it when parents come up to me with their kids and say, '*Isne* Student of the Year *chaar baar dekhi hai. Hume bhi dekhni padi.*'

As a film-maker, I love to observe what is happening around. I'm always looking at what people wear, how they speak. My sense of observation has always been my biggest strength. I'm not a great person for watching all kinds of global content, and hearing all kinds of music.

I don't do that. But I look a lot at people. I observe young kids in my company who've been ADs. I observe how they speak, what they wear, all those little things. So if you see *Student of the Year*, it's not wannabe, it's young. I fear being a wannabe.

In fact, I didn't think Sidharth Malhotra, Varun Dhawan and Alia Bhatt were from another age bracket when I talked to them. Actually, they are my friends today, all three of them. Two of them, Sid and Varun, were my ADs on *My Name Is Khan*. I remember Ravi Chandran, the director of photography (DoP) on the film, using Varun and Sid for the lighting of Shah Rukh and Kajol. Every time Ravi had to do the light, he would make them stand in the frame. At one point, there was a close-up of Shah Rukh and Kajol that he was lighting. I wanted a pretty light. He put these boys in that light and I stared at the monitor, and said, 'They are movie stars.' Good looks don't always translate to the screen. Off-screen, Sid is a great-looking guy but when he comes in front of the camera, he looks even better. You see him in real life and you think what a great-looking guy. You see him on screen and he's a movie star. Varun looks ten times better on screen. He comes alive on screen. I heard about Alia from my friend Niranjan. He told me that Mahesh Bhatt had a young daughter, seventeen years old, who wanted to be in the movies, but maybe she was too young. Alia came, chubby, from school, in her uniform. She did an audition. I had auditioned 400 girls by then. She was not thin, she was not conventionally beautiful. She was cute like Pooja Bhatt, but her audition! She danced like she was the slimmest girl in the room. She was not even aware that she was large.

She said, 'You find me chubby?'

I said, 'Yeah, you are. You should lose weight.'

She said, 'I never thought I was chubby.'

In her head she looked great. I loved that about her, that she wasn't carrying her weight around as weight. She was so confident.

I called her and said, 'Lose weight and come back in three months.'

I got her on to a dietician and to a gym, but I knew that she was the girl for the film. I knew it, I just didn't want to confirm it to her till she had lost that weight. She came to me after three months and she had lost weight. We did a photo shoot with the boys, and they looked great together.

I had such fun shooting *Student of the Year*. The actors would come on time. We actually started the day at 9 a.m. That had never happened to me. Stars always come late.

I remember I was the most senior person on the sets of *Student of the Year*. I had a young crew of ADs, my DoP was younger than me, everyone was young. I thought, oh god, I'm like an uncle on this set. But it was great. We shot in fun locations, we had fun music, and we made a fun film. Everybody who saw the film asked me why I was being apologetic about it. It was a blast. Happy, good-looking kids, all well dressed. My friend Manish Malhotra told me, 'You'll slap me, but I prefer *Student of the Year* to *My Name Is Khan*.' He said it was my kind of film, so energetic and youthful.

I feel as though my personality also kind of changed post *Student of the Year*. My decision to do *Jhalak Dikhhla Jaa* happened that year. My life literally started changing after forty. I had this big bash to celebrate my fortieth which I called 'my wedding bash' since I'm not getting married. This was my big party. I called everybody who'd been a part of my work life, and my personal life. It was a black-tie event, and I felt very excited. *Student of the Year* hadn't launched as yet, but the three kids were there. I'd been in the movies for fifteen years, and I thought, it's been a great innings, so why not make this like my wedding party because *shaadi toh hone wali nahin*. I resolved I would do this every five years—at forty, forty-five, fifty, fifty-five, and so on. I would celebrate it like that because life is about celebrating with people. It was my instinct that in my fortieth year, things were going to change at least work-wise, and they did. Everything kind of opened up after my fortieth birthday. *Student of the Year* released in my fortieth year, and it did well. The company expanded even further. Dharma had two humongous successes after that, *Agneepath* and *Yeh Jawaani Hai Deewani*. Everything got energized. I believe my forties will be exceptionally important in my career graph eventually. I have another six years to go in the decade. But something instinctively tells me that this is going to be a great decade.

In the future, Dharma will be doing all kinds of films. But I won't make films that I don't understand. I don't get horror, so I won't make a horror film. Films about creatures—I can't relate to them. Personally, I don't love animation. I don't get it, I won't make it. But a taut action thriller, a comedy, a romance, a drama, a saga, a trilogy like *Meluha*—I would love to make. Wherever there is an emotional thread, I'm on board. I made a film called *Brothers* which is about mixed martial arts; while I know nothing about the sport, it had such a strong emotional thread. When I saw the original, *Warrior*, I was moved by it. I cried at the end of that film. I go by emotional motivation. I can't make a junk-food thriller. It has to connect with me on a human level. I loved *Agneepath* because it came from a very angsty place, and Karan was the right director for such a film. That angst comes through on celluloid. For me, the human, emotional connect is the most important factor in greenlighting a film. I can't do it otherwise. I have to feel that tug at my heart.

I love music. And I listen to only Hindi film music. I don't know what's happening in music in the rest of the world. I pick up sounds when I travel abroad, but that's it. You ask me what Britney Spears is singing or what Justin Bieber is jamming to or what the hell Beyoncé is up to, and I know nothing. They pop up on my iTunes chart sometimes, and I think, what are these songs? I now know what EDM stands for and I know what house music is, but I know this only because of my shopping. Because, when I go from one shop to the next, I hear a certain kind of sound, and I think, oh all right, this is what is doing the rounds these days. It's again a sense of observation. Otherwise, my iPod and iPad have only Hindi film music, music from the forties, fifties, sixties, seventies.

My best times are when I'm travelling abroad and I'm walking around listening to 'Mera Kuch Samaan' from *Ijaazat* on my headphones. I listen to the songs of *Masoom* or I listen to '*Lag Ja Gale*', and it would always get me teary. I just love the melody of those times. They are immortal. I understand melody. So even the item numbers in my films must have a proper tune. If I don't feel that my feet and heart are connecting to that tune, I don't say okay to it. Sometimes, I've bounced about twenty tunes because I was not happy with any of them. Sometimes, you let go because the film is due for release; so you say, '*Chalo, kar lo.*' *Aaj ka daur hi kuch alag hai*, in terms of the songs that work today. You have to update your sense of music. When Yo Yo Honey Singh came on to the scene, I thought, okay, this is the order of the day. You have to understand that rap is now liked. I don't get rap. I think it's crap. But I know that at the end of the day, you have to adapt your understanding of music to the times. That's why I go on about my relevance to the youth. You can't trash what you don't understand. You have to integrate what you don't understand with what you do.

Songs like '*Sajda*' and '*Mitwa*' did very well. But when you're doing a *Humpty Sharma Ki Dulhania*, you can't do a '*Sajda*' although you can have a '*Samjhawan*' which you understand. But you also need a '*Saturday Saturday*' for the pop culture kids to dance to. So you have to know that this kind of song is nice too. There's beat and rhythm. Also, when you want to dance in a party, you can't dance to '*Sajda*'. So you have to have a '*Balam Pichkari*'. You have to integrate Hindi film music with coolness. The lyrics have to connect somewhere with the new generation. I always give hook-lines first. Like I gave the line, 'Where's the Party Tonight?' Or 'It's the Time to Disco'. Then the lyricists work around the lines. Javed saab is so funny. When he was writing, 'Where's the Party Tonight?', he kept saying, 'Why are they singing "where's the party tonight" when they're already at a party?'

So I said, 'Javed saab, you don't understand, you can party at a party.'

He still didn't get it.

I said, 'Javed saab, the word "party" is equivalent to fun. You can ask this question at a party.'

Then Loy wrote some rap, that 'it's down the road'.

So Javed saab said, 'If it's down the road, then why are they singing "where's the party tonight"?'

He was very funny. But he gets the youth. He is the youngest man I know. He wrote the song around it then. It's important to give a line that becomes like a catchphrase, something that will play on the mind. You have to think like a marketing person when it comes to selling a song.

I go abroad when I have to write my scripts. I go away to London to just be in a different time zone. It's as simple as that. When you are in the same time zone as Mumbai, you are always harassed and harangued. When you are in a different time zone, you are less harassed by people. In fact, when I go to New York, it's even better. When I wake up in the morning there, I just address one or two calls. Everyone is asleep through the day in Mumbai and so I get the day off.

As far as the creative process is concerned, with me it's a bit ad hoc. I don't write. It's very strange, but in all my years I've never put pen to paper. I dictate and somebody else writes. When I'm there, in London or New York, I'm just thinking. I can narrate my whole film—say *Ae Dil Hai Mushkil*—to anyone without a single piece of paper. I don't forget what I create.

When I go abroad to write, I keep walking and thinking. Even while eating in a restaurant, I'm thinking. While shopping, I'm thinking. I walk a lot. I walk blocks in New York. It's my favourite city actually. I walk 100 blocks in a day maybe. I like to go out in the winter too. I'll wear my jacket, put my hands in my pockets and walk, sometimes with my coffee in hand. I walk aimlessly, looking around me, going into a shop sometimes, walking out, coming back to my hotel, lying down, watching random TV, ordering in sometimes, meeting a friend for dinner perhaps, sleeping early, waking up late. It's my time off.

Every year I do it for at least a month. I love it. It's my time to myself in a country that's far away.

I don't meet hundreds of people when I am abroad. It's cool. First of all, everyone's not dying to meet you; they all have a life of their own. There's also such a strong weekend culture in the West, so you land up meeting people only on the weekends. Nobody meets you midweek. And there everything is early, you meet at 7.30–8, and you are done by 11 p.m.

I love going out of the country and just being. Thinking. Then I come back and narrate the story and make somebody put it down on paper. I have ADs whose job it is to put it all down. I've always done that. *Ae Dil Hai Mushkil* has been written by me after *Kuch Kuch Hota Hai* and *Kal Ho Naa Ho. My Name Is Khan* and *Kabhi Alvida Naa Kehna* were co-written by me and other people. *Student of the Year* was written by Rensil D'Silva, I directed it.

So this is my process when I write. I wrote *Ae Dil Hai Mushkil* in September 2014 when I went abroad for my mom's treatment. I wrote it in a month. I was on the Emirates flight, Dubai to New York, it's a long flight. I did a lot of thinking and suddenly it came to me. This is how I want it, this is what my characters will be like. And it evolved into a narrative. One fine day, I remember, I called my friend Aarti Shetty. We spoke for two hours and I told her that this was the film I would be making, these were the scenes. Then I said I had to make it into a screenplay.

And she said, 'But, Karan, you've just narrated the entire screenplay to me. You have the whole film in your head.'

And I thought, yes, it's true, I do have the film in my head!

I remember I took Niranjan Iyengar for a walk in New York once and I said these were my ideas, but he said, 'You've just told me the whole film! You have called me to New York just to jot down what is already there?' I thought then, yes, it's true, I do have it all in my mind. But then you do have to write the screenplay and dialogues.

I don't know what kind of films I would like to make in the next few years. It always depends on my headspace at that point of time. *Bombay Talkies* was out of my comfort zone. It was something that came to me in three days. I jotted it down and shot it in six days. I enjoyed it. It was great fun, something that was off the cuff. I don't believe I have completed a film so fast, from inception to shoot. I thought of it in December, shot it in February, it was ready to release in May. I thought, *chalo art house bhi bana dete hain, thodi slow rakhenge, thoda intellectual hona chahiye; Anurag aur Dibakar aur Zoya ke saath blend ho jaye.* There was always a fear I would stick out like a sore thumb. I spoke to Rani and Randeep and Saqib about it, and it all came together, though there was much ado about the kiss between Randeep and Saqib. They were anxious about it. More than Saqib, Randeep was nervous. I told them to trust me—'the way I've designed it, it'll never seem cheesy'. But Randeep was horrified about shooting the scene. He said, 'I've never kissed a man in my life.' And I said, 'It's okay, you can kiss one on screen.' We had one take of that scene and that was it. It's a film about a repressed man and his need to live a lie and how he puts his wife through all that. I had a lot of people tell me that they suspected their husbands were gay after they saw the film.

There is a scene where '*Lag Ja Gale*' comes—when I described that scene to Randeep, I told him, 'In your head, you were in love with your friend in college and he got married and then you got married. But he was your big love and "*Lag Ja Gale*" is the song that reminds you of him.' That was my backstory, though it was not mentioned in the film anywhere. He asked me why I was connecting to this child, and I said, 'You're connecting to the song, and the innocence of this child is reminding you of your love.' That was what I was trying to show emotionally at that point of time. It's just a moment when he feels something. I think I sometimes tend to surprise myself. When I narrated the film to people, they said, 'Er, you've written this script?'

The funniest story was about the beggar child. Tarun Mansukhani was my first AD on the film—I needed familiar faces around me—and he came to me huffing and puffing, and said, 'Karan, what is this?'

I said, 'What?'

He said, 'About your costume requirement.'

I said, 'So?'

He said, 'There are three costume changes for the beggar child. A beggar can't keep changing her clothes, she's a beggar.'

I said, 'Oh, I'm so sorry.'

It became a big joke in the office that I gave the beggar three costume changes!

Much as I would like to project reality, there are some things that just don't come naturally to me!

I get clothes. When kids were reading *Tintin* and *Archie*, I was buying *Harper's Bazaar* and *Vogue* from the *raddiwala*. My father was a garment exporter and he had some connection with clothes. I had heard about these magazines and I used to see them at the raddiwala. My eyes would literally pop out. My mother found it strange that I was buying these fashion magazines, but never questioned me about it.

With Dharma, I've known when a film is not going to work. And I will never lie to a director of this company. When I see a film I don't like I will tell them honestly. I may not feel proud but I will always acknowledge that it's my film. I will support it. You have to acknowledge success and you must acknowledge failure. The other day somebody asked me about my film *Baar Baar Dekho*. I didn't like it and I had told the people involved. The film bombed but I'm the only one who didn't suffer that weekend because I had expected it. I felt terrible for the first-time director, terrible for the lead talent, terrible for my co-producers but I didn't feel terrible for myself.

Puneet Malhotra's last film *Gori Tere Pyar Mein* was a flop. But I have immense faith in his abilities as a commercial film-maker. He had made *I Hate Luv Storys*. He is really a pop culture kid. He knows what he's doing. He's directing *Student of the Year 2* now. He's taking a huge Dharma Productions franchise ahead. That's what I tell him—films go wrong sometimes and I will never hold that against you. That is not a reflection of your talent

I knew *Ungli* wouldn't work either. When I saw it, I knew it was awful. I delayed it by a year and a half. I tried to salvage it in the edit.

I somehow always know. I pre-empt failure. I think like the audience, not as a film-maker. That's why I detach myself from the making of a film made by someone else in my production house. So that when I watch it, I think to myself, was I moved? Did I like it? Was I entertained? I have never ever been surprised by the success or failure of any film of Dharma Productions. It's an instinct I have. It's my only strength—my instinct to choose the right people, the right films. I remember Shashank Khaitan came with the script of *Humpty Sharma Ki Dulhania*. I didn't know him from anywhere. The script was lying on my table with that title on the first page. And I thought, what a strange title. There were four scripts lying in front of me, but something compelled me to pick up *Humpty*, because of the title, I guess. I read it and thought what a funny, well-written script. Who's this writer? Subsequently, when Shashank came to see me, he said he was the writer but that he realized that he wouldn't be able to direct it because I didn't know him from Adam. He was a Whistling Woods graduate and he had been making the rounds of the studios with this one script in hand. I met him three or four times and I told him, 'You direct it.' I felt he would be the right person. And he made a wonderful film. Actually, what are you without your instinct? We all have it. We don't act on it sometimes because we underestimate it. But it's a gift given to us by the universe. Your instinct is never wrong. The ones who work on their instinct through meditation or inner peace are actually the most evolved souls in this world. They're the ones you call 'spiritual beings'. That's what spiritual evolution is—acting on your instinct. The higher the level of acting on your instinct, the better the result. We all have an instinct—in our relationships, in our professional zone, we're all born with it, but we all have to act on it. I tell the people in my office, 'Never be deluded about your product. You must know what you have. You can't pretend that what you've released is great.'

I always get a sense of things. I remember what happened in *Student of the Year*. I had put out a promo that everyone loved. It was young, these three kids were fresh. But when the trailer released, after four days I realized something was amiss. I went to Apoorva and said that this trailer was not working. Something had not created the stir it should have. We overestimated the fact that I was launching three kids and people actually knew who they were. I said we needed a very big hit song to flag this film off or we would be fucked. Because we had put in a lot of money into the film. We needed a song that already had a resonance. '*Disco Deewane*', the eighties cult song, was what I had in mind. I said, 'I need to get that song. People have heard of the song, it's kind of lost in the archives, but when it comes, people will say, "Oh shit, we loved this song in the eighties."' I said I needed to get the new generation to listen to this song. I needed to bring that song back.

But the problem was that the song was with Sa Re Ga Ma. If you sell your music rights to Sony Music, for example, you can't put in a song that's with Sa Re Ga Ma. They have a policy; they don't allow you to put it on the album because you've already sold your music rights to another company. They don't want that song to be leveraged. Sa Re Ga Ma didn't mind exploiting it for themselves but that wasn't okay with Sony because they had paid a big sum for the rights of the music.

I know Sanjiv Goenka, who runs Sa Re Ga Ma, really well. He is a friend of mine; he lives in Kolkata. So one morning—I didn't tell anyone—I took the six o'clock flight to Kolkata, and called up Sanjiv. I said I had come to meet him and that I would have breakfast with him. I reached his house and said to him, 'See, I've never asked you for a favour before this and I will not ask you again. But this is a favour you have to do for me. You have to give me "*Disco Deewane*". I have to put it on the *Student of the Year* album. I know you have a policy that says you can't do this. But you have to help me. I need that song.'

Sanjiv is very fond of me. I, too, am very fond of him.

He looked at me and said, 'Yes, it's a company policy, but you've come all this way . . . I'll bend that policy for you. But promise me, you won't ask me again.'

I said I wouldn't.

So I recorded that song with Vishal Shekhar, and that's when *Student of the Year* got a buzz around it. I knew the rest of the music was great. But I needed that one song that had a recall value. It would break through the clutter. And it did.

9

The Karma at Dharma

Zoya Akhtar told me one day, 'People are saying I'm the new Karan Johar.'

I told her, 'Don't take it as a compliment. They don't mean it as a compliment. They mean you're making films about rich and frivolous things that don't matter.'

I feel no matter what kind of films I do, I never get credit. It gets forgotten immediately afterwards. I'm still associated with popcorn, bubblegum, frivolity, NRIs and rich people.

In the film industry if you don't make a social comment, if you don't talk about the middle class and their issues, then you're frivolous. 'Oh my god, you're talking about rich people!' It's almost like a curse. You can't talk about rich people. It's as if rich people can't have any problems. But you're making a film about emotions. You are making a film about life. I'm sorry I can't make a film about what happens in the slums of Dahisar and Dombivli not because I don't empathize with them—of course, I do. I feel terrible with what happens when people have to live in poverty and suffer from lack of education. I feel very strongly about how women are treated in our country, and I have opinions. But tomorrow if I offer these opinions, they'll say, 'Oh, you shut up, you frivolous fool. You're sitting in your expensive designer wear, who are you to have an opinion?'

I think this is totally wrong. How dare you say that about me? I'm willing to have an opinion because I have a heart. Am I not allowed to feel because I'm rich? Because I drive a designer car and wear designer clothes, I'm apparently not meant to have an opinion about anything that is Third World. I'm supposed to be this frivolous film-maker who makes films about rich people and their issues. I get so angry with certain intellectual voices. I want to go and tell them, 'Just shut up! What have *you* written? What have you done? I work very hard. I work twenty-hour days to run my company. There are lives I have created, careers I have curated. I have done all of that out of the bounds of what is expected of me. What do you know about my life? So you don't like my films, I don't mind that. You don't have to love me or my work, but don't judge me unfairly. Don't compare me to somebody else.'

Yes, I get a lot of love as well. I have people supporting me in what I'm trying to do. There are people who say he's the best and then there are those who say he's overrated. I've heard everything. Say all that, but don't say things like xyz was better than watching a crappy Karan Johar film because you've definitely gone to the cinema hall and watched it, and got some guilty pleasure out of it. You've definitely danced to my music in your bloody bedroom or at a wedding or at a party when you got drunk and high. So how can you judge me?

Anupama Chopra says, 'Give me a Karan Johar film any day.' I've read her reviews. Once she wrote, 'I wanted to run out and watch a Karan Johar film.'

The truth is critics and intellectuals are not my only audience. There are more innocent viewers out there who respond to my films because I have actually given them happiness through what I've created on screen. When somebody reacts to my film or my music, I just believe that I've made their lives happier. These intellectual voices do annoy me after a point. It's on my bucket list to slap some of them. But I won't. I shall allow it to pass. Because I don't want to be angry about some stupid intellectual banter of people who know nothing, and can't create anything themselves. I understand that you're meant to have an opinion in your job. But I also can't help getting annoyed or irritated. The only critic I read and take seriously is Baradwaj Rangan of *The Hindu*. He is fantastic. He has not liked a single film of mine except *Kabhi Alvida Naa Kehna*. One day, out of the blue I got an email from him. The irony is that he wanted me to write a foreword for his book. I told him I loved his reviews and would write the foreword in a heartbeat, which I did in spite of being all busy. He still doesn't like my movies, but it doesn't bother me. I don't care. That's who I am.

Anupama Chopra called me once—she had seen *Ek Main Aur Ekk Tu* and she liked it. There's one scene where Imran has this board, he organizes his life on it, and Anupama wanted to know if that board was available in the retail market. I told her, 'Anu, I'll find out because finally there's something you've actually liked in my film.'

I also find this fascination for what's in the West so annoying. They look at us like we are cringeworthy. I don't think that is right. I hate that level of condescension. I read Rangan for academic reasons and Shubhra Gupta of the *Indian Express* for entertainment reasons. She so seriously doesn't like anything. I like the fact that she's not attached to anyone in the film industry. She doesn't know anyone, and she doesn't care about anyone. I love that she hates every film, including mine. When she liked *Baahubali*, I was so excited that she liked a film. I wanted to say you liked a film that I am connected to!

I've watched a lot of Hindi films, right from the VHS phase onwards. I took to the old classics first. I've watched the films of Bimal Roy, Guru Dutt, Raj Kapoor and Yash Chopra. I didn't watch a lot of contemporary films. I had heard all the music through my mum, so I wanted to know the films that had those songs in them. At age ten I was watching *Do Bigha Zameen* and *Pyaasa* (which I didn't understand the first time I saw it, then I watched it again). *Kaagaz Ke Phool* I understood probably because it was about the film industry.

I had a bare understanding of it. Actually, *Pyaasa* took me a third viewing to completely comprehend it. I watched *Mother India* and *Mughal-e-Azam*.

While I enjoyed the pathos of Guru Dutt and the angst of Bimal Roy, I was most influenced by Raj Kapoor and Yash Chopra for their opulence and urban stories. I loved Raj Kapoor's films. I saw *Prem Rog* many times—I was fascinated by the haveli, the grandeur. *Bobby* because it was so youth oriented. I loved the way Raj Kapoor presented his women. I loved Yash Chopra for his 'society' films, the way tea used to be served in his movies. There were always flowers in a vase, everyone was so well dressed, and the women wore exquisite chiffon saris. I was obsessed with these two film-makers. I think I've seen *Kabhie Kabhie* a hundred times. Every time I had nothing to do I would watch *Kabhie Kabhie*. I felt I was a part of that family and their lives.

I remember I saw *Love Story* fourteen times, with every maid and driver of mine! My mother would get really fed up with me. Sometimes, I had to lie to go and see it! She thought I was mad.

I feel everything in Hindi cinema is emotional. Your investments in the character are emotional. Hindi cinema tugs at your heartstrings. I've wept through so many films. There's nothing like a good Hindi-film cry. Boys my age would not cry at the movies but I used to weep.

I loved the 'angry young man' movies, and Amitabh Bachchan was the best actor in the world for me. But it was not my preference to watch *Deewar* and *Trishul*; I was not into that anger. Amitabh Bachchan was larger than life, and I happened to know him personally. He was Amit uncle to me. He was someone I had known since I was a kid. But that macho phase of cinema was not my favourite. I did enjoy *Amar Akbar Anthony*, but that angst, that whole 'angry young man' phase was not my thing. I was very happy watching Rishi Kapoor singing in his lovely sweaters. I was more tilted towards the popcorn cinema of that time. *Jhoota Kahin Ka*, *Doosra Aadmi*, *Khel Khel Mein*, I was obsessed by those movies. I was really into *Khel Khel Mein*. I loved Rishi Kapoor and Neetu Singh. They were my favourite actors. I felt like they were my friends. They were so happy and cute and glamorous. Then I loved the social dramas. I cried watching *Basera*, *Yeh Vaada Raha* and *Kasme Vaade*. I liked social dramas, high-society entertainers like Yash Chopra's films, and that cute pop romcom space. High-octane, angry, angsty dramas were not my cup of tea at all. I was very ditzy about my choices in mainstream films. But I'm a Gemini and there are two sides to me for sure. One part of me enjoyed this ditziness and the other was watching Guru Dutt. There was a parallel cinema movement in the eighties, and I was also watching *Tamas* on television, as well as *Arth* and *Ardh Satya*. Actually, I liked everything that had to do with Hindi films. I had to see every film, whether it was the most idiotic B-grade film or whether it was the finest alternative cinema or the vintage classics that cinema is archived by. I watched everything.

But *Hum Aapke Hain Koun . . !* was a turning point for me. I thought it was like sunshine. I thought it had a group of great human beings, it was about family values, love, music, romance, emotion (I wept when the bhabhi died). I was totally absorbed by the film. When I first watched it, Sooraj Barjatya was there in the theatre.

I went and held his hand and said, 'Sir, you've made the best film ever.'

I don't even think he remembers that! Cool kids in my college would say, 'Are you mad? You liked *Hum Aapke Hain Koun . . !* You've lost the plot. It's like a wedding video, it's like a *mithai ka dabba*.'

I would say, 'Don't you dare talk about the film like this!'

I walked out of groups, I would take it personally. Everyone who bitched about *Hum Aapke Hain Koun . . !* was not a good person for me. It was my way of judging them as people. The most memorable moment for me was going and narrating the script of *Kabhi Khushi Kabhie Gham . . .* to Sooraj-ji. I went to his office and told him I wanted to narrate my family film to him. He was very helpful and supportive, and gave me a couple of suggestions. He probably never realized what a great moment it was for me! I think I bored him to tears with my four-hour ramble. But he listened to me so diligently, making notes, giving me pointers. *Kabhi Khushi Kabhie Gham . . .* was actually

Kabhie Kabhie meets *Hum Aapke Hain Koun . . !* It was that poster of *Kabhie Kabhie* and the family values of *Hum Aapke Hain Koun . . !* The two big influences of my life came together in that film. Which is why I said that that film is not me, it's my love for Hindi cinema, it's a reflection of my love for these two movies.

I know human dramas, and I'll always make films on them. I don't know that other space. I don't know how a serial killer thinks. If you give me a great script, I might be challenged to direct it, but I'm not sure if I'm really up for that. I would like to do a thriller because I like the greyness of the human mind, and I would like to write it myself. But I'm not challenged by it right now.

I do watch all the big international films. I watch everything important. But I won't watch those cult films that are hidden away somewhere, though I watch the art-house films that are revered and respected at the time. I love watching the Oscars and I watch every nominated film because when I'm watching that show early in the morning in Mumbai, I need to know about all the films. And I need to have my favourites.

If our films reach out to audiences abroad, it should happen organically. I don't understand crossover. If I'm crossing over, then I'm not leveraging it here. I make a Hindi language film—if it works, very good, if it doesn't, fine. I would love to go and stand on that stage and make that speech: 'This one's for you, India,' is the way I'll end it—but it's not the be-all and end-all of my life. If it happens, it's part of my life and destiny, but I can't plan for it. The only thing I plan for is commercial success in my terrain. Anything else has to be an upside on the content created. I'm not interested in going to Hollywood and sitting there for two hours and rubbing shoulders with Hollywood celebrities. I'm happy meeting the Hindi film industry. I would rather sit with Sridevi and Madhuri Dixit, and talk to them about how they wore chiffon saris in the eighties, rather than go and rub shoulders with Blake Lively. I'm happy to watch them at the Academy Awards or Golden Globes and see what they're wearing on the red carpet, but I have no interest to be a part of that world. They won't know me. I'll be one in a million. I'm very happy to be one in two here! I'm very excited about where I am. I love Hindi cinema and I love my industry with all its insanity and madness, negativity, delusion, all of that. I don't want to leave it and go anywhere. Put me in a Beverly Hills mansion with eight bedrooms and three swimming pools, and I will get bored very soon. If I go there, I won't see Mehboob Studios, and I won't walk in the dirt of Mumbai to go into some vanity van and sit there, and have the call sheet in front of me. It's just the magic of what we do.

I'm not an immensely politically motivated person, so I don't have strong political beliefs. That doesn't make me disinterested in my country's ethos, it just makes me unaware, which requires me to shut up and not exercise my political point of view too much. Sometimes, I feel I'm not on the same page vis-à-vis the beliefs some people have about how cinema is impressionable, about how sexual projections on screen can have deep social ramifications. I don't catch that layer sometimes. I feel like I should but I don't. I take some things frivolously which I later feel upset about in the larger scheme of things. Every time I've had detailed discussions with Aamir and Kiran, I realize how passionate they are about these things. How we project our men and women on screen can actually change the DNA of our society in a certain sense. I watched a film with Zoya, and she walked out of it, saying the hero was stalking the heroine. She said, 'Stalking doesn't amount to wooing her, it doesn't amount to love. There are people out there who will take a page from this and stalk women, and that perhaps leads to rape sometimes.'

I was not used to looking at life like that. I would think, *arre usko toh beinteha mohabbat hai*. Or people say, 'These item songs should be thrown out of movies! It's exploitation and objectification.' But I think, oh, she's hot, yaar! And I've objectified more men than women in my movies. I've even shown them in their *chaddi*s!

Actually, I detach cinema from reality completely. My organic thinking process doesn't veer towards a certain social consciousness.

Does that make me dumb? Does that make me frivolous? Sometimes, I've fought with my inner demon about it. Maybe, I'm just so stupid that I'm not catching this layer, but it's not bothering me. However, I don't have a natural reaction to this emotion. So should I fake it? Maybe this makes me irresponsible. You can judge me but this is the true me. What to do? Since childhood, I've seen Helen do the best cabarets, men pursuing women with flamboyance, it's in my DNA as a film watcher. I can't suddenly start being the moral police for the same things I grew up watching and loving.

Shabana Azmi once called me from Birmingham. She'd seen *Kuch Kuch Hota Hai* at some film festival and she said, '*Main aapse sawal karna chahti hoon. Chhote baal the toh pyar nahin hua, lambe baal ho gaye, sexy lagne lagi toh mohabbat ho gayi. Iska kya jawab denge aap?*'

I thought for one second and said, '*Main bas yehi kehna chahta hoon ki* I'm very sorry, I have no answer to give you. *Ladkon ko khoobsurat ladkiyan achchi lagti hain. Toh main kya karoon? Maar dalo mujhe*, that I like beauty. Kill me.'

She said, '*Kya jawab doge?*'

I said, '*Koi jawab nahin hai.* Sorry it didn't appeal to your sensibilities.'

But that's what it was. When Kajol looked dumpy and wore sports clothes, he wasn't turned on. When she became hot and sexy and evolved and beautiful, he fell for her. How can anyone dismiss the fact that there's something called attraction? It's a huge part of love. Isn't it stage one of love? You fall in lust, then you fall in love.

Actually, there was a lot of conflict and contradiction in *Kuch Kuch Hota Hai*. Shah Rukh says, '*Ek hi baar jeete hain, ek hi baar pyar hota hai.*' But he got married again, he fell in love again, so why was he saying these things? It didn't make sense. It was the conviction of the film-maker that pulled it all off. Rani is writing eight letters to her daughter. What did she write in the first three letters? Gagagoogoo? What would a child know? *Ma ka pehla khat* is to a child in a cot! What did Farida Jalal read out? What could possibly have been told? What did that toddler of two or three understand? *Main yeh aath chittiyan chhod ke ja rahi hoon, isme woh sab cheezein hain jo woh apni ma ke bare mein jaan payegi.* And how did she know Kajol was going to be free and available? It was just conviction. I love the film because of that conviction. I'm envious of the conviction I had in 1997 when I wrote it and in 1998 when I shot it, because today that conviction has got too logical. Today, you think, oh my god, *log kya kahenge, critics kya kahenge.* But we never cared about all these things then, we were like, *Hindi picture hai, banao!* Now I'm bothered about 35,000 people—*censor kya kahega, moral police kya kahega, Twitter kya kahega, Shabana Azmi kya kahegi, Shobhaa Dé kya kahegi, PIL kya kahega . . .* That time it was only *distributors kya kahenge, audience kya kahegi.* Simple, just make the picture.

Yes, Dharma is my life. Pretty much. It's my identity, it's my strength, it's my day-to-day routine, it's everything to me. And it's the one thing I created, not from scratch, but it's a maintenance of my father's legacy, it's what actually makes me feel emotional and strong. I don't know what to do if I'm not in my office—this cabin, this room, this chair, sitting with my ADs. I love the vibe, I love the people, I love the fact that the people who work for me work for me, not just the entity but the human being. My favourite days in office are Sundays when I come to work. Sometimes, I just come here on Sundays to think. I don't like to sit at home, I like to sit in my office. I feel the energy in my office is great for my headspace. We have a peon called Vishnu who is like my shadow. Sometimes, there's not a soul here. And I happily sit here and sometimes just stare at nothing. I'll stare for three or four hours, then I may go home or visit a friend. I don't like to do nothing. I think in that sense I'm like my father. He could not handle holidays.

People think I'm rolling in money. But there's more money in perception than money in the bank. To me, money means having enough to afford my luxurious lifestyle. Yes, it is not a necessity-based lifestyle, it is luxury based. I love the best hotels, I love the best airlines. I'm not apologetic about it because I feel I've earned it. But I don't want a private jet or yacht or three homes in London, New York or Dubai. I love hotels. I love shopping, I love spending on myself and my mother, and buying presents for my friends. I love giving people things. Birthdays for me are a big deal. As long as there's money to pay my bills, I'm fine. If I can afford to live in the manner I do today for the rest of my life—I'm absolutely fine. I'm ambitious about the prestige that my company creates for me, not the money. So many of my decisions have been profile decisions or prestige decisions, not money decisions. Like when I decided to release *Baahubali* in another market. Yes, it did very well but I also did it because I wanted my brand to be stronger. Like I backed *Lunchbox*. It was not about the money.

As for the films I make, I spend a lot of money on them. Sometimes, people curtail budgets and still charge a lot for music or satellite rights, but I actually put in a lot of money. I'm that person. I believe in brand over wealth. Always. Reputation over income. People think I have much more money than I actually do. If they really saw my balance sheets, they would be surprised. *Itna hi hai?* There's a lot of reputation and brand value. But there's not that kind of income. I've had to make it in stages because I spend a lot on the movies I make. Even in *Student of the Year* where I had three newcomers, I spent humongous amounts. I did recover the money because it did well, but I didn't make pots of cash on that film. I had spent so much on the songs and sets and outdoors. I went mad; nobody spends this kind of money on a newcomers' film.

Somehow I think that conviction pays off. I'm putting money into the film, into what you the audience will see on screen. I'm not penny wise, pound foolish. I'm not stupid about money. I feel money goes, money comes. It's my simple theory. I've always realized that I will have wealth. I feel I'll never lose it all because I'm not a gambler. I don't gamble to an extent even in work. But when I believe in something, I go all out. I don't have the need to be on any list of millionaires. I don't want to be on the *Forbes* list. I don't want to be public listed. I don't want all that. I feel I'm a larger entity without all of that. I have belief and confidence in myself. I will be remembered for the things that I have done. I don't need the financial validation of a *Financial Times* or *Economic Times*. I don't want any of them to tell me that I'm the most powerful or the richest. Because I believe I am. And I don't believe it in an arrogant way. I believe it very strongly. When I walk into a space, people know who I am. They may like me or hate me, but they can't ignore me. Because, I danced on a reality show or I was roasted on *AIB* or I've done a talk show or I've done a feature film.

If you have a private plane, take me on it. I'll come. You have a yacht, call me. I may arrive. You have a big home in the south of France. Invite me. But I don't want to own any of it myself. I don't want the headache.

There's no place like a hotel. It's such a great concept. I want to have enough money that I can stay in the best of hotels for a month or two if I want to. I want that wealth. I love travelling. I love shopping—it's a big disorder. It's my only vice. I'm not much of a drinker. I'm not a drug consumer. I'm a big shopper—online, offline, every which way. I'll buy ten pairs of shoes on every trip I make. I'll buy all kinds of jackets, I love jackets. I love scarves. Even if I buy hair products, I'll buy twenty of them. If I want to buy a messenger bag, I'll buy five. If you come and see my closet, it's full of shoes and clothes, all neatly organized. I don't buy clothes for occasions. If I buy a jacket, I wear it.

10

Shah Rukh Khan

My first proper meeting with Shah Rukh Khan was on the sets of *Karan Arjun* with my dad. Then I met him on the sets of *Dilwale Dulhania Le Jayenge* where I told him that many years ago, I had sat across him in Anand Mahendroo's office. He said he remembered being there but didn't remember seeing me.

Now when I look back, it was a really weird first meeting. Who knew what life had in store for both of us?

My father had taken me along to the sets of *Karan Arjun*. I knew Kajol was going to be there; she was somebody I had known as a child (she was one of the few people who lived in South Bombay, on Carmichael Road). I was a bit nervous because my father had started taking me around a little (he said I should go out there and meet people). He wanted to sign Shah Rukh for *Duplicate*. This was before I started to assist Adi in *Dilwale Dulhania Le Jayenge*. So I called Kajol and said, 'I'm coming for the shooting of your film. Will you be there?'

She said, 'Yeah, I'm doing a song sequence, "*Jaati Hoon Main*" [which went on to become quite popular].'

I had this preconceived notion about Shah Rukh. I thought he was this young brat, borderline arrogant. But within five minutes of that meeting in Film City, my opinion of him changed. He was warm and chatty.

I remember my father got out of the red car we had and Shah Rukh came up to the car and opened the door for him. It was meant to be a ten-minute meeting, but they had broken for lunch or something and Shah Rukh spoke non-stop for two hours! He was so accessible, friendly and respectful of my father that he won me over in those two hours. I was very sensitive about how people treated my father because I knew what he had gone through.

He said, 'I've heard so much about you, sir, and such wonderful things about you as a human being.'

Then he talked at length about what we should make with Mahesh Bhatt. My father had signed Mahesh Bhatt to direct the movie. Shah Rukh said he thought he should do a double role, something he was excited about. Then he turned towards me and asked, 'What do you do? You should be a part of this movie.'

I said, 'No, no . . . I'm not interested.'

That was my first meeting with him. I remember coming back and telling my father what a nice guy Shah Rukh was. He was so different from what I thought movie people were like. I had seen my father dejected and disappointed with so many of his fraternity people. I was not cynical but I was apprehensive about them. But Shah Rukh was an outsider and he was new. His syntax as a human being was very different from others in the film zone. I remember being completely enamoured by how he connected as a human being. He was so charming. He was not my favourite actor; I was a big Aamir Khan fan. But somehow in that two-hour meeting, my entire perception of him changed. I felt he was magnetic, charming, funny and sensitive. All these qualities came jumping out at me.

There's so much that's been said about Shah Rukh and me. Yes, there was definitely a distance between us in recent years but that was because we were not working with each other. There's no other reason. And there were a lot of people who broadened this gap. There were people who said things to him, and who said things to me.

I sent him a message to come on *Koffee with Karan* in the last season, for the New Year episode, to which he didn't reply. But he replied to every other message I sent him, about everything else. Maybe, he didn't want to come for the show. I understood he didn't want to come, and he expected me to understand. I didn't ask him after that. It's not that I called him and said, 'Why are you not replying?' But I called him when there was a problem or a situation I needed his advice on. Or I would go and have a drink with him in his house.

When two people are so close, when they've done six feature films together and then haven't worked together on the set for a while, there's bound to be a gap. That's the way the industry is.

The fault is mine because I went on record to say I would never make a film without Shah Rukh Khan. I should not have said that because I put that seed in his and everybody else's head. I don't blame people for saying things because I went on record and then didn't live up to my promise. So it's my fault. I don't blame him. Also, you get attached to somebody, and Shah Rukh is a very possessive person. He's a possessive friend. I think I may have hurt him when I made a film without him. And I think I got hurt because when I did, I felt he didn't give me that paternal or fraternal feeling that I had from him otherwise. I think we were two hurt friends for no reason.

Shah Rukh and I have the most awesome chemistry at work. When we work together, it's magic. And when the right film is to be made, it'll be made. But it has to be something that we both love.

Even when there was this minor or mild distance between us, on many levels, he was still my first go-to person in a situation of distress, or to seek help or advice.

When I had a falling out with Kajol, the first call I made was to Shah Rukh. He came to meet me, spoke about it to me. Then I called Adi, and we discussed it. But my instinct was to call Shah Rukh first. He had nothing to do with the problem. But I still called him because somewhere Shah Rukh, Kajol and I have been so close. We've built a very solid part of each other's careers together. I called him to discuss the situation, to know whether what I was saying was valid and right. And he was very helpful. He called me right through every day that week to check whether I was okay. When *Gori Tere Pyaar Mein* bombed—and I was not used to having that kind of a big failure—he called me to ask, 'Are you okay?'

I said, 'Yeah, things happen, shit happens. Once in a while you have to deal with a film that doesn't work.'

So while admittedly there was a distance between us, it did not take away from the largeness of our relationship.

This industry is full of all kinds of people. The messengers are the worst. The Chinese whispers really ruin relationships. Sometimes you say things in a certain tone. I could say, 'Oh, he's retarded,' and I could mean it in a fun way. But if you quote me and say, 'Oh, he said that X is retarded, and really stupid,' it would be perceived in a completely different way.

I find people are so happy to tear other people apart. I feel people thrive on other people's unhappiness. Bollywood has enough people who have nothing better to do than say things about people to other people. It's all about riling you up.

People would say things like, 'Oh, Karan has become really friendly with Aamir.' Or 'Karan is doing a film with Salman.'

Sensitivity and tact are not just token qualities; they should be a way of life. It's like this: you've lost your spouse, and I keep talking about mine. It's something one shouldn't do. Or talking to someone about a friend you've been spending time with when that someone is no longer in touch with that friend. There are many ways in which people are insensitive. Sometimes, it's the warped human mind that makes you so insensitive.

I'm not that person. I'm exceptionally sensitive about what I say to people. I think the grey layers people operate within make them do things like this. What happens is when two people are not communicating with each other, your life becomes a bit of a playground for other people to play on. When you're communicating, you can easily absorb all this and dissolve it. But when you're not, people can take advantage of that fact.

If someone tells me, 'he said this', I'm not going to call that person and ask, 'Did you say this?'

But honestly, now this doesn't bother me at all. Hearsay doesn't affect me. I never base my opinions on hearsay.

I think Shah Rukh and I are aware of the fact that people are envious of our relationship, which is why we've never had a blowout with each other. There was a simmering, silent, respectable distance between us. But there's also an equal amount of love and affection we have for each other. That's never going to go. I have a huge amount of respect for him. He can ask anything of me and I will do it. And I know that if I were in dire straits, and if he could do something to change that situation, if it was in his power, he would do everything to help me. There's a big layer of love and respect still, and no one can come in the way of that.

Shah Rukh might have been angry with me, but I can never be angry with him. I respect him too much. I think he just went silent because he is not confrontational. I think when he hurts, he becomes quiet. I could have hurt him, he may have hurt me.

We never had any ups and downs in our relationship before. Never. It's only been when we haven't worked together. And I think that's the way of the world, in this age and time, in this industry. Like Ayan and Ranbir are very close today. I always say I'm not cynical, but if you feel inseparable from someone today, there could be a time when you may not feel that way. When you don't work together, you don't meet each other regularly. It's as simple as that. When you meet, you get involved in each other's lives. When you don't meet, there is a distance. Then you work with other people, he works with other people. That separation creates a distance—the geographic separation and the professional separation create an organic distance which then starts being perceived as a problem, though actually, Shah Rukh and I knew there was no problem. There was not one incident, fight or a 'situation'. If the media were quiet, maybe we wouldn't be where we are today. We would be better off. But somewhere the written word, the industry talk, the people, they all spoil things. I always feel that even though you know the truth, when you read it in black and white, it can irritate you. And you get irritated even though there's no reason to get irritated.

Success has many friends. Failure has distances. People who want you to fail when you're successful are not your friends, they are your competitors. But then, there are those friends who don't want to see you rise to that extent that you slip out of their hands. Those you have to eliminate. I feel two achievers are more capable of being friends with each other. I feel Shah Rukh and Salman can be friends. There's genuine love between them. Salman's family was the first family that welcomed Shah Rukh in Mumbai. There is a strong friendship, but life and circumstances came in the way. As difficult as it might be for people on the outside to feel it, there is a certain love that causes this hate. Gauri always says that Shah Rukh and Salman behave like they're in love with each other, bro love. Reshma Shetty, who handles Salman, also always says this. No matter what the dynamic around them is, they understand each other.

Adi and I can still hold our ground as friends because we're both successful. There is no insecurity between us. But when you find a friend who's working in your field and not doing as well as you, fear, insecurity and jealousy get in the way. I find the theory that two competitors can't be friends is not true. Shah Rukh and I can always maintain our friendship because both of us are doing really well in our individual capacities.

I'm kind of back in Shah Rukh's life in a way. When the origin of a friendship is so strong, it just cannot die. I've not allowed it to either, and neither has he. It happened organically. We met at Deepika's party celebrating *Piku*'s success.

At one point when we were talking, we looked at each other. I hugged him instinctively and said, 'I've missed you.'

And he said, 'You've no idea how much I've missed you.'

We had this moment. We've actually always been there for each other. Even through the years when we were not entirely at our best, we were connected. So when I told him I missed him, I felt it was all back to before. It took just that. I wish I had said it three years ago. Because, I had missed him even then. I feel I let the past few years pass for no reason.

Even through the low years in our friendship, I was in touch with Gauri and his kids, so I wasn't feeling the disconnect. It was not that they were out of my life, they were very much part of my day-to-day existence. I was in touch with Gauri every day. I think Shah Rukh and I come from a very emotionally hypersensitive space. I think both of us get hurt very easily and then we back off. And we backed off not because of venom or vindictiveness; there was no fight, it was just an emotional separation. Then you realize that the emotional separation was for no reason but emotion. And that same emotion has to be expressed for you to come right back on track. And that's what I did. He was hurt that I didn't work with him. I was hurt that with *Student of the Year*, there was no acknowledgement from him, there was no love or support given to me. Then it just grew. It was like he thought 'after everything I've done for Karan' and I thought 'after everything I've done for him'. We both felt like we had contributed to each other's lives so tremendously.

It was just two people sulking. Even through these five years, he always knew he could count on me. Whenever there was any big issue, a health issue with Gauri or something to do with the kids, I was the one he called. 'Gauri's not well.' Or 'Aryan's going to school and Gauri's getting hyper, talk to her.' It was all happening but it was not happening with that same affection.

Suddenly, we had become formal with each other. We were never uncivil towards each other. We were overly formal and that was the problem. He was not backslapping me like I wanted him to. And I was not cracking that odd joke like I would have. We call each other 'bhai'. It began with me telling him, 'You should have macho studs walking around you like real gangsters have, but who do you actually have? Me.' He said, 'Okay, I'll call you bhai and you call me bhai too.' It began as a joke and then it stuck. I call him 'bhai' all the time.

From being so close it transformed to: 'Could you please call me when you have a minute?' Once, just last year, he got so angry with me. I called up his manager and said, 'I really need to meet Shah Rukh.'

He called me and said, 'When did you start calling my manager?'

I said, 'Oh, I didn't want to disturb you.'

He said, 'Achha?' And he fell silent.

Like that had hurt him more. I was trying to do the right thing, but I had upset him even more by doing that. I wanted to say that if I had sent you a message, you might have replied the next day or two days later, it was faster this way.

I think that was the first effort he made which made me say, 'I've missed you.' With that, he opened the door a little bit.

Yes, I was upset he didn't come on *Koffee with Karan*. I was very hurt. But you get hurt only when you love, so even in that phase, the love was very much there. You feel pain only when you love. And there's a lot of love we have for each other and that love is beyond any kind of rift people might have tried to create, or the circumstances we found ourselves in. He knows I will stand by his family through thick and thin, whatever happens.

I am very close to his children. I talk to Aryan like I talk to a friend, he's like my son. Shah Rukh's wife is my closest friend. His kids are my family.

We went through whatever we went through. But when we had that moment, the love was back—and how. Because, it had never gone away. Sometimes we don't express the feelings in our heart, and when he said, 'You have no idea how much I have missed you,' it meant everything to me. We're back to doing what we were doing, talking about work. He can call me and tell me about a problem and I tell him what to do or what not to. It just took that one moment. It just needed communication. And it's not that Shah Rukh is someone who calls you every day. He's very busy. I'm busy. Then I went and sat with him in his home—he, me, Aryan, Suhana and Gauri—like we used to. At one point, I said in my head—this is my family; this is as good as it gets for me. I was asking Aryan some naughty questions about his personal life and he was getting very harassed, and then we started laughing because I used to hold Aryan by the hand and walk with him, and now he's eighteen! He's as old as my career. He was born right after the first schedule of *Kuch Kuch Hota Hai*. And Suhana has become this pretty young girl doing her hair, and I'm giving her fashion tips. And I thought, oh, I do have parental skills. I have that maternal or paternal feeling—I feel it for Gauri's and Shah Rukh's kids. I go to Gauri's house now just to play with AbRam. Even if Gauri is not there, I go and sit with him. And he comes and spends time with my mum all the time. My mum loves him. He's like a toy that you want to own. He came to the office the other day and the entire staff came out to see him. Everyone was behaving as if Brad Pitt had arrived. He was delighted with all the attention.

So yes, Shah Rukh and I may go through our ups and downs when he doesn't work with me or I don't work with him, but he was and will always be family for me. We are working together now, not on a film directed by me though. Gauri Shinde is directing it for me, and there's another one we're talking to him about.

But I did direct him recently, in *Ae Dil Hai Mushkil*. Directing him after seven years was both exciting and surreal. There was a part in the film of Aishwarya's ex-husband, the character who voices the ethos of the film, the concept of the film. I felt that it required a big movie star of gravitas, so I just went to him. There were no questions asked.

He said, 'When do you want me to shoot?'

That was it. That's how it is with Shah Rukh and me. He got the scene when he arrived on the set and he just did it. And I felt like those seven years had just not passed. He knew exactly what I wanted, I knew exactly how he wanted to go about it. I wrote the scene keeping him in mind. When you see the performance you will see that that's the synergy only he and I can bring to a film. There's a certain kind of romance and love and the display of that on celluloid that he has done for me and I have created for him—it's a magic only we can create. I felt a kind of ownership of that kind of portrayal.

Ranbir, who was in the scene, came and told me, 'It's bizarre, I've worked with you for about sixty-five to seventy days, but I felt that what you have with him [Shah Rukh], you don't have with anybody else.'

I told him that that rapport comes with having worked for 500 days on sets together.

He said, 'You both have such an easy understanding of each other as actor and director.'

That's something that comes from love and respect. And from a space of family love. I know he's got my back no matter what. He may have been angry and upset, we have been through our ups and downs, we both know it, but that love felt so strong on that day. When I hugged him tight at the end of the shoot, it felt like it all came back. That's why, with him, when people conjecture about a fallout, I feel like saying, dude, you don't know, there's so much love there. When we were on the set, both he and I understood that what we have is special and it's always going to remain so.

11

Friends and Fallouts

I don't have a relationship with Kajol any more. We've had a fallout. Something happened that disturbed me deeply which I will not talk about because it's something that I like to protect and I feel it would not be fair to her or to me. After two and a half decades, Kajol and I don't talk at all. We just acknowledge each other, say 'hello' and walk past.

The problem was actually never between her and me. It was between her husband and me, something which only she knows about, he knows about and I know about. I want to keep it at that. I don't really want to say what transpired. But I did feel that she needed to apologize for something she didn't do. I felt that if she's not going to acknowledge twenty-five years of friendship, if she wants to support her husband, then that's her prerogative. At some outer level I understood it. But I just couldn't see myself in her life any more. It's been months we haven't spoken to each other.

Prior to the release of *Ae Dil Hai Mushkil*, there's a lot that happened. Things were said, crazy accusations were made against me, that I had bribed someone to sabotage her husband's film. I can't even say that I was hurt or pained by it. I just wanted to blank it out. When she reacted to the whole situation and put out a tweet saying, 'Shocked!' that's when I knew it was completely over for me. That tweet validated the insanity, that she could believe I would bribe someone. I felt that's it. It's over. And she can never come back to my life. I don't think she wants to either. I never want to have anything to do with them as a unit. She was the one who mattered to me but now it's over. I told my mother that she could have a one-on-one relationship with Kajol if she wanted. That's my mother's preference and if Kajol chooses to, but she's out of my life.

I wouldn't like to give a piece of myself to her at all because she's killed every bit of emotion I had for her for twenty-five years. I don't think she deserves me. I feel nothing for her any more. I've been told by my friends that it's still my hurt talking but I'm so indifferent to the situation now, what with everything that's transpired. There was still a bit of me that wished we would get back to what we had, but that one-word tweet that she put out—that was the most humiliating thing she could have done for a person who loved her deeply. That broke me. Once it broke me, it angered me and then I went into indifference. Now no matter what happens, I'm never going to be there for her. Maybe it doesn't matter to her at all. I don't even want to speak about her husband because that's inconsequential to my life now. He doesn't matter to me, he never did. I still don't want to say anything about her husband because I want to respect the history she and I shared.

But yes, it hurts me that she's still close to people I'm really close to, like Manish and Niranjan. Somehow I wish she wasn't. When they talk about her, it angers me. I know it's not fair for me to impose my feelings on them but it bothers me. I can't be dishonest and say it doesn't. I can't help it. I'm human. But I don't want to be that person who asks his friends to take sides. I'm not territorial normally, but about this, I feel very strongly.

It's very difficult to keep relationships going in the film industry. Consistency is the problem, not creation—the creation of a relationship is easy. The consistency, maintaining it, is impossible sometimes. The cynic in me feels that. But more power to those who keep them afloat. We live from one project to the next. All our investments are in the films that we make. I work as a producer with many people, so the ones I don't work with, I don't end up having a dynamic with. The ones you work with, you have a relationship. You stop working with them, the relationship goes on hold, it's as simple as that. And you meet socially, it's all superficial and *upar-upar se*, like how you meet people and say, 'Hahaha, great, great', but there's no depth there. And I have stopped creating depth in any way. I've done my bit of having in-depth relationships, and I think I'm not interested any more because where is the time? There are too many people around; there are so many young actors now. I can't create relationships with all of them. I don't want to. I've had my share of relationships, I've had my solid bonds. I'm close to Manish Malhotra, I'm close to Niranjan Iyengar, I have Shah Rukh and Gauri. The Bachchan family. I've known Rani and Kareena very closely. At some point, they've all required my presence in their lives. Kareena and I have deep-rooted love for each other. I always say if things were different in my life, I would have married her. She is the only person who makes me laugh. She has a terrific sense of humour. She's really funny. I call her 'Jagga Jasoos' because she knows exactly what is happening in everyone's life. I told her that she secretly writes for Pinkvilla.

My non-film friends are my college friends. I have a couple of college friends I'm still in touch with. Two of them are girls, and we meet once every two months. Then I have a couple friend in Delhi that I'm close to.

In Bollywood, I have a few strong friendships. Adi is somebody I don't see very often, but our bond is thick. I would say Manish, Niranjan and Adi are my closest friends. Manish and Niranjan have been my friends for twenty-five years. And Aditya Chopra, ever since I can remember. The level of love, affection, accountability and dependency is as much as it was, if not more. And now Manish, Niranjan and I, we talk about growing old together. We're all single, unattached, and professionally focused. Niranjan says that he'll outlive both of us. I can actually imagine him at ninety attending everyone's funerals.

He keeps saying, 'That's the biggest curse you can give me'—being alone.

I think Manish is perpetually young. He's forty-eight now, but he has the spirit of a twenty-two-year-old. I've realized he's the most positive person I know. He's such a self-energizer. When we go on trips or holidays together, we walk. He's almost fifty, yet he doesn't look it. He's got the spark and zest of a teenager. We have our coffee, walk in the park, talk about life, sitting together on a bench like two aunties. He's different from me but we have a very strong connection. We've had a deep friendship for years. He's the most loyal and loving person I've known. He's really there for me. Sometimes he's emotionally inexpressive. He doesn't understand pain, heartbreak and hurt. He's such a positive, happy person that he doesn't get the other side of life. He doesn't see the grey in a relationship, he sees only the white. Or the black. He doesn't understand the concept of grey which is where we all operate from actually.

I tell him, 'Manish, you're almost ditzy sometimes.'

He'll say things like, 'Why's that person sad, she's so pretty. Why's he so depressed, he's so rich.'

I say, 'How are these parameters or barometers of emotion?'

But he's a stress-buster. He'll make your problem sound so trivial to you that you think, yeah, why am I getting so wound up about this?

When my heart was broken and I would talk to him about it, he'd say, 'What's the problem? Go have sex with somebody.'

He'll give you the most simple remedy. And that can make you happy.

He'll say, 'Go and work, you have so much work to do, and movies to make. What's all this rubbish?'

And suddenly I think, yeah, he's right!

He's so funny about problems. When you talk to him about a problem, he'll listen to you, then he'll give you the most ridiculous solution which actually makes the most sense. And I've realized that sometimes, somebody else's happiness is a sponge you can absorb from. He's that sponge in my life. He's the sunshine on a gloomy day.

He'll praise me, he'll say you're such a big film-maker, people love your movies, what are you getting so wound up about all these small things? You're powerful, you're famous, you're this, you're that, and I think, yeah, maybe I need to hear these things once in a while.

I've grown to have a soul connect with him. We've had the closest friendship for twenty-five years, but in the last five years I feel our friendship has really found feet. He's been a discovery for me. Sometimes you understand the value of a friend at a certain juncture of your life. I've understood his value now. He'll tell me about his sex life and I'll tell him about my lack of it. He's always telling me, 'You're a bore!' And I'm always telling him, 'You're the opposite of me.' Let me say he's a lot more colourful than me. I love hearing about his life because I feel I can absorb it like a sponge, perhaps even live vicariously through him.

I also feel we're in the same situation. We're around the same age (he's five years older than me). He lives with his parents, I live with my mom. We're both single and successful, and now oddly enough, he's moved into the same office building. He's on the seventh floor, I'm on the second. I bought a new house, he bought his new bungalow on Pali Hill. I feel he's a friend I can grow old with. I can see myself at eighty, sitting down with him, like two old friends who've had a whole life together, sharing our day. Me going from my house to his Pali Hill bungalow, two tottering old people talking about our life.

Adi is the big weakness of my life. His opinion matters to me. He's someone I may not speak to for two months because both of us are busy working, but my love for him is at another level. I owe everything in my career to him. The amount of love and affection I have for him is really deep. Perhaps that is why I know he has power over me. Adi calls only to fire me. That used to happen before, and it happens now. He hasn't changed. He cannot bring himself to change his dynamic with me. When he got married, I was the best man and had to give a speech. There were eighteen of us and I made the speech and got very emotional. He got so teary, so did his mum, Rani, everyone. Our entire life flashed by in front of me. I felt, my god, he's the one person I've known for twenty-five years of my life. And he's been so much a part of my journey. People think we're competing companies—there's Yash Raj and Dharma—but it's never come in our way. He'll call me to tell me, 'You've made a fuck-all film' or 'You've made a really good film.' I can't do the same to him. I'm his assistant. I never forget. Even today, my body language is of being Aditya Chopra's assistant. When he's angry with me, he addresses me by my full name.

He says, 'See, Karan Johar, don't argue with me.'

Then I reply, 'Why are you calling me Karan Johar?'

And he says, 'That's because you've become Karan Johar now in what you're doing.'

If he feels very strongly about something I'm doing, whether it's right or wrong, he'll call me. And he'll hear me out. But it's a one-way street. I can't do the same. If I think he's made a terrible film, I'll not say it. But I'm completely open to his criticism. And it's been like that, and that's not going to change.

I do feel, however, that we've lost touch in the last couple of years. I think it's to do with our schedules. Also, I think he feels that today he doesn't have the right to say things to me the way he used to, because he feels I've grown wings. I wish he wouldn't feel like that. I wish he would still treat me the same way because I like it when he fires me! He used to fire me earlier: 'Why are you doing this event?' 'Why are you doing *Koffee with Karan*?' 'Why are you giving so many interviews?' Now he says, 'I've lost you. You used to be Karan, now you're Karan Johar. You've become this monster!' I love it when Adi gets angry with me because then I feel that the *apnapan* is still there. He lectures me a lot less now, and I miss it.

Along with Adi, my other deepest friendship is with Shah Rukh. They're my left and right. One of the two people has to have no ego in this dynamic. I decided that that person was going to be me. I was junior to both Adi and Shah Rukh. Even if I've been hurt by them at certain junctures of my life and I'm sure I've hurt them too, I decided to be the one to compensate, irrespective of anything. Shah Rukh and Adi are two men I deeply love. They are responsible for my career, for giving me the chance when I was totally new. I don't think I can give any third person that kind of credit, and that includes my own family.

I could have allowed these relationships to dwindle into nothingness but I won't; I choose not to because I want to hold on to the emotion I feel for these two people. It's not been easy, and people around you make it worse. People have gone and fed them things about me—because nobody enjoys age-old friendships. Everybody enjoys and revels in the fact that there can't be any friends in the film fraternity. People feel this is the norm. When I go through a deep level of failure in my life, how many people will still be around? I don't know.

Hearsay is one of the biggest problems. We are in an industry where everyone says things frivolously. It's the tone that's important. I always say, 'Please don't ever text serious things. Say them.' Text messages are the biggest undoing of human relationships because they never come with the tone. Without tone, things sound much worse than they are. The emotion is not there in the message, they are just words. I always believe—speak to people. Confront.

Confrontation is such an underrated concept. But it's so important in any relationship. It's an Indian thing I think, of not sitting across and sorting a problem out. People won't say I have a problem with you. They'll insinuate, they'll back off, they won't message, they won't call back, and they'll sulk. It's such a stupid waste of time. I used to be non-confrontational, but I've become confrontational because once too often I've been scarred by the lack of communication in a relationship. Always confront. Don't allow things to fester. If you continue to suppress the emotion, it will explode in your face one day.

Over the years, I've made some unlikely friends in the industry. I love Anurag Kashyap. He's like a big teddy bear walking around with his satchel and his angst, his issues and his madness. But I love him; he's got a really clean heart. Anurag is a giver, full of love, affection and largeness of heart, which I didn't realize till I met him. I love the fact that he supports so many other film-makers. He's really created a space for them; he's given them a platform. His production house, Phantom, does that. My regard for it is because it push smaller films; it will make sure a film-maker who's not on the radar but has written a great film comes up to the surface. They're encouraging of talent. He's the pioneer of that belief. He's made people from nowhere come to the forefront. And he stands tall with them. Anurag has pioneered the alternative movement in film-making in this era. *Bombay Velvet* notwithstanding, you cannot dilute the impact he's had with so many films and film-makers. We're totally different people, we don't like the same films, we don't like the same people, we have nothing in common barring the fact that we both like to push and promote talent selflessly. I think that's our strongest binding factor.

My fight with Ram Gopal Varma was all fun actually. Both of us were playing to the gallery. He doesn't care about me and I don't care about him. Sporadically, we would say something about each other for other people's entertainment, but now he's bored of me and I'm bored of him, and so we're both silent. It's just that the perception has lasted so long. It's good fun to take on somebody or the other once in a while. It's entertaining. How can life be so sterile? Sometimes, you need to shake it up a little. With Sanjay Leela Bhansali, I think he was being silly, and I was being stupid. Sometimes alleged stories and reports can cause a lot of damage, because they make people start thinking in that direction even if they are not true. Sometimes, reportage can ruin relationships. People get very conscious when the written word is out there. By the way, I don't think anyone is quoted out of context. The problem is when you make a comment loosely which is then misinterpreted and highlighted.

Apart from Adi and Shah Rukh, the most important person in my life is Apoorva. He's been like an elder sibling to me. Sometimes, your brother can't be your friend. And that is what Apoorva and I have become. I spoke to my psychologist about him and she said, 'You know, the way you talk about him, he's your brother.' We have differences of opinion, we have social distance, but actually, he's my one point to call at any moment of emotional duress or professional anxiety. We're clearly siblings. We're running the show together. He takes total charge of the finances and the commercial aspects, and I look after the creative side of the business. We fight like siblings, we hurt like siblings, we keep things from each other, and then there's this one big explosion.

Then there's Kajal Anand who's been my friend since I was ten. We're family friends. I've known her as a kid, and when I was eighteen or nineteen (she's four years older than me), she kind of introduced me to people and became like a sibling. My dad and her dad were friends. My dad died of cancer, her dad died of cancer a year later. We're both without siblings. We go through similar emotional traumas. We discuss our mothers with each other, and our mothers discuss us!

There's a lot of commonality.

If I am in hospital or my mother is in hospital, she's that one person who will be there the whole day. When there's a medical crisis, there's that one person you call, she's that one person for me. My mother has a back injury, she'll come to New York with me. When I'm taking my mother to the hospital for an MRI, she'll be there.

I have lots of women friends. But I'm not the classic hanging-out-with-a-group-of-women guy. I have one-on-ones. Or I have one-on-twos. I have these units of friends where we meet in twos. It's very strange. Like Gauri and Putlu. Two college friends, Simeen and Sunaina. We meet every one or two months. I have a lot of these twos. They all have one thing in common—they're all intelligent, and all exceptionally modern in their approach. I can't talk to bimbos for long. I can be amused but I can't hold a conversation with them. Someone who doesn't have emotional intelligence bores me. For me, EQ is much more important than IQ.

I have stronger connects with men. Them I know one-to-one. Wholesome, grounded, solid, long-term friendships. Shah Rukh, Manish, Niranjan, Apoorva and many others.

Reshma Shetty has been a big support to me and I feel deeply connected to her. Today she has emerged as one of my closest friends and someone with whom I chat about my work issues a lot. She and Apoorva are the two people with whom I talk a lot about work. She's a celebrity manager; she runs a company called Matrix. She handles Salman, Katrina, Kareena, and my three kids are with her. She's the biggest celebrity manager and her company does strategy much more than management. She's a very bright girl. We've had a strange connection that has strengthened over the years. I've known her for twenty years. I'd gone to her for *Dilwale Dulhania Le Jayenge* looking to cast Shah Rukh's and Kajol's friends. She was at that time a model coordinator. Then I ended up playing the part of Shah Rukh's friend. Over the years, we have had a civil, cordial, friendly relationship but it's only in the last six years that we've really connected. She's been my most recent close friend and I consider her family now. Actually, it started eleven years ago when my father passed away, and one evening, I was sitting alone and she came (she had not been in town when my father passed away). She walked in and said, 'You know, your father passed away on the same date as my father and they died of the same cancer.' So it was strange how we had this freaky commonality of memory. I think we have a karmic connection. After that we were in touch and we always had this deep connect. And then I requested her to represent my talent. From then on, she's been a big support. She's very close to my mum as well. She's my age and we're both unmarried, and I keep teasing her, 'If I don't find anyone, I'll grow old with you.' We're both very driven by our work, we have single mothers who we're very into; it's also very much like with Putlu, my other friend who lost her father and has a mother. These are the two women I feel very connected to. As for Reshma, I don't meet her socially at all. She doesn't meet anyone. I just meet her one-to-one for dinner. She doesn't socialize, she doesn't go to parties, she just works. She's very close to Salman and his family. She's not in the social zone, so nobody even knows that Reshma and I have this special connection. I take her advice on professional decisions very seriously. I'm very dependent on her take on work and people. I've built a bond with her over the years and it's very solid.

My Papoo maasi's two daughters, my cousins Priyanka and Anushka, are my only family. They will be in my will. These two girls are like my daughters, though technically they're my second cousins. One is thirty-two and the other is twenty-eight. Priyanka works for *Vogue*. Anushka styles and designs, but not for films. They're not very connected to the industry. But they're my daughters.

And that paternal feeling I have for my two cousins extends itself to Sid, Varun and Alia. Recently we went on a Dream Team tour and I realized how protective they were about me. I was the only older person in that group of youngsters, and on the chartered flight they were always so thoughtful. Alia would come and give me a blanket if she thought I was feeling cold. Sid and Varun would make sure I got into the car first. I always used to feel like the parent but they took charge of me as if I was their child. It was all about me and I realized that actually we have an organic parental bond.

Then there's my comfort group—Dharma and a group within Dharma. That includes each director in Dharma, whether it's Tarun and Puneet who came in earlier or Karan and Shashank and Shakun, who joined a little later. I feel very attached to all of them. There's also the comfort I get from Garima who handles my life. Garima and Niloufer are these two strong women who look out for me. Apart from my mom, if I have two maternal figures in my life—though one is older and the other younger—it's these two. I see them huddling around when they know I'm in a bad mood. Sometimes when I'm working late night, Garima is still there because she knows I've had a stressful day, though she has a husband and daughter waiting at home for her. I can just see the protective instinct they have for me.

Then there's another whole group—Ayan, Abhishek Varman who's a director in the company, Aarti and Pooja Shetty. We have a

WhatsApp group we call the 'A List', and since Pooja is the only one whose name begins with P, I decided to call it 'AAAP'! I feel like they're my monitors. Every day I get messages like 'Have you slept?' 'Have you eaten?' 'Karan, that's ridiculous, you're dancing on *Jhalak*!' They're my police. Then I get messages like 'Where are you?' When I was at the Toronto International Film Festival, I got a message saying, 'Send us a picture of what you're looking like right now!' This policing makes me feel emotional. I feel like someone cares.

And there are so many other people, kids who work here. I'm someone who brings people together. When people from the outside come in, they get enveloped in my zone. Like, say, Reshma who is so antisocial, but she will make an effort with the people I know.

Zoya and Shweta are the other two girls from my childhood I'm very connected to even today. Farhan and Abhishek were the brats. Shweta and Zoya are still very much part of my day-to-day life. Shweta and Putlu are very close now. Gauri and Putlu are best friends. People from my past have integrated with my present.

I feel lucky to have some good friendships which I've tried hard to maintain over the years. My friends love me unabashedly. I know it!

12

Love and Sex

I lost my virginity at twenty-six. I had no sexual encounter before that. Yes, it is true. Why would I say this on record if it were not? It's not something I am proud of. It was in New York. Up till that point, I was sexually completely inexperienced. Even when I was a kid, I was very backward in this department. I didn't know things. I still remember the first time someone told me about blow jobs.

There was a kid in class who was pulling my leg and he told me, 'You know what a blow job is?'

I said, 'No, what is it? I've heard about it though.'

He said, 'You take off all your clothes and put your fan on high speed, and that's a blow job.'

I said, 'I can do that. What is the big deal in that?'

And at twelve, I remember, I removed my clothes and put my fan on full speed.

Later, I told him about it and he said, 'You did it!'

I said, 'Yeah, yeah, I did it three times.'

He said, 'You had three blow jobs yesterday!'

I said, 'Yeah, I had three blow jobs.'

I know it sounds hard to believe but for a very long time, I didn't know what the words 'fuck' and 'masturbation' meant. There was a big age gap between me and my father, and no one else told me about these things. I had a very square group of friends; we were all very good girls and boys. We were the Gujarati bunch who would go to picnics. We were the most uncool, unaware and innocent lot.

While growing up, I was combating a hundred issues in my head. The thought of sex made me awkward; it almost rattled me. I thought, am I asexual? Why am I not feeling this? Why am I not doing anything? There was a lot of turbulence in my head. For me to address it, talk about it, discuss it, was a big no-no. I brushed it under the carpet all through the making of *Dilwale Dulhania Le Jayenge* and *Kuch Kuch Hota Hai*. At that time, I was also very large and was grappling with my weight issues. I felt physically undesirable. Post *Kuch Kuch Hota Hai*, I had actually started working a little on my looks. I had lost some weight and had groomed myself a bit. Finally, I had developed a little spring in my step, a little confidence. That's when my first encounter happened, after the release of *Kuch Kuch Hota Hai*, out of the country. Right after *Kuch Kuch Hota Hai* released, I went to London. I was twenty-six then. In passing, I had heard about a high-end, safe escort service. But because I was still overweight at that time, I was very self-conscious about my body. When you're younger, you're a lot more nervous about removing your clothes in front of someone. But then I thought, if you're paying for it, then who cares what they think?

It was a very nerve-wracking experience for me. I did it twice. The first time I ran away. I paid the money and then said I can't do this. I was so stressed, I couldn't do it. One week later, I mustered up my courage and went back again. This time, I walked out with guilt. I felt miserable. Why have I done this, I thought. It's not that the sexual release was fun. It just seemed a bit stupid; it seemed fake because obviously the person assigned to please you is going to please you artificially. It's a job and that's what they're paid to do. It seemed like I was in a film with cameras on. I thought, what am I doing? It's not giving me happiness and nobody else knows about it anyway, so who am I really doing this for? It's not something you tom-tom about, you can't go around telling people, 'Oh, I paid for sex today.' It's something you would want to hide which I did. It didn't do anything for me. Even though I was young, paying for sex was something I couldn't understand. I felt, how can I fake this part of my life? I can't be paying for something that's giving me pleasure; I have to work towards it or create it for myself or not indulge in it at all.

Then I remember in my late thirties the thought occurred to me once more in New York, and I did make an appointment but I cancelled it an hour before. It's not that I got moralistic about it or ethical, it's just that it didn't make sense to me. It's like Twitter, why should I give my opinions to seven million people I don't know? Why am I doing this unless it's for effect? Similarly here—do I have to say I've had sex with a certain number of people because everybody else has? But if I'm not getting it of my own accord, should I be paying for it? It's not the money that bothered me; it was just that it didn't add up.

I'm old-fashioned about love. I have a bit of romanticism in me that I want to hold on to. I believe in protocol, even in love. I still believe in chivalry. I would let a woman go ahead of me, open a car door for her, I would give a senior gentleman or lady my space. Some of these things are inbuilt in me because of my father. I've seen him do it always. I believe in respect for elders, and treating women well. Some of these things are in my DNA.

Today, people think that I have all the possible avenues to have all the sex in the world. But that's not who I am at all. To me, sex is a very, very personal and a very intimate feeling. It's not something that I can do casually, with just about anyone. I have to invest in it. I am very protective about that part of myself. My entire body becomes tense if I feel someone is hitting on me. And if I am not interested, I become like the stern principal of a school. I am people friendly but I am very awkward in that zone.

I've always handled the rumours that came my way. There has been so much conjecture about my sexuality. For heaven's sake, for years there were rumours about Shah Rukh and me. And I was traumatized by it. I moved from anger to indifference and finally to amusement. I was on a show on a Hindi channel, and I was asked about Shah Rukh. *'Yeh anokha rishta hai aap ka,'* the interviewer said. He worded it in such a way that I got really angry.

I said, 'If I asked you if you are sleeping with your brother, how will you feel?'

So he said, 'What do you mean? How can you ask me this question?'

I said, 'How could you ask me this question? It's the same thing, *agar main aap se puchoon ki kya aap ka koi sexual rishta aap ke bhai ke saath hain toh aap kya kahoge mujhse?'*

He said, *'Yeh kaisey bol sakte hain aap mujhse, yeh kaisa sawal hai?'*

I said, *'Toh aap ne jo mujhse pucha woh kaisa sawal tha?'*

For me, no matter what ups and downs Shah Rukh and I have been through, in my head he has always been my father's friend. He is a father figure, an older brother to me. He is the first person I would talk to about anything, because he has replaced my father in my life in a way. For me to look at him in that way or be subjected to those rumours was just ridiculous. I used to get appalled at the stories. I have heard stories that I was making out with him in the Concorde room of the British Airways lounge in London. Even if we had to, would we choose such a public spot?

But it didn't bother him. He said, 'People talk nonsense, and if a man does not have an extramarital affair, he is supposed to be gay.'

Is that what the perception is? If you are not sleeping with a woman, you are sleeping with a man? Here is a man who is committed to his work and he is close to me. And he hugs me, pats my head, it's that kind of a dynamic; he's always treated me like a younger brother. Shah Rukh made a joke about it on *Koffee with Karan* once.

I asked him, 'What if you woke up as Karan Johar?'

He said, 'My chances of waking up as him are less but waking up with him are more.'

It was on national television. And we laughed about it.

I have always been surrounded by such rumours about my alleged affairs. I get scared of being spotted with any single man now because I think they are going to think that I am sleeping with him. I mean, firstly I have never ever talked about my orientation or sexuality because whether I am heterosexual, homosexual, bisexual, asexual, it is my concern. I refuse to talk about it. Even if I was banging 100 men or 200 women, I would not talk about it. I have not been brought up to talk about my sex life. I know I am the butt of many jokes, pun intended. I know how my sexuality is discussed. I have become like the poster boy of homosexuality in this country. But honestly, I have no problem with people saying what they want about me.

Twitter has the maximum amount of abuse. I wake up to at least 200 hate posts saying, 'You fucking homo, leave our country' or 'Get out, you're polluting our nation, you're dirtying society' or 'Shove [IPC Section] 377 up your arse.' I get this on a daily basis and I've learnt to laugh it off. I am not bothered. I have developed an iron armour which protects me from all this shit. Sometimes, people are just rude and ask me to my face at airports.

Like one man came up to me once very cockily at Heathrow airport and said, 'Is it true that you are a homo?'

He was with his wife and child, and he asked me this.

I looked at him and said, 'Why, are you interested?'

And he said, 'Hey, what what what!'

And I said, 'Don't what what me.'

And I walked out.

I always come up with a retort. Some major sections of the English media are very sensitive in the way they approach this question.

I'll be asked, 'Oh, there is some conjecture about, you know, your sexuality.'

Everybody knows what my sexual orientation is. I don't need to scream it out. I can say it in this book—everybody knows where I come from. And if I need to spell it out, I won't only because I live in a country where I could possibly be jailed for saying this. Which is why I will not say the three words that possibly everybody knows about me in any case. I've given hints. I've stood on a platform like *AIB Roast*, and I had half of the people supporting me and the other half dissing me for doing this. But at the end of the day, I did what I did, and I did it with my mother in the front row, and screw you if you have a problem with that. The only thing that bothered me was when people stood on the high moral ground and said, 'Why was your mother in the front row?'

But she's cool. Do you know the discussions I've had with her on this? Do you know that I tried to stop her from coming but she insisted on coming?

I said, 'Okay, if you're cool enough to endure what could be said about me on that stage in front of 5000 people, then hell, yeah, come! And be in the front row and laugh.'

The other thing I told her was, 'Mum, laugh. Do not squirm and do not be embarrassed for me because I'm not embarrassed for myself.' If they're going to make jokes about my sexual orientation, I'm okay about it. I'm not embarrassed about who I am. I'm not apologetic. I'm embarrassed about the country I live in vis-à-vis where I come from in terms of my orientation. I'm sad, upset and disheartened with the trolling that happens on social media, when every morning people say, 'Wake up, you want it in your ass.' I read things like this on a daily basis, at least 3000 of them in a week. It saddens me how people just don't understand that you could be more messed up even if you're a straight, completely heterosexual individual than a not-coming-in-your-way homosexual.

At the end of the day, this whole homophobia is so disheartening and upsetting. And then they say, 'Why don't you speak about your sexuality? You could be iconic in this country.' But I don't want to be iconic anywhere. I want to live my life. The reason I don't say it out aloud is simply that I don't want to be dealing with the FIRs. I'm very sorry. I have a job, I have a commitment to my company, to my people who work for me; there are over a hundred people that I'm answerable to. I'm not going to sit in the high courts and the Supreme Court of this country because of ridiculous, completely bigoted individuals who have no education, no intelligence, who go into some kind of rapture for publicity. I'm not doing this.

I've reached a point in my life where I am not going to conform to what people think I should be saying or doing. I think I've gotten away with it because I have a level of decency and humanity that comes as a coating on top of who I am. I've never offended people, never hurt people, whether it's my family or my relationships. I've always been there for my fraternity, been there for my company. I've always done the right thing. So if you have an opinion about my sexuality, then screw you. I don't care. My life is my life and I have to think ahead about what I have to do.

My one major relationship was overseas, with someone who lived in Los Angeles and then finally moved to New York. It didn't work out. It lasted for just over a year. And that was the only relationship I've ever had in my life.

Of course, I've fallen in love in the past. But I always end up falling in love with unavailable people. Whoever I've fallen in love with, they've always known, but I've always protected my broken heart. I'm practical like that. Like they talk about Oscar winners, I'm a three-time heartbroken person. But I've always emerged from it, fought back and continued to live my life. There was not even a single element of physicality in any of these three times. I communicated my love to the people but nothing ever came out of it. It was just selfless love, almost sacrificial in some strange, romantic Hindi film way. But it was something that nurtured me. The best pieces of writing I've ever done were when I had a broken heart. I wrote *Ae Dil Hai Mushkil* post a broken heart. All that energy went into the script. The heartbreak was completely justifiable; it was nobody's fault but mine and I completely take the onus of that emotion. But at the end of the day, I transfer a lot of that into my writing. And then I think, chalo, at least a film came out of it, if not a relationship. And maybe, a film matters to me more at this stage of my life than a relationship. Strangely enough, heartbreaks can also be satisfying.

There have been a series of unrequited love situations. There have been two instances that have been heartbreaking. One in college, and one after that. Both of these were largely about unrequited love which I will take to my grave because there are very few people who know about them. Only I know and the person involved, who I was silently and madly in love with. And it never worked out. But it nurtured me. I suffered the heartbreak just like in *Kuch Kuch Hota Hai* because through my college years and after that for about seven or eight years, I was in love with someone unconditionally, completely and madly. And it broke my heart and there were tears. But I understood why the love was not reciprocated. On both occasions, we were not on the same wavelength, emotionally, physically or sexually. That's why it was unrequited.

But where it was reciprocated, where I felt I was in love, I was with someone and we dated for over a year. But I remember breaking it off because I felt like I was in it for the wrong reasons. I was more in it because it was the first time I had had a lover. For the first time, I could say—this is my relationship, I am dating somebody. So I felt I was doing it more for that tag, for that tick in the box than for the feeling of it. Actually, it was a little boring. The idea was more exciting than the relationship itself. It was not something I enjoyed. I was not invested in it the way I should have been. My unrequited love has absorbed me much more than the one relationship I had.

There's a Faiz Ahmed Faiz line:

Gar baazi ishq ki baazi hai jo chaho laga do dar kaisa
Gar jeet gaye toh kya kehna haare bhi toh baazi maat nahin.

It is actually the most beautiful thought—you can win even when you've lost in love, and I think everybody should go through it. Falling in love is the most beautiful thing ever. Sometimes, not getting that love back can break your heart into tiny little pieces. But heartbreak has really strengthened my core. It has made me feel alive. When I was going through the deepest angst and was losing the zest for life, heartbreak woke me up. I felt in touch with a beating heart. It happened to me after very many years. It happened to me once in my twenties in college, once when I was in my late thirties. The reason I'm not going to expand on this is that it's not fair to the other people involved. It's like self-pity, which is a luxury. It can be beautiful. If you don't live in it forever, sometimes self-pity is great. So a half relationship and three heartbreaks. Like four weddings and a funeral! So the longest relationship in the forty-four years of my life lasted for just one year. People can choose to believe this or not, but it's the truth and I can swear on my life, career, family and everything that it's true.

Here I want to add that nobody has ever fallen in love with me first! I would be screaming from the rooftops if people were in love with me; everyone loves being loved. But I've not had one person who's been madly in love with me, whose heart I've had to break. I've never had to reject somebody's deep emotion for me. I feel terrible about it. Even I want to be loved. I too would love to break someone's heart, just to have that story to tell. At one point, I thought I was going to develop a low self-esteem about it. Maybe, I'm just not putting myself out there in that way and allowing somebody to fall in love with me. I'm so busy protecting my core, and I'm so aware. Awareness is a disease.

There have been a series of sexual encounters, passing phases, but not as many as somebody in my situation would have had. But I didn't enjoy them. They were very fleeting, very few, very far between. I am not a very sexual being. I am a lover. I am about love. If I don't feel it's a relationship or something intense, I am not aroused. I am aroused by emotions. I am not aroused by physicality. I am not aroused by a body; I am more about hug-and-cuddle affection and intimacy than I am about sex. I can do without sex if I get that love. If I love someone and that person loves me back with equal intensity but cannot have sex with me, I am okay with it. I am not a very sexual being. It's not that I don't have the feeling or the ability. It's just not who I am. I think all my energies are channelized towards my work. I probably moulded myself like that. Everybody says, 'Oh, you don't have a relationship.' I've gone through that phase of feeling bad for myself, and trying to put myself out there. People say you have to go out there, meet new people, you're so in your own clique. But where do I go, whom do I meet? I am a famous person in India, I have to accept that. So in India I can't date random people who are not from the industry. And the ones who are from the industry, it's just difficult. I can't leave my company and move to the mountains. So, what do I do?

I actually did join a high-end dating service last year. I was in London and I was told about this service which takes on a lot of well-to-do single people. They choose you, you don't choose them. They go through your profile. You have to have a certain balance sheet to even be part of that dating service. You could meet anywhere in the world. They called me and said there was someone interested in meeting me in Tokyo. But I really can't be going to Tokyo to meet someone! I know about overseas relationships but Tokyo was taking it a bit too far. I may not find any happiness through this dating service. But I have to go through the beats before I realize whether I want a relationship or not. I was missing that excitement about somebody new. Meeting a new person in the capacity of a relationship is exciting. Maybe, it's a little toy that I've found that I want to play with for a while; maybe, I'll fall flat on my face and say I don't want this. But I want to go through the experience of it.

Sometimes, it's wonderful to go through even the beat of a break-up or heartbreak. But right now, there's nothing. I hear from the whole world and their uncle about their love stories, relationships, break-ups, trauma. I've had nothing. I too want to be dramatic, I want to be traumatized, I want to bang phones down, and then make up with the person I'm seeing. I want to have break-up sex and make-up sex.

I've only heard of all this. I hate it that people don't know that about me. They probably think I'm in some secluded relationship in London or New York. But I'm walking all over these cities on my own. There's nobody I'm dating over there. People keep telling me knowingly, 'You keep going to New York, huh? You keep going to London. Somebody tucked away there, eh?'

And I want to say, no one is tucked or fucked away anywhere! I wish there was! But there isn't. There's only *main aur meri tanhayee or aksar woh dono baatein karte hain.*

The experience, the exposure to a new emotion and feeling is what I'm really wondering about. It's a way of re-energizing my existence and I'm really waiting for it.

The dating service is a great inroad into a potential new experience. I'm dying to go on a blind date. I've never been on one. This will be like a version of a blind date. Meet someone and say, oh, what do you do, etc. Just have a new conversation with a new person from perhaps a new culture. It's the excitement of that interaction. Even if my fame comes in the way of my love life, and it has come in the way in the past, I will never diss it for anything. My fame has given me so much. Sometimes, it can be a roadblock but it's not such a big problem. Fame coming in the way of a relationship is such a self-involved kind of statement. It should be an asset most of the time. I'm not putting aside my personality, my individuality and my identity for anyone. No person is worth sacrificing who I am.

The truth is that after so many years, I'm really used to my independence, and I'm very afraid of losing that. I'm so much a master of my day that I don't know if I'll be happy to be answerable to anyone else. I want a relationship but I don't think I'll be able to deal with it. That's my fear. But I want the feeling of it. I want the accountability but I fear it at the same time. So I'm being a little on the fence about it only because I don't know what the outcome will be. But I know me. If I fall madly in love, then I might be capable of becoming like a doormat. I fear that sometimes. I'm so needy that I might become like a completely subservient, mad person. The dichotomy is that in my workspace, I'm a powerful entity. I give instructions. I delegate. But in a relationship, I might become like a subservient carpet. I might become that red carpet I've walked on all my life. I'll be walked all over.

I feel I can't be accountable to anyone but my mother. Now I feel if I have a relationship, and this person asks me, 'Where are you going?' 'What are you doing?', 'When are we meeting?', I can't do it. I run this company entirely on my own. I run my life entirely on my own. I travel when I want to, work when I want to, sleep when I want to, wake up when I want to, and plan my meetings of the day when I want to. I fill my days with work to such an extent that I don't give myself time. The only time I sleep is when I'm really exhausted. Maybe, I'm running away from something. But now that I have run for so many years, I'm so used to it that I can't stop became I'm in a relationship. I can't. It's like I've put myself on the 'play' button all my life. Now 'pause' doesn't work for me. Now I have to eject the possibility of anything else. I have to just continue running till my health allows me.

My work is my biggest orgasm. A hit film is a multi-orgasm. A blockbuster venture or a big film being made is the sex that I don't have.

13

Koffee and a Roast

The other big thing that happened in my career along with my films was, of course, *Koffee with Karan*. It all began in 2004. The show finally went on air in November 2004.

There was a man called Sunil Doshi, who had worked very closely with the Bachchan family, and I knew him. I told him I would like to do a talk show. You know, just for fun, like a hobby. He had worked with Star TV. So he had an association with television. It was always something that I wanted to do. And I wanted to do it in twos—I wanted to call two people at the same time.

I thought I would call an actor and an actress or two different actors or two different actresses. I wanted a freewheeling chat, which wouldn't be about just one person. It becomes more fun when you bring in another individual in the room. Actually, the combination of two people has never been done anywhere. In most talk shows, one person comes or you talk about your film. I wanted to call two people, who may be part of the same fraternity so that the energy in that conversation doesn't become specific to one life. I had the name ready too: Koffee with Karan. Casual, irreverent, fun banter: that's what the thought was. I wanted to make it look like a drawing-room conversation. But when it is watched by other people, it gives them a sense of voyeurism. That was my idea. So I told Sunil Doshi and he came back with the money. He said, 'We'll do fifty episodes per crore [rupees].' And my father said, 'A crore is a lot of money to get.' Then my dad passed away in June. And for three months, there was no conversation. Then in the month of August, Sunil Doshi came back to me. At that point of time, I was advised, and I can't remember by whom, that the money was too little and that I should ask for more because I was bringing in the stars. I was told, 'It's your concept, you are doing everything!' So the contract was made and it turned out to be four times that amount. That's how we launched *Koffee with Karan*.

The first episode that I shot was not the first in the sequence of the telecast. It was with Saif and Preity. We shot it on Saif's birthday on 16 August 2004. He was going through a bit of turbulence because he was on the verge of splitting up with his wife. But he had given me a commitment, so he reached the studio. It took us six hours for a show that normally takes an hour and a half to shoot. Saif had to be perky on television and talk about his wife as if things were kosher. On top of that, we had lighting problems. It was a bit of a strange first episode.

Koffee with Karan is a five-segment show and we shoot pretty much in real time. We shoot a little extra so that we can edit it later. I actually don't take very long to shoot it. Once the stars have come and sat down, we get started and wrap it up quickly. The stars are not briefed about anything I'm going to ask them (contrary to what people may think). The Rapid Fire round is never shared with them because their instinctive answers when they're put in a spot is what makes it exciting. In my entire *Koffee with Karan* history, there's only one person I ever gave the Rapid Fire questions to, and that was Sanjay Dutt. He was going to come in with Sushmita Sen, and I knew she would really bite his head off with her answers, and he would just come across looking blank because he was really nervous, and it was the very first season. I gave him the questions in advance and he won the hamper. It was cheating on my part. But I haven't done that with anyone else, not Mr Bachchan, not Shah Rukh and not Salman. In fact, no one has ever asked me to.

In *Koffee with Karan*, I take four breaks. I have a system I devised with the producers, Fazila and Kamna, who are from a company called Sol. So the green light is a warning, and when the red light comes on, I take a break. That's the only way I know that the conversation needs to go towards a break. The only challenge was to make sure that we didn't overshoot too much. Unlike other shows where people just ramble, my breaks are designed. I'm not afraid of the camera or an audience. I'm not shy like that. Give me a camera and put me on stage, and I will make an impact in whatever way possible. I'm confident about that.

There were some odd episodes, like when Rakhi Sawant came. She left me hysterical. I remember laughing so much. In fact, I used to laugh a lot in *Koffee with Karan*, sometimes so much that I would be all tearful. Rakhi said some really weird and wild things.

I remember the Deepika–Sonam episode. They were just wild, and went off at a tangent. They took off like a train and just didn't stop. They were so funny but I knew there would be some repercussions. But I just enjoyed the episode so much. Of course, Shah Rukh and Kajol were great. But many of the standout moments on the show were unexpected. Salman was great fun, and I knew that line about 'I'm a virgin' would work. Then there was Kareena and Rani. Nargis and Freida Pinto. Whenever there are two girls, I have had the most fun. Those have been my favourite episodes. Nargis was really funny. Nobody knew she had such a wicked sense of humour. Her fan base really increased after that episode. I never even get into the ratings but with every season, mainstream media and social media awareness kept increasing. So I actually don't know which is the better season because the last season always seemed like the one where the most noise was created.

Somehow, *Koffee with Karan* always does well. People like to watch it. Guests are repeated but everyone has a new lover, new enemy, new controversy. And I ask everyone everything that's out in the public domain. I never ever cross the line of friendship. If I've been told something in complete privacy by the celebrity, I would never ask a question about it. But I'll ask about whatever is in the public domain. I'll ask about who they're dating, the argument they supposedly had with some person. It's just the way I roll out the questions. I can keep badgering them, which journalists don't have the luxury of doing.

I can say, 'No, tell me, you're lying.'

No journalist can say that. But my guests will take it from me. If any news channel reporter says to a star, *'Aap jhhooth bol rahe hain,'* he or she will say, 'How dare you!'

We do get requests from PR to feature some newer actors, but I say no. There's a bit of prestige attached to being on *Koffee with Karan*. Alia not knowing the President's name worked for her. Sometimes, even something like that can endear a star to the audience in a strange way. Then she did that short film with All India Bakchod and that just cemented it. She made fun of herself. Everybody found her cute and sweet. Alia Bhatt became a household brand. It's all about brand building. Sometimes, negativity can also be useful to build a brand. Suddenly, everyone was talking about the fact that she didn't know who the President of the country was. I think it worked in her favour. She agreed to do it and make a jackass of herself. Actually, she's not dumb at all. She's one of the brightest bulbs there is. It's just that she's politically unaware of certain names. She's just not aware of who's running this country, which is ridiculous I know, but she's street-smart, she's bright, and she'll think before a scene. She reads books. She's Mahesh Bhatt's daughter, so she's living with a book of quotes.

I had equations with all the actors, so to get them in pairs was not a problem for the first lot of twenty episodes.

I had always wanted elements like the Rapid Fire and the hamper. Sometimes, the hamper has a computer, sometimes there's a phone, then there are chocolates, all kinds of fun things. It's quite a happening hamper.

But I had never imagined that *Koffee with Karan* would take off in such a big way. Simply because I took it as the extension of a hobby. I was getting paid to talk, which is great, because I do it anyway.

Four seasons later, it emerged as a huge brand. I didn't realize what it could do to my brand equity. Even today, I mostly get asked about the show. I've made so many movies but it's all about *Koffee with Karan*. I didn't realize that this casual, irreverent banter between me and the fraternity members would be of such global interest. What worked is this exact sense that I had when I planned the show—the sense of voyeurism. You feel you are almost prying into a private banter. That is how I kept it. So it was fun and gossipy. It was not at all about doing a cerebral show.

I remember some directors coming up to me and saying, 'Are you sure you want to expose yourself so much? A film-maker has to have a sense of intrigue.'

And I said, no, it didn't have to be that way.

Interestingly, now everybody is on television. Every other celebrity began judging reality shows or hosting something or the other. I think I just got the ball rolling.

The show has mostly stuck to its original script. While it has become different in terms of the texture, the essence has remained the same. I was more careful in my first season. With every passing season, I started becoming more and more wacky. It also progressively became more sexual for some strange reason. It was as if I grew wings with every new season. I guess the show has become more 'sexy' now because I'm more 'sexy' now. If you see the four seasons of *Koffee with Karan*, it shows my own evolution, it shows me changing as a person. I was actually like a vulnerable, innocent child in season one, and I come across as a horny midlife victim in the fourth. And I'm doing all this for fun. I am no nymphomaniac. Far from it. The opposite possibly. But I just don't care any more. It's gone from polite conversation and reverence to not giving a fuck. So if you really want to know of my evolution, you have to go from the first to the fourth season. If you pick up just any one episode of season one to any episode of season four, you will see the difference. Because, it's been a decade and I can feel the change. Anyway, we talk a lot of nonsense. Some parents have even told me that they wouldn't like their kids to watch this kind of rubbish. I had become like *Stardust* or *Cine Blitz*, but with a touch more dignity.

In *Koffee with Karan*, I'm naughty, funny, cute. The problem arises when the two people sitting across start talking about a third person. At one point, Shobhaa De got upset with me because Sonam and Deepika took off on her.

So I said, 'They took off on you, it's not my fault.'

Then she understood.

I said, 'They have an opinion.' But these things are temporary. They will meet at some event and patch up. There are no big wars.

In the first season of *Koffee with Karan*, there were a lot of freewheeling chats. People said plenty of things because after a point, they forgot that the cameras were on. Now everyone comes more prepared because they have seen the impact of the show. Some people said some controversial things, and a few fights happened. Suddenly the media had all the fodder in the world to play with, because in the Rapid Fire round, I would make people rate actors. I must say it's quite a Narad Muni thing for me to do. Many of the guests ask me, 'Can you cut this out? I've said something I shouldn't have.' It didn't happen so much in the first season. It started happening more from the second season onwards. It was because in the first season people just came and spoke; they didn't realize that there would be ramifications. But by the second season, people would say, 'Oh god, can you not ask me about this?' And I would say, 'I'll ask you and you deny it.' But I would make the denial fun. Even if they were saying no, I would say, 'Shut up, you are lying.' I made Anushka Sharma's life miserable by asking her about Virat Kohli. I traumatized her. But she was laughing by the end of it because I went on and on, and she didn't even know how to deny it any more. I said she was like the first lady of cricket. I made a lot of puns.

Koffee with Karan also became about who was coming for the show and who wasn't. But it never affected any of my relationships. Well, yes, Rishi Kapoor got very offended, and that too right before we did the maximum work with him in the company. He and Neetuji got really upset about the comments made about Ranbir in the Deepika–Sonam episode in the third season. Ranbir was cool but the parents—rightfully—got offended. They felt I had egged on the girls, though the girls seemed to have come equipped with what they had to say. So Rishi Kapoor went on record to say, 'I will never work with Dharma Productions again.' But he worked with us immediately after that because I met him and said, 'Look, I am sorry. I didn't mean to offend you. It's a fun, irreverent show. If you watch the show, you'll know that's the vibe. And no one means any harm.' Ironically, Ranbir was sitting there when the girls were recording the show. He kind of knew what they had said. But he didn't realize it would blow up like this. There's always this madness that surrounds us in the industry—'How can these girls say this? *Karan ko kuch karna chahiye tha. Karan ne kyu nahi roka.*' I also met Neetuji and sorted it out. They're seniors. I have great respect for them. Ranbir told me, 'You sort it out.' However, despite all the controversy, I worked with Rishi Kapoor in *Agneepath* and *Student of the Year* right after that. So it was all good. This was the only problem I got into with the show. Internally, I'm sure everyone must have had some problem or the other with each other. The media also fuels the fire.

I have all these strong equations with people in the industry. Even if I have not worked with them, I know them well. By the fourth season, I said to Aamir, 'You have to do it for me, otherwise I'll be most upset.' So then he said, 'I can't say no to you now.' So he and his wife, Kiran, came. When I asked Aamir in the interview why he hadn't come earlier, he said it was because he didn't like me. And then he said he realized that he was wrong. He was quite candid about it. I did have a feeling he didn't like me. He had great regard for my father but somehow, there was something about me he didn't approve of or didn't like. I have a great amount of respect for him though. He said he had an impression about me, which was wrong—that I was a slightly frivolous, flaky socialite film-maker who would go ha-ha-he-he at a party without showing any depth, sincerity or conviction. I am not that person. But this talk show has given me the reputation of being slightly flighty, frivolous, campy, gossipy and chatty, like a kitty party queen. It has taken my depth away. There's a certain urbane, affluent, snooty air about the show. People enjoy watching *Koffee with Karan* because it's got that tongue-in-cheek humour and irreverent vibe. So the big damage has not been to my relationships with the people who appear on my show, it has been to my own reputation. Nevertheless, I still love the show. It's put me out there in the limelight.

And now I'm doing the fifth season, in which we'll reach 100 episodes!

The truth is I did regret being part of the AIB Roast. Not because of what I said but because of what happened afterwards. After the controversy broke, I was sitting with cops, commissioners, lawyers. And dealing with all that for six months and more—that's why I regret it, not for any other reason. I was appalled at what I had to put my company, my lawyers, my legal team through when they should have been fighting about contractual clauses in studio deals. They were fighting about me on a roast!

When I agreed to host the AIB Roast, I knew what I was doing. The four boys of AIB—who I find very funny—came to me because they said they couldn't think of a better 'roast-master'. They sat in my office, all four of them, nervous, thinking I would throw them out. But I told them I would be happy to do it. I'm impulsive. I didn't think too much about it either before or after. I'm not embarrassed about anything said about me.

During the show, I never made fun of anybody else other than the people on that stage. Everybody knew what I was going to say. They said things about me, I didn't care. I said they could make all the fun they wanted to about me but they shouldn't make me mention any person who was not part of the Roast. I would never talk about anyone else, because why should I do that?

I was told, 'You're a big film-maker. Why did you need to do this?' But why should I take myself seriously? Why am I supposed to be this big film-maker who is meant to maintain mystique and mystery? Maybe, I'm not interested in being in the archives as this legend who was mystical. Maybe, I don't want to be Rekha. Maybe, I want to be out there. I'm a pop culture boy. I regret AIB only because of the legal ramifications, not because of what happened during the show. I would do it again today if someone told me that there would be no legal hassles.

Frankly, I don't know what I'm capable of doing. My mind has become like an open space today; it's a maidan where I'm allowing all sorts of thoughts to creep in. I curtail myself because sometimes my sense of humour can offend you. So I make sure my joke is always about me. I don't want to hurt anyone. If I haven't liked a film, I will not say it in an interview. It's not fair to that person. But if I'm talking about myself, I should be allowed to.

My mom came for the Roast; she sat through it, but didn't say anything. We came back home and we had dinner together. We didn't talk about it. So I don't know what her thoughts were on it. She hasn't spoken about it to anyone. She's modern, evolved, and above all, she's my friend and partner in life. She knows that my heart is in the right place. I'm a good son, I'm a good friend to people, I'm a good boss, and she's immensely proud of me. She's proud that I carried forward the legacy of my dad quite well. I've never had my mother sit me down and say that I've done something wrong. She laughs at me. When I told her not to come for the Roast, she said, 'You've danced on national television, what can be more humiliating than that?' She has the same sense of humour like my father and me. We're a family of funny people. My mother has a very straight-faced kind of humour. And people love her because she mainly bitches about me. My mum is very popular with my friends. She's very nasty about me in her own funny way.

She disses most of my achievements; I think she does it to keep my feet firmly on the ground. If I tell her I got the Most Stylish Person award, she'll say, why're they giving you this award? You're far from stylish! She says things like this. I know she's saying them purposely so that I don't get carried away by anything. I know she talks about me with great pride—but behind my back! Sometimes, I'll say something mildly arrogant—mildly because I'm not arrogant by nature—and as if on cue, she'll tell me five greater things that five other people have achieved, and that'll shut me up.

People say that I make fun of and stereotype homosexuals. But I say, 'No, I've brought homosexuality to dining table discussions. I've received over a thousand emails and letters from gay boys and girls thanking me for making *Dostana* because, they said, now at least people know what the concept is. I also made *Bombay Talkies* which dealt with gay married men who are actually hiding and repressing themselves, owing to social and parental pressures. That was the backstory of the film.'

I've not made fun of homosexuality; I've addressed it with humour, but all for a reason. Now a lot of people talk openly about it. I've even flirted with the anchor Manish Paul on the dance show, *Jhalak Dikhhla Jaa*. I'm flirting with a man, right? How come it's become so believable and acceptable? Families say, *'Hamein aapki aur Manish ki nok-jhok bahut pasand aati hai!'* I've had a very traditional lady come up to me at an airport and tell me how much she loves my banter with Manish. Doesn't the moral police of the country realize that the only way you can penetrate a thought in this country is with humour? When you lace it with seriousness and make it like fighting for a cause, it achieves nothing. You take a step back.

There's a way of communicating sexuality in a country such as ours. It's very sad but we need to have different ways of communication. When that lady told me that she liked the banter between Manish and me, I thought, how great is that? She's not offended by it. She's probably more progressive than her husband who actually could be gay. I always feel that the biggest homophobic men and women in this country are definitely oppressed homosexuals. We're a country full of divided sexuality. I know from personal experience that the lines are very blurred when it comes to sexuality. Everyone's experimenting. Every single person has done so or wanted to. The thought has crossed their minds. They are no longer just the usual thoughts that pass through the human mind. Everyone has tried all kinds of things in their heads if not in their bed.

To go back to the AIB Roast, it was only when I was on that stage and I saw those 5000 people laughing loudly or going 'Oh!' in a shocked way, that the enormity of it hit me. I don't overthink these things. I've never sat and strategized my own brand value. I've never projected a certain kind of image which is the reason I think a lot of other directors in this profession don't take me seriously at all. I've done a variety of things in my career. I've danced on a reality show, I've done a roast and I've hosted a talk show. I'm not taken seriously by the industry nor by the audience beyond a point. I don't know why. Maybe, I'm a victim of my own image. Maybe, I'll never be given the credit even if I create a piece of brilliance on celluloid, like Raju Hirani gets, for instance. I think every other film-maker is far more easily forgiven than me. I'm just this person who is always assaulted because of the things I do. I dilute the importance of being a serious entity. I don't stand seriously, quietly in a corner like Raju Hirani does or project mad insanity like Sanjay Leela Bhansali or have the seriousness and Sufism of Imtiaz Ali or the intellectual capacity of Zoya Akhtar. I'm this *bhaand* who entertains.

The simple truth is that I do things that make me happy. I'm not here to create a structured legacy. I'm here to live in the moment. If in that moment I feel like I want to do something, I'll do it. If I feel like I want to dance in that reality show, I will dance even though I may look crazy. I never go back and watch myself on TV. If I'm acting in a film or on a show, you'll never see me going to the control room to see what I'm looking like. I don't care. I'm done with the shot, I've danced spontaneously, and that's it. Now it's for the world to see and judge. I remember Anurag Kashyap was totally shocked by this. He had a completely different impression of me. When he was directing me, he thought I would come rushing to the monitor. I never went once, till they forced me one day to come and see for myself. If I'm at a photo shoot, I don't go and check the images. I'm very confident in my skin and I'm very happy that way. That's why I don't care where my name comes in the film credits. I notice how some film-makers put their name in every department. I don't feel the need to do that. Give me my credit as a director, that's all I want, even though as a director, it's your job to contribute to everything. I'm not insecure about my professional life. I'm insecure about my personal life, that is how I am.

14

Midlife Angst

I've been through something in the last couple of years which I call 'urban angst'. I feel the pressure of delivery. Sometimes, I feel the need to be the human being I'm designed to be and sometimes, I could not care less about everything around me. I feel like saying, just fuck off.

Since last year, I've started going to a psychologist. I was wondering what I was going through and I was finally told that it was an anxiety attack. Call it work pressure, the stress of handling people, the fear of emptiness, loneliness, and probably the feeling of growing old alone. My mother has been going through health issues and every time she doesn't answer her phone after three rings, I think the worst thoughts. As I'm growing older, I'm getting more vulnerable. I fear losing the only family attachment I have. This last year has been actually the most turbulent for me emotionally and there's no particular reason for it.

Then I realized I'm going through the quintessential midlife crisis a little earlier than others perhaps. My sessions with my psychologist have meant a lot to me. Dropping my guard with someone who has no connection to my life. She's a lovely lady and is very sorted. People don't understand that there's a difference between therapy and psychology. Therapy is when you go back to your childhood, etc. But psychologists actually prescribe medication and I've been on medication for the last year because I felt the need for it, to calm myself down, to understand why my heartbeat was racing the way it was, and why my lack of sleep was eating into my daily output level. That was what was happening to me. I was not being able to focus. So my psychologist prescribed medication for me. I'm a strong believer in allopathy; I'm not one of those who believe in homoeopathy, etc. If I have a headache, I pop two pills. Yeah, it's wrong and it'll eat into your system later, but screw it. You're living for the moment. I could die tomorrow. Why should I have this headache and go for herbal therapy and homoeopathic medicine? No. Pop a pill. I'm a big pill popper. If I can't sleep, I'll take a sleeping tablet. I know it is not the most healthy thing and I don't prescribe it for other people. But I don't do drugs (though I take Restyl which is a sleeping pill). Once in my life, I took something when I was in Goa which is supposed to increase your serotonin level and make you happy, but instead it made me sleepy. It did nothing for me. It was the most wasted drug experience of my life. The one and only experience. But you walk around in the industry and everyone thinks you're sniffing charlie. I flew with somebody—an affluent banker—on a Mumbai–Delhi flight once, and he said, 'Oh, all of you must do a lot of drugs.'

And I asked, 'All of you means?'

He said, 'You and your industry.'

People think we're a group of retarded aliens who are debauched, decadent and doing everything that is incorrect and jail-worthy.

He said, 'You don't sniff charlie?'

I said, 'No!'

He said, 'Don't be silly, you're always on such an upper, you always look so energized, so you're not doing coke?'

And I said, 'Not at all. I don't do drugs. But I've done MDMA once.'

I don't know why I told him. I felt the need for him to believe me. I know I'm in an industry where people apparently do drugs, but then the whole world does things. It's never done anything for me and I'm not doing it again. What's worked for me is the medication my psychologist has prescribed. She's weaned me off it and now it's a minimal dosage. But the eight months that I took it, I realized that there was a chemical imbalance that had been caused with all the anxiety, stress levels, fears and insecurities. My professional zone is intense; I have a lot of love around me, though I'm trying to sieve and find out who really matters and who doesn't, but nobody realizes that.

When Deepika spoke about her depression, I completely empathized with it. I don't want to sound like a poor little rich boy. It's not that. Sometimes the grass is greener on the other side and nobody sees what you're going through. I project a lot and there is a fatigue that creeps in because of such projection levels. You're expected to be happy. You're expected to be sociable. You're expected to be there for the people. These expectations can drain you.

Last year has been a period of self-realization for me. Nobody knew I was visiting a psychologist once a week. My office didn't know. My mum didn't know. She thought some lady was coming for corporate meetings.

I called up Putlu and said that I needed help. It was a vulnerable moment the night I called her. I told her that I was going through something. She's somebody who's medically informed, and she's been a friend to so many people. I said, 'Putlu, I need help.' She said I needed to meet this lady. She got it because she'd been sensing it herself. The very next day that lady came. Now I'm sorted, I'm much better. I'm at least 50 per cent better and that's a big improvement. I was just going mad in my head.

I feel it's such a misconception when people attribute personal happiness to wealth. Actually your work, your creativity, your commercial output, whatever, is separate from what you go through within. When you're in your bedroom, those minutes before you go to sleep, the day or your thoughts about the next day flash in front of your eyes; so much goes on in your head that is not going to be perceived by people unless you put yourself out there on a daily basis. I'm a Gemini; I can swing a different face as soon as I get out of my house. I can play the part of being me. I can walk into meetings, be charming if I need to, show vulnerability if I have to, show overconfidence if so required, show power if I have to. I can do all of that. I can play a part. But you cannot stop being your own person in this industry or any other place in the world. I run a company and I have people working under me; you can't be showing your vulnerable side to your accountant, can you? You can't show your marketing head that you're lonely that day or that you feel sad or let down by a particular individual or that you've been hurt in love or that you're heartbroken or alone. How can I show that to the people in my organization? I can't show it to my mum either because it will worry her, and she's already combating medical issues.

So who do I show it to? You show it to your friends who then feel the need to check on you regularly and that annoys you as well because you're an independent person. So where do you find solace? With a doctor. Some go to psychics, some to pandits, some to gurus. I have a psychologist. I feel mine is a modern-age way of dealing with inner stress and issues. I went for medical help straight away. I didn't go to a babaji. I didn't go to a mandir. I didn't go to a tarot reader. I felt I needed medical attention.

You know they say the heart is racing faster . . . that's exactly what happened to me. I found myself taking deep, shallow, noisy breaths. That's anxiety. You feel like the oxygen from your system has just been sucked out. You feel like you're in Ladakh. You feel you need acclimatization. Your mind is running, your dreams are running. You dream, you wake up, you dream, you wake up. That's anxiety. We don't realize it, but depression or anxiety are medical conditions. They're not because you're mad and losing your mind. It's the serotonin level that shifts in your body. We're all born with a serotonin level. Some people have it in abundance, those are blessed souls. Some people have a balance and they're blessed souls too. Some people have low levels of serotonin; they tend to veer towards sadness. But sadness and depression are totally different things. Sadness can be dealt with but depression needs medication. It could be your serotonin level, the chemical imbalance in you, which is something no one gets. The West overreacts to it, and I feel in India we under-react to it.

I don't feel I'm a depressed person. I feel I'm an anxious person. And my anxiety level was eating into my day-to-day functioning and I needed to address it. My anxiety was coming of course from layers of fears and insecurities that were on a personal, not professional, level. I can deal with professional failure, I know how to. I've been there. But the anxiety about personal issues is not easy to deal with. It's not that I was recovering from any kind of crisis. I had been through this about six years ago when I lost my father but I had not self-diagnosed myself at that point of time. I had not realized what it was. I spoke to my psychologist and she asked whether I had been through this before and I said I had felt this strongly about six years ago. She said it was a late reaction to my father's death. She said if I had addressed it then I would have probably not gone through it.

So when I read about Deepika's admission of depression, I completely empathized with her. I've been there. There was a section that thought, oh, how brave of her to talk about it. And some were like, is she seeking attention? This latter type is the kind which believes that everyone has an agenda. Then there are those who don't know sadness. My friend Manish Malhotra—he's one person whose serotonin level is very high—doesn't understand why people get sad. He doesn't understand the concept of sadness.

He said to me, 'Why is Deepika going through depression? She's so pretty! So beautiful, she has everything, career, success, beauty.'

I tried to tell him, 'It means nothing.'

When she sleeps at night or when she wakes up, she could feel like the loneliest person perhaps, I don't know. She and I have spoken about it on several occasions. I totally get it. Beauty has nothing to do with your inner self. The most beautiful people could be the most messed-up individuals on the face of this earth. Beauty can be a curse as much as it can be an asset. She's alone in a city, running her home, running her career, away from her parents. It can get to you. Even success can. Nothing fails like success sometimes. So at the end of the day, expectations increase and living up to them is so stressful. Failure can be a beautiful place because there's a way up then. Success is like holding on. How do you keep holding on to something that can easily slip out of your hands? You're holding it tight, but when you hold something tight your entire body is tense. That's what success is. It tenses you to the extent that your mind, body, heart, soul, everything is tense. But when you're a failure, it has slipped out of your hands. So there's an ease. There's a certain comfort in it—oh, I failed, I'm sad; three days later I'll rise again, I'll try again. But when you're holding on, gripping, every nerve in your body is tense. Success is a huge, huge burden to live with. It's not easy. I get it. I get it on a subliminal and deep level.

15

Bollywood Today

There is a certain kind of newness in Bollywood today—a new energy, new film-makers and new writers. It's a new age of thought that is slowly taking away a lot of the old nonsense. The quintessential movie, the typical masala potboiler is not really getting the kind of warm welcome that it once did. There is a divide. There is a mass–class divide, between multiplexes and single screens. There is still a certain kind of business that's garnered by mass films but we're heading towards interesting times.

Bollywood is going through a kind of meltdown. There's a dip in footfalls because the multiplex pricing is high. The 1990 *Agneepath* had more footfalls than the 2011 *Agneepath*, and the latter was a hit. Do the maths. Also, cinema is tackling digital media, television, so many other platforms of entertainment. And it's not just about Bollywood; Hollywood is combating all this as well. Television is becoming like that annoying mother-in-law, while digital might be the new patriarch of the family, and I think film is going to be the troubled child who needs therapy.

In India, international studios are realizing that producing Hindi films is not bringing in the kind of profits they had thought it would. Stars charge too much money, directors spend too much money, footfalls are dropping, and cost-to-profit is not making sense. So let's just release Hollywood films. But all this is going to make our content better because eventually people are going to make better films. Because, only those will eventually make money. These big-set films with big stars that are made just to bring in the money—well, there are very few stars who can bring in that kind of money, and with bad films they don't bring in anything. There used to be an assurance that a star gave you a certain amount of money on the opening weekend. That's not happening any more. Akshay and the three Khans are the dependable stars. But how can you run a movie economy with four stars? And very few directors guarantee you that opening. Some people have made Herculean errors, including myself; sometimes we've spent too much money on a film that did not warrant it. But we've made fewer mistakes; other studios have made many more. You can't blame any one person, it's just the order of the day.

But I feel this is an interim zone we're going through for the larger good of cinema. One will find the money to make films but we will have to cut costs. It's not like cricket. The country will always be obsessed with cricket. Cricket won't have to fight kabaddi to emerge as the sport that drives the nation crazy. But we are combating the Internet, piracy and television. The satellite market has dipped only because they decided they were paying the film producers too much money. So, what do you do? You have to bring your budgets down. But on the other hand, there's excitement because there's a lot of new, young energy and talent in the industry. There is no nepotism any longer. Film-makers are bringing in new cultures with their own style of film-making. The whole North Indian invasion that's happening in Hindi cinema is actually not an invasion, it's an inclusion. The whole texture of films like *Tanu Weds Manu* is new; there's a different syntax that has suddenly evolved in the last decade. A new kind of content is being made and appreciated. While there's still the junk that does well, there's also a *Piku* that wins your heart. *Tanu Weds Manu Returns* got the character so brilliantly, and Kangana was beyond believable, like she was in *Queen*. These are the films that have actually garnered a lot of interest. In fact, *Tanu Weds Manu Returns* has been a big success commercially as well.

In the coming years, Indian cinema is going to be more relevant on the global map. Already there is a noise about Indian cinema that wasn't there earlier. That's why all the big studios are here. There is a certain kind of excitement we are causing in the global arena. When a film like *PK* rakes in 20 million dollars in China, it wakes up studios. That's a lot of money. Films don't do so well even domestically. But it did that in another country. When a film like *Lunchbox* does such phenomenal business in Europe, it makes people sit up and notice. You will see a lot of co-productions, collaborations, and integrations taking place in the future. All this has happened in the last five years. In world cinema if there are two countries that are making a noise besides Hollywood, they are China followed by India. I'm not talking about the Golden Globes or the Academy Awards; I'm talking about pure commercial business. Eventually, the only art that resonates is when it's commercial, whether it's a painting or a film. It's always valued in wealth. Even the parallel films that have made money are the ones you recall. Unfortunately, it's always like that. In this world, your only barometer is wealth and money. What your value is comes from a value. It's as simple as that. You could make the most amazing film but if no one saw it and no one gave it money, it's not going to be remembered. Not even in the archives. Today what is archived is wealth. Eventually when *Lunchbox* does business in France, Germany and Spain, you think, oh, this film made a lot of money.

Shah Rukh Khan, Salman Khan and Aamir Khan are not going anywhere. They've gone through their transition phase, and have emerged hugely victorious. They are not leaving any time soon and they should not. People often say, 'When will these guys stop?' But does anyone know why they're still here? Because they didn't overanalyse their careers. Of course, they made mistakes and went through ups and downs. If you want to be a big-ass motion picture star, you have to fall to rise. The audience has to go through your journey. You have to do five films and three could be crappy and two could be great. You have to see that fall.

Most stars are worried about failure. But you can't worry about failure if you want to be great. You have to fail to succeed. And these men have failed. They've given flop after flop, then hit after hit, then flop after flop. You have to go through a graph to sustain yourself for twenty-five years. You can't just keep going up. That happens only in death. You have to go through that ECG kind of fluctuation to have a solid heart at the end. But this younger generation does not want to fail. That's their biggest problem. They are ultra-cautious; they want to choose every film extremely carefully, they want every film to be a hit, followed by another hit, then another hit, and so on. No, I say, make a flop film. Take a decision on an impulse, do a bad film. I tell all of them, whether it's Ranbir or Ranveer or Sidharth or Varun, that you guys are being too careful. When Ranbir was upset after *Bombay Velvet*, I said to him, 'It's a good thing. You've given your flop. Now when you give a hit, people will give you more love, it'll be like he's back, he's re-energized his career. You're bound to fumble and fall. So you have to do brave things. You did a *Bombay Velvet*. It may not have been liked, it may have been a global disaster, but you took a chance, didn't you? It's a good thing. You didn't play safe. You played a slightly off-character in an off-mainstream film and the studio might bleed, but as an actor, you took a chance. You took a chance on *Barfi*, you took a chance on *Wake Up Sid*, you took a chance on *Rocket Singh—Salesman of the Year*.' I tell all of them, please go ahead and take a chance. Do many more movies, do a lot of work. Do what Hollywood does. They keep working, they go from one film to the next. Not every film has to be a spectacle, not every film has to be opulent. You have to fail to learn. Only when you fail and learn, do you learn to sustain. Longevity comes with failure and success. It doesn't come with success alone.

The three Khans have worked consistently and they have kept themselves relevant in the way they look. They have a magic. They seem different but I think their minds are very similar. Two of them get love and one gets respect, which is as important if not more important than love. All of them were born in the same year, all turned fifty at different months of the same year, but they're still around, working in the biggest motion pictures. And they're going nowhere for the next five years as lead actors. After that too, they will be doing films which will revolve around them.

All three of them have what I call 'practical ego', that's what keeps them going. Their ego allows them to be relevant and it never makes them fall off the brink and self-destruct. Another way of looking at it is that they have controlled megalomania. It operates in the right way and they know when to let go of it; they know when to be accessible and amiable, and when to be the star. They just know it. These three men are unique. They know how to be movie stars and yet they know how to be endearing personalities in their own way.

Is there a superstar in the younger generation? To be honest, I don't see one. I don't see stardom any longer having longevity. The consumer is also so fickle nowadays. You get support because of the people, and the people are fickle. They shift like quicksand. Stardom has a lot to do with the aura that you create off-screen. Salman has made mistakes and apologized for them. He's 'redeemed' himself, whether it's following the Being Human path, or how he is with his family. He has always put his personal feelings very naturally across. People see the bad boy being good, and they feel protective about him. Shah Rukh has talked about his angst as a result of the loss of his parents; he's spoken about his relationship with his kids. Aamir has broken down on television because he feels connected to issues. He's shown his emotional energy. The younger generation don't show themselves. They don't allow you to get to know them. You don't know what they really are as people. You react to them based on how you see them on screen. I know them personally, so I know what they are like, but you as a consumer do not know them. What is Ranveer really like? Do you know his vulnerabilities? Do you know his weaknesses? His soft spots? His strengths, his insecurities? You don't. If you don't know him, how can you continue to love him? You know Shah Rukh somewhere. You can feel and touch him. You know there is a certain integrity about Aamir. You know Salman as the bad boy with a big heart. But you don't know this generation. I wish they would allow people to know them. You think Varun is fun because he's done fun films. You think Ranbir is charming because he's been so on screen or in reality shows. He'll hold a woman's hand nicely, he'll escort her out, he'll be chivalrous. You know that Ranveer Singh is crazy and energetic, but for all you know, he's a depressive. For all you know, his energy is a release from his inner sadness. I wish these people would open themselves up a lot more. That's the way they will find a connect with the national audience. The irony is that we're in an age of media and communication like never before, so everyone is so aware of the eyes on them that they clam up. Shah Rukh, Salman and Aamir broke through because they gave interviews and spoke during a time when the media's presence was not this heavy. Today they are reaping the benefits of all the impressions that were created in the past. Whenever someone spoke in those times, it was taken a lot more seriously. Nobody does those archival interviews any more; everyone's tweeting, instagramming, talking nonsense, lying about their personal life, and being cute about everything. It's so stupid.

I like that Anushka talked about Virat. I like that she opened herself up. Or that Deepika talked about her depression. I wish she would talk about Ranveer. I wish Ranbir and Katrina would come out and talk openly about their relationship. I wish these things would happen. I don't know why they don't do this. Maybe, they think that stardom as it is perceived has to be like this: We should not talk because it's our personal life. But I say to them, 'Come on, yaar, you're now public figures. Acknowledge it, envelop yourself in it, accept it, embrace it, put yourself out there and talk about yourself. You chose this profession, now you're public property. Open yourself up. You can't allow your gates to open only on weekends. You can't say Monday to Friday I'm shut, you're only allowed to visit me on Saturday and Sunday. No.

You're not a monument. You're a celebrity, you're a star, the public must know you. How else are they going to continue to love you?'

I don't understand this anonymity. Unless they genuinely feel that way—but they don't. They'll be upset if they're at a public place and nobody takes their photo. I've met some Hollywood stars in my life who genuinely hate the attention. I was at dinner with Christian Louboutin who is a friend, and he brought along this British actress Kristin Scott Thomas (she was in *English Patient* and *Four Weddings and a Funeral*). She walked in wearing a T-shirt and jeans, and she really didn't want the attention. After the dinner, she got into a cab and left. Some of them just treat it as a job. But our movie stars want the attention. They all desire it. I don't know a single movie star here who wants to shun the attention.

Kangana is a great actress but she's decided to make this her thing—staying away from the limelight. She will not go to an award function. She's made a branding out of her absence. (She went only to the National Awards.) People have a magnificent presence; she has a magnificent absence. It's worked so well for her.

I come from the school that says, speak, talk, communicate and convey. People cannot love you merely because of your screen presence. Everybody loves Shah Rukh Khan because they have felt him and loved him as a human being. The only one person they have given love to without knowing what is going on in his head is Amitabh Bachchan. He breaks that myth. His mystique and mystery are paramount. But he just has this presence. And I feel it's best no one knows what's happening in the genius mind of Amitabh Bachchan. He's made an entire career out of silence and diplomacy, and a fascinating mystique. Amitabh Bachchan is a superstar beyond superstars because you really don't know what goes on in there. I think he's too big a man for me to know. That's his calling card. But in this generation it will not work. If you clam up, you're out. If you start protecting yourself too much, it's not going to work either. Amitabh Bachchan came from a different time. But he's relevant even today. You see him at an event today, you feel you can go up to him and talk to him about something cool.

I use Twitter more as a professional tool. I have about seven million followers and I want those seven million to see the promos and posters of my films. I was one of the first people who joined Twitter. In fact, I got a whole lot of people to get on it. But I don't feel the need to write my daily thoughts on it. There's something attention-seeking about it which began making me feel awkward and uncomfortable. The idea of me expressing my opinion on something random, and to get reactions from people I don't know does not appeal to me. In Instagram, you put up photographs because you want to share them.

Today it's become a done thing. Since you've seen a movie before its release, you must support the film, and say nice things about it on Twitter even if you're lying about it. And I've lied many times. Now there are people who are beginning to see through my tweets! Trolling can be fun; at least, they're venting, ranting, and writing things about you. Sometimes I laugh at the hysterical things they say. But mostly I'm bored and find it pointless. Even now, though, once in a while, if I have a thought for the day, I will write it. Once in about twenty tweets there will be some stupid philosophical thought that I share. But I can't bear the day-to-day engagement. It's not something that interests me. Like, 'Oh, today is a lazy Sunday, staring out at the sea . . .' I don't feel the need to write it.

Earlier, I had more tweets about my life. Then I realized I was being stupid. Why should I care about millions of strangers hearing about my thoughts? What am I gaining out of it? Yes, when I don't want to give a quote on something, I just put it out on Twitter. If there's a controversy, during the AIB Roast for instance, I just wrote, 'Not your cup of tea, don't drink it.' And you know it's going to be quoted everywhere. So make it crisp so that it becomes a headline.

Acting in *Bombay Velvet* was a tick in the box for me. I was more disappointed for Anurag Kashyap, and for Ranbir when the film flopped. It didn't affect me. I was playing a cameo, I did my bit, and people who saw the film seemed to have liked my performance. I was not considered to be an error of judgement. In fact, I was well reviewed.

I was very happy that the critics who mattered to me liked my work. I don't know if I will get any acting offers after *Bombay Velvet* but I'm open to them. I enjoyed the experience of being on the set as an actor, and working with Anurag and Ranbir. I feel that I had drawn and leveraged from it in some manner.

I realized when I faced the camera that I can act. I felt happy that I am capable of doing yet another thing in my life. I would love to do it again given a chance. But I can't direct myself! I don't have that level of megalomania. I'm a practical person. I'm a director, I'll make films. But everything else I do, I have to be paid for. Then it's somebody else's belief, it can't be my own. And that belief has to be stronger than mine. Other directors tease me and say you were in a flop film. I laugh and say, 'I'm back to claiming *Dilwale Dulhania Le Jayenge* as my debut.' Yes, I felt terrible on that weekend when it was being slandered, but personally I was not surprised. I understand why the film didn't work commercially. I get it. When I saw the film, I knew it wouldn't work. But this extent of negativity? I think Anurag invites it because he's so out there. I feel there's a lot of parallel between him and me in certain ways. I feel if I had made a disaster like that, I would have been assaulted the same way. If I make a failure, I think people will celebrate that failure with abandon. That's what happened with Anurag. He made a very expensive film that was not mainstream and got lambasted for it.

I would have liked Ranbir to open up after the failure of *Bombay Velvet*. Happiness is a very common emotion. It's how you deal with sadness or depression or angst or anxiety or failure that you learn from. That's what life is full of. Life has more downs than ups really. It's like this song in which I love the positivity in sadness:

Rahi manwa dukh ki chinta kyun satati hai, dukh toh apna saathi hai, subah chhaon dhalti hai jaati hai, dukh toh apna saathi hai . . .

If you make sadness your friend because it's part of your life, then you'll be able to deal with it. I wish these movie stars would open up about their failures, their insecurities. I don't read a single interview of any of

these movie stars. I flip through the entertainment pages because I find
it all so boring. I feel no one has anything to say of any relevance any
more. They all talk so badly in interviews that I want to slap them. They
come across as cute caricatures of I-don't-know-what. They all sound like
Paris Hilton. What's happened to these women and men? Where has that
depth gone? You turn to a Shah Rukh interview and you think, thank
god for men like him. Why is he a journalist's delight? Only because he
has things to say. He's intelligent, he's communicative and he's coherent.
I find sometimes when you ask this generation a question, there's no
coherence in the answer. You've asked a question and they've gone into
something else altogether. And they laugh at their own jokes, which are
not funny. They have nothing clever to say. It's so sad. Some of them are
supreme talents, yet they have nothing to say.

So much has changed in the film industry. I'm one of the few people,
along with Aditya Chopra, who have seen the transition in the past twenty
years. We were the cool kids in the late nineties and saw the advent of
the new way of moviemaking, the discipline that came into cinema, the
marketing changes, single screens turning into multiplexes . . . All of us
film-makers in our forties have seen black-and-white turn into colour,
television go into video, video go into LDs, and LDs go into DVDs.
Soon I think it's going to be some little things that you put into your
ear to watch movies! It's reached a point of technology that everything
is becoming smaller. I remember the days when the Walkman was so
exciting and now it's become a mini iPad; soon it's going to become a
little device that you put into your underwear!

I've seen all the changes. Today when I'm on a set, I see an
entourage with some stars—a manager, a publicist, a fashion designer
and a hairstylist. It reminds me of how my father used to go mad about
make-up and hair, and wondered why men needed hairstylists (he
would say, *'Mard hai, apne baal kyon itna kanghi kar raha hai?'*). Today

men are blow-drying, they're setting their hair. Everyone has stylists, managers and publicists. Suddenly, there's a loop of nine people you're going through, and I think, oh, so this is wannabe Hollywood? Or is it about projecting ego? Is it insecure stardom? Or is it the order of the day? I don't know. I'm confused because I'm somebody who walks alone into a party even today. I don't like having my managers with me. I don't feel insecure going alone to a party. I don't say, hey, you want to tie up and drive together? I like my independence too much. That's who I am. I'm with Matrix, which is Reshma Shetty's and Vivek Kamath's company that handles Salman, Katrina, Kareena, and my three kids, Sidharth, Varun and Alia, only because they take care of the legalities and modalities. But if you ask me, I'm happy with no one being around me. I don't like a manager answering for me. I'm all about one-on-one equations with people. So when I'm on the set of *Jhalak Dikhhla Jaa* or *India's Got Talent*, I understand the need for that manager to be there but I actually don't leverage that need at all. I walk into airports on my own. Yes, there are people who come up to you, yes, it's annoying that I have to click selfies, the big bad new word of being a celebrity. People don't even know what it means but they use it. I've had families who say, 'We'll take a selfie,' and then give the camera to somebody else! That's not a selfie, that's a photograph. But now, 'selfie' has replaced the word 'photograph'. And when they take selfies, *tedhe-medhe* pictures of us come online. But so what? I like walking into stores on my own. I go to this place called Neelam Foodlands where I pick up low-fat *khakra* and other such nonsense. Twenty people will stare at you, probably wondering why Karan Johar is shopping in a grocery store, but I like to do certain things on my own. I like to go into Starbucks on my own, grab my coffee and yes, people will stare at you, but what is the big deal? You're in this profession for the adulation and attention, isn't it? I get so annoyed when I see all this wannabe stardom. The greatest people in this industry are those who actually pick up their phone and speak to you. Amitabh Bachchan, Yash Chopra, Shah Rukh Khan, Aamir Khan, Salman Khan, these are the people I've dealt with and all of them have picked up the phone when I have called. Yash Chopra used to be up at seven in the morning, making his own calls even for costumes.

Then there is the middle order of actors. I think it's the worst place to be in as the insecurity level is rather high. I tell the three kids I've launched that I would slap them if I found out that their manager was calling senior people and fixing appointments.

I've seen where cinema was when I got into Bollywood and where it is today. It's more structured, more disciplined, but it's become completely soulless. Yes, the younger generation get along more with each other, but they're also indifferent to each other. They'll party, they'll drink with each other, they'll have fun, and they've probably slept with each other's girlfriends and boyfriends at some point of time. I'm not judging, I believe in live and let live, do what you want to, and sleep with who you want to. It happens in every industry, but only Bollywood is more spoken about because we're more out there. Everyone's on Pinkvilla and Miss Malini and a hundred other sites.

Now who's wearing what at each party has become a very big deal; the paparazzi has reached your bathroom literally. It's all out there for public consumption. I have no judgement on all of that but I just feel that it's such an overtly ambitious, soulless and cut-throat industry today. So do you adapt? Or is it that if you can't beat them, join them? Or do you just ignore it? Be a part of it and also maintain your own individuality? There's always a dilemma.

Epilogue

I have been thinking about having a child for a long time. It is the biggest emotional thought in my head right now. I am not growing any younger. You know that you have lived half of your life at least. So you assess all the things you have done or not done. All the things you have done are great, because you are done with them. But what about the things you haven't?

These days, I find I am always staring at old people. I never used to do that before. I am always looking at men and women on wheelchairs and at the family that surrounds them. I am in and out of hospitals because my mother sometimes keeps poor health. I am drawn to these visuals much more now than I ever was. Previously, when I was younger, and looked at a person in a wheelchair, I might have stared a bit but then looked away because I had my own life to deal with. Now I think, would I be on that wheelchair two or three decades later? And if so, who's going to be wheeling me in and out? These thoughts are scary. Then I wonder—do I want a child just because of my needs? Then I realize the truth, yes, it's just for me—my big emotional investment that hopefully will pay rich emotional dividends when I need it. That's the only way I am looking at it. I am looking at it the way people look at it when they are hiring CEOs or domestic staff. I am looking at literally getting a child as my old-age insurance.

I think it's self-acknowledgement. It's coming to terms with everything. It's not living a lie any more. It's not living a fake existence. It's acknowledging your issues and addressing them for yourself, if not to anybody else. I think that's what I've done. I've let go. Like when I spoke about Kajol. I've let go. I'm removing a lot of emotional clutter. There were some people absorbing my life, I don't want them around any longer. Out.

Coming clean is my dynamic. First I used to end up saying things or doing things because I was trying to protect the other person, but actually I was harming them more. Now I'm just honest. If you don't like a script, just say it. Don't let it fester.

My health has suffered. I had developed medical issues apart from the psychological ones. I developed haemorrhoids which is a blockage. My father had fourth-stage cancer, a tumour in his throat, and I think he kept a lot of things to himself. But it does manifest in your body. I'm a big believer in the fact that health has everything to do with your mind. I feel like you have to start easing out on everything. Like things that come out of your mouth. We've been given two eyes and two ears. The human body has been made in a way where you can see two different things—you have two eyes. You can see something and you can see something else as well. Similarly, you can hear one thing and hear something else as well. But the mouth is only one. So, what comes out of your mouth should be really what you're feeling. I'm not saying be a loose cannon and say what you want. But definitely say what is bothering you. And sometimes, we see something else, but perceive something else altogether. What I'm trying to say is that we should communicate more freely. We should start saying what we feel. I've certainly reached that stage.

When I told Shah Rukh 'I miss you,' it was something I should perhaps have told him eight months ago. Or two years ago. I did miss him then but I didn't say it. Then I didn't know how he would react. All sorts of fears. That's what I mean by communication. Sometimes it's important to tell people that you love them. I came back recently from London, and I met Ayan. We were having a glass of wine and talking, and I told him I felt so happy talking to him. These things were not usually said between us. But I'm in a different zone right now. I think it's a Zen mode to be in. Communication is Zen.

Of course, I worry about my health. I don't have any pressing issues. I don't want to jinx this, but I've never spent even a single day in a hospital. The only night I've spent in a hospital is when I was born! I've been around for everybody else in my family. I mean my mother and father. My mother has had nine surgeries. My father had had many health issues. I have a long-standing relationship with the ICU, though I've never been in it myself. And I hope it stays that way. I'm not a worrywart. I know it may start worrying me when I reach a certain stage. But right now, I don't think about it a lot. My relationship with the gym is very sporadic. In one year, I do three months. I'm focused on something else. I feel now I can't give that any attention. *Kyunki main pagal ho jaoonga*. When I'm abroad, I love it because there I walk all the time. I feel exercise *ho hi rahi hai*. I'm very active like that. My mind is active and I'm capable of running around and doing three things at one time. I never feel like I'm exhausted. I've never had a massage in my life. I don't like massages. I don't like spas. I don't like facials. I don't like manicures and pedicures. The only time I sit in a chair and get something done is when I colour my hair. That's a big torture. People have this impression that I am this diva. When you do public appearances, you do hair make-up and reach the venue. Actually I can't bear it. It annoys me. I love facing the camera, but my problem is the whole prep for it. I keep wondering about all the skin treatments— what are people shoving into their faces? Why Botox and collagen? I don't want to do it. When vanity and madness hit me, maybe I will, I don't know. I'm very self-assured and confident like that.

With my mother, it's quite a lot of guilt now. I feel I'm combating it on a daily basis. I feel I'm not giving her the kind of time I should be. She's alone and gets lonely, and I don't know what to do about it. Sometimes I try and run away from the sadness of it. Sometimes when I see my mother looking sad, I feel if I sit there I'll get sad too, so then I avoid it, which is not right. I'm not giving her the kind of support she needs. Yet, I'm the best son in the world, according to her, because I'm always there. I live with her. I'm forty-four but we live in the same house. So there are always the morning and evening chats. I probably give her more time than any other son gives his mother in this industry, but it's still not enough for her and it's certainly not enough for me. Recently, I've been trying to address it. I keep complaining to her: 'Mum, you've lost that zing and that zest which you used to have.' I don't blame her at all because all she now has to live for is me. And if I tell her about my stress she'll get really stressed, so I always act happy around her. Sometimes when you reach home your guard drops, but I can't allow my guard to drop in front of her because the moment she sees me vulnerable, sad, low or fatigued, she will get very disturbed. If I tell her I have a bad stomach, she'll call me five times a day. So I can't tell her anything. I hate being sick, because the three days I'm in bed with a viral or whatever, she's really stressed out.

My relationship with my mother is exceptional. We're very close. My love for her is very emotional. She doesn't like to get out of the house much, so I feel very bad that she's not able to enjoy the happiness that my life can provide for her in terms of, say, travel. She travels rarely, her health issues restrict that. She travels with her friends when we're on film shoots, and stays with us, and becomes part of the crew.

But there's a lot of guilt from my end, and I feel that guilt makes it worse; it distances me even more and I feel very sad about it because I feel like I should be there for her much more. She still misses my dad a lot. I don't think there's any reduction in that feeling. Over time, you become habituated to living without your partner, but they had such a good, strong marriage, and they were so close to each other, such good friends and such soulmates and companions. They both laughed at the same jokes, and watched the same shows on television. He would talk to her in a certain way which even now she recounts. She talks to his photograph almost every other day. She has a big photograph of his in her room and she talks to him. She complains about me, I think! But she also tells him how proud she is. I've walked in many times when she's in mid-conversation with him.

Actually, the new house has brought a certain kind of renewed vigour, and we entertain much more. People come, friends come, and all my friends love her. They come and sit with her. She's also quite cool. She's seventy-three but she's got quite a youthful vibe, and is very connected in terms of technology. She's on Facebook, Twitter; she's on the iPad, she downloads and watches stuff; she's very clued in. She knows who was wearing what at which event; she has a comment on all of it. She reads Internet jokes, she's online all the time, on WhatsApp, BBM, email.

I like the fact that I have a beautiful new house. It was designed by my friend Riteish Deshmukh; he's a trained architect and interior designer. He doesn't do it professionally; he does it as a hobby. He was amazing through the whole process and made this beautiful house for me, so I'm very grateful to him. He put a lot of himself into it. My mother always wanted a house with a terrace, so this house has one that's sprawling. I wanted a humongous walk-in closet because I'm obsessed with shoes and clothes. Actually, I don't have a closet. It's a room that houses my clothes. And I wanted a huge bathroom. I take fifty-five minutes to get ready—I've timed myself. By the time I get up, read the paper in the loo, have a shower, and so on, it takes me some time—I wanted a big bathroom. Those are the kind of things I wanted.

But attachment to the house? No. There is no attachment. I'm not proud I bought the house or anything like that. I like the fact that friends can come; it's the kind of space that's conducive to entertainment. I don't feel it's a symbol of my success. I don't take it that seriously. We moved in on 9 April 2014. There is no immediate memory that I have of this house. I never grew up in it. I haven't yet created a life in this house. There's no hallmark memory so far. I might be here for the rest of my life, maybe it'll happen. But right now, the energy hasn't given me a memory which leads to attachment.

I am not in a serious relationship, and marriage is definitely not on the cards. Do I want to die alone? I do not really have any immediate family other than my mother. We don't have an extended family. I have two cousins and an aunt who I am really close to, and that's it. So I think, oh, I am building a company and this production house, and this studio. I would like it to be taken forward, just like the way I did for my father. Before he passed away, his big dream was to take his company to a higher level, which I have tried to do to the best of my abilities. But what next? Who will take it forward for me? I will soon be old, and in less than two decades, I will be in my sixties. Work will slow down. I would like to leave what I have created to someone. It was very scary when my CEO who is also my oldest school friend, Apoorva, told me that I should make my will. That is when the thought came. You think you are invincible. In my head, I am always in my twenties. I still feel like I have the energy level of a twenty-year-old. I am always combating the process of ageing. I don' like it. I don't like feeling like I'm forty-four years old. I hate the feeling, because I don't feel it in my head or heart, but the reality is that I am going to have to accept it.

So this is the zone I'm in, where I am thinking about having a child. It will, of course, have to be a surrogate child, or I will have to adopt. These are the two options that I have in front of me. I have all kinds of decisions to make, such as: Am I ready to be a father? Am I ready to slow down and take care of another life? Obviously, being a parent comes with a huge amount of responsibility. Am I ready for that? Am I emotionally ready? Am I pragmatically ready? Am I professionally ready to slow down and make that space? More than anything else, how will I be as a parent? The only one thing I feel is that because I have nurtured so many young careers, a sense of parenting has crept into me, so I may be ready. So am I thinking of my life as my career? But I am not one of those who rests on his laurels. I always say, move ahead! When one job gets done, you move on to the next one. I am that kind of person. I have never sat and re-evaluated my life or my career. It's like how I am thinking now about what's going to happen. I don't want to die without a sense of family around me. And selfishly, I want to have a child who will take care of me because I am afraid of growing old alone. That's my greatest fear. Death doesn't scare me, life sometimes does.